A Boy's Eye Norfolk Village Life

AS SEEN BY

Derek Bumfrey

Robert Boyd
PUBLICATIONS

Published by
Robert Boyd Publications
260 Colwell Drive, Witney
Oxfordshire OX8 7LW

First published 1997

ISBN: 1 899536 16 7

Printed and bound by The Alden Group, Oxford

Contents

Preface

The real object of my book is to take a look at life on a large Norfolk Estate through the eyes of a farm labourer's family in the years leading up to the Second World War, throughout the war years and on to post-war changes. In the main it is a diary of my own life as I was born and bred on the Estate and take it as a privilege to be able to record the happy and contented days of my early life as well as the struggle and hardship my family often endured to give me such a wonderful childhood and later a good education.

The one point I would stress from the beginning is that there is no axe for me to grind on behalf of the underprivileged working men, as no bitterness between man and master clouded my early life or that of my parents. Life was what you were born to, and if, as I was, you were of working class stock, the answer was to make the best of it and enjoy the things you had and not worry unduly about things just out of reach. I'm not denying that life was hard for all, because it was, very hard indeed, but for all that life was good, very simple but full of love and caring for one another. The toughness required to survive kept one's priorities right at all times.

Acknowledgements

I would like to take this opportunity of thanking Alan and Celia Comber for all their technical help in getting my story into print. Without their unstinting work and encouragement this book would have remained a collection of near unreadable longhand sheets.

Without the facts gleaned from Aunt Ivy I couldn't have accurately written the first chapter so my appreciation goes to her.

Last but not least a thank you to sister-in-law Heather, long ago workmate Leslie Richardson and Jean Little for diligently seeking out most of the photographs we are able to include.

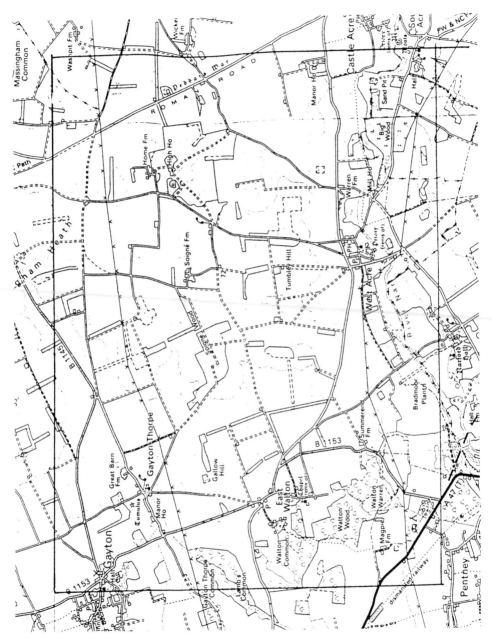

A roughly squared off boundary showing the wide extent of Westacre
High House Estate in north west Norfolk.

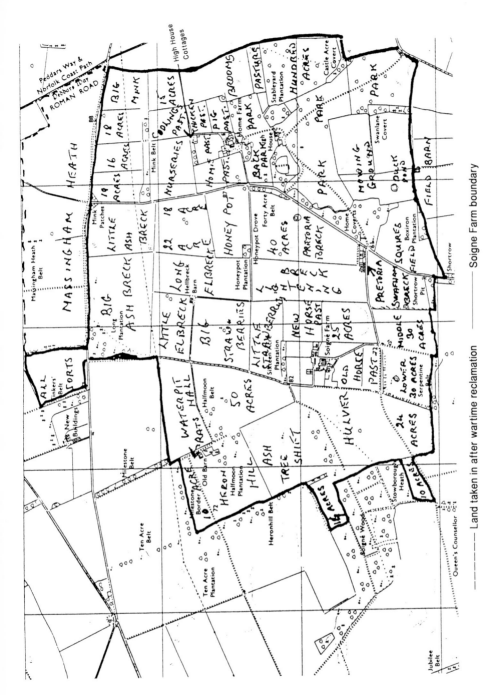

Soigne Farm

——— Land taken in after wartime reclamation ——— Soigne Farm boundary

Chapter 1
Rats Hall

The real story opens almost six years before I was born. It was in 1927 that Grandad Alfred Bumfrey moved his family from Baconsthorpe in north Norfolk further west to the very edge of the Westacre High House Estate. Without confirmation I am fairly sure the move took place on October 11th because farm workers in Norfolk always moved job and house on Michaelmas Day and as they exchanged tied cottage for tied cottage the big change around took place on the same day. For some strange reason our Norfolk Michaelmas day seems to be different from other parts of the country, but there, Norfolk people have always been a race set apart. Anyway I digress and must return to the main theme.

Grandad was coming to work for Alfred Lewis, a very good, but very demanding, tenant farmer renting Soigné Farm on the Birkbeck Estate at Westacre. At that time the Estate belonged to Henry Birkbeck who was born in 1853 and died in 1930 and most of the farms were rented out to tenants at the time when farming was in the doldrums and many farms made a loss on all their hard work. Consequently the lot of the farm labourer was pretty hard to say the least. Alfred and Rosa Bumfrey had a family of nine, ranging from Jack born in 1902 to Stanley born in 1920. As you can see the family followed a typical pattern with an average of a baby every two years stretching finances far beyond breaking point. At the time of the big move both Jack and Will the eldest sons had joined the army, Jack as a batman in the Royal Norfolk Regiment and Will in the Royal Dragoon Guards which was a cavalry regiment. Jack spent his life in the army but Will returned to the land after nine years most of which were spent in India. The rest of the family came to live and work at Westacre: Fred (1904), Archie-Roy (1908), Jane (1910), Cyril (1912), Marjorie (1915), Ivy (1917) and last of all Stanley who was born in 1920. The furniture, family and outside fittings travelled in the back of an open lorry. Aunt Ivy tells me that Grandad almost lost his hat in the overhanging trees as the vehicle slowly made its way up the incline to the Milestone gateway and on to the cart-track beside the whin border leading to Rats Hall, their new home.

Just imagine their trepidation as they all waited the sighting of their destination. As the lorry dragged along the last two miles of narrow country road they would see large arable fields on either side with no signs of human habitation. A group of bullock yards on the right of Patch Corner may have held their attention possibly to catch a glimpse of the

Rats Hall

lone cattle tender feeding his charges. The lorry would turn almost back on itself leaving the Litcham to King's Lynn road to follow a by-road that really came from nowhere but proudly boasted a milestone that gave information now long lost to time.

After regaining his headgear Grandad would have directed the driver to turn right at the Milestone and head up the sandy track with an open field to the right and a narrow belt of deciduous trees on the left. At the top of the track along the skyline was another wind break of whin bushes and silver birch trees looking decidedly scrubby and rather neglected. On grinding to the top of the incline they would all look down into a sheltered hollow and see only a couple of hundred yards ahead the tiny settlement of Rats Hall which was to be home for most of them for the next twenty years: a row of three flint-walled cottages with their tiny wooden lavatories at the bottom of the long garden, a large barn, and cattle yards in the central position and two bungalows further on, almost hidden by the woods which ran along the entire south side. Large rough grass areas at the front would make lovely playgrounds, giving ample room for long washing lines as well. It was the middle cottage that was to house the seven offspring along with Mum and Dad. Set in deepest Norfolk it was literally miles from anywhere and Grandad Alfred didn't even ride a bike. I expect the eldest sons had bikes but not their parents. Was it any wonder my dear, soft and gentle grandmother sat down and cried after being transported to such an isolated spot.

I wonder who opened the door first to find all the muck and wood shavings the builders had left after putting down new floorboards in the bedrooms, and who found the brushes on the lorry and set about cleaning up. Let's hope that many hands made light work. I'm sure Mrs Rye, the next door neighbour, would make a cup of tea for them because this was the country tradition in those days, but did she have the nine cups to go round plus the one extra for the lorry driver?

I believe there were only two bedrooms so it took some organising and a large shoehorn to get everyone to bed that night; I know that downstairs they had a large living-room, kitchen and walk-in larder plus the cupboard under the stairs. A wooden shed on the end of the row completed their covered accommodation if we discount the vaulted lavatory down the garden. A fire-heated copper was built in a corner of the kitchen, I believe, at Rats Hall - although often a copper would be confined in a shed or outhouse.

My Aunt Ivy kindly furnished me with all the relevant information I needed for this first chapter and I am grateful to her for it. She was just ten years of age at this time. She gives me to understand that John Rye, Lydia his wife, and son Geoffrey lived next door on one side and the

Rats Hall

Cooper family on the other. The bungalows were occupied by Grandfather Welham who held the post of head gamekeeper for the Estate and the other housed a Miss L Seaman of whom I know nothing except her name.

Well the Bumfrey family had arrived and was destined to play quite an important part in the workforce of Soigné Farm in the years to come. As I mentioned previously the man renting the land was Alfred Lewis. A farmer in every sense of the word he expected a very good day's work from his men and carried no shirkers for very long. Alfred Bumfrey was a big man in all ways, tall, broad and very strong, he was a labourer, shepherd and stockman rolled into one. In 1927 he was exactly fifty years of age. His sons still at home were Fred twenty-two, Archie or John, as he was known, nineteen, and Cyril or Sos as he was to us from now on, was fifteen. All went to Soigné with him - a fine catch of workmen for any farmer and all housed under one roof as a bonus.

Two years later Will left the army at the age of twenty-five to join the workforce as well. In later years Fred became cowman, Will and John horsemen, and Alfred a shepherd, so you can see they all held key positions. The only exception was Sos who didn't really care for farm work and joined the Tank Corps in 1938, but that is rushing too far ahead.

Let us then send Alfred, Fred, John and Sos off to work at the farm some half mile along the field footpath. Jane, then seventeen, was taken into service, first I believe at Westacre High House or the Hall as it was called locally, then on to Mileham Hall where she met and married Wilby Dye, raising three sons and a daughter. Marjorie twelve, Ivy ten and Stanley seven were of course still of school age. It was to Westacre school their weary feet led them that first Monday morning, two and half miles along the fields and footpaths down into Westacre village. There they met Miss Cross, head teacher, Miss Wiskerd and Miss Ellen Cross the infant teacher. The first and last ladies I only know by name but Miss Minnie Wiskerd was still there when I graduated into her care in 1938. My knuckles felt the edge of her ruler as did my aunts' and uncles' before me.

It has been rumoured that Ivy got the cane the first day, but it is hard to believe that such a sweet and inoffensive person as she could be treated so. But those days were hard for young and old alike so we ought not to be surprised. Anyway, she has always been a model citizen since so perhaps the rod helped to shape the child - in her case at any rate.

Let us, just for fun, follow those three intrepid young explorers as they set off to school on a misty October morning in 1927. Watch them as they waved goodbye to their mother, carefully carrying their dinners in three little snow-white muslin bags, probably made from bleached flour bags with a draw tape in the top. (Baking flour used to come in muslin

3

containers holding three pounds with a picture of a windmill on the front.) Did they stop just out of sight at the foot of Donkey Hill for a peep to see what was in them? A good guess would be jam sandwiches and cake, home-made of course, and perhaps an apple from the tree in the garden. On then up the short, very steep hill and out of Rats Hall kicking the wet, sweet chestnut leaves as they might uncover the prickly chestnut cases and provide a few shiny brown nuts to eat on the way, then a long trek down a narrow footpath between Fifty Acres and Ashtree Shift, over the corner of the Hulver and into Soigné farmyard where the men would be working with horses, feeding pigs and milking cows - no time to tarry except perhaps to join with the children from the farm cottages who trod the same path to the village. If on the way their father was working one, two or three fields away he would shout to them (Alfred could make his voice carry from one side of the farm to the other - and further even than that if some stray dog came near his sheep. He would have been the undisputed town crier if Westacre needed one). On they went, up the farm road to White Gate Corner where once more they would strike out along the cart-track-cum-green-road footpath, between Lower and Middle Thirty Acres towards the unseen village almost two miles away.

By this time their socks and boots would be soaked through with dew from overhanging grass and would have to dry out on their feet during the day. At last they came to a long slope down the path leading past the school, the bell started to ring and they all ran the last few hundred yards, with the little ones trailing, into the playground on the stroke of nine.

Who would be the lucky ones to sit next to the coke-filled tortoise stove (if there was one) and be able to dry their feet? (If it was always the same as when I went in later years then a large open fire warmed a tiny bit of classroom and the heat never got past the teacher's desk and the only heating we received was from the cane on numerous occasions for minor indiscretions.) So after a hard day at their desks our pupils set off up the incline home with empty dinner bags neatly folded and empty stomachs beginning to gnaw and groan. A handy field of swedes or turnips helped to stay the hunger pangs (and one or two less for the sheep didn't seem be classed as stealing, although my mother as a girl had to appear at the Magistrates' Court in Holt charged with stealing a turnip. So you see already that I am sprung from a family of near felons who would have been transported a few years earlier).

They arrived back home as dusk was falling, back to the appetising smell of stew and dumplings with such a tale to tell their mother, omitting of course any misdemeanours at school and the swede or turnip snack on the way home. The soft lamplight, warm fire and family love soon set those little heads nodding, so off to bed to rest in readiness for that same long trip tomorrow. Let's pray for a fine day because if it rained they would sit in damp clothes all day before another wet trudge home.

A very important question we may ask ourselves at this juncture is how did the isolated families obtain their food supplies whilst living so far from the shops. Well, with the coming of the motor car, tradesmen's vans quickly replaced horse-drawn vehicles and came as a boon to country housewives. At Rats Hall the bread supplies came from Gayton Mills who would call about three times a week providing also flour, yeast and meal for chickens. These chickens in turn kept the family in fresh eggs for most of the year. Howard Brothers were the butchers and also hailed from Gayton a medium-sized village some three miles away on the King's Lynn road. The grocery van called each Saturday providing the most exciting highlight of the week. All the children would be on hand hoping Mother would be able to spare a farthing or halfpenny for sweets. These were weighed out loose and poured into a three-cornered bag twisted at the top and given into the hand that could reach the highest to be shared with brothers and sisters. Often the grocer's hands still carried the smell of paraffin oil which was dispensed from a tank under the van and was such a vital necessity for heat and light. It seems as if the paraffin scent added that special ingredient to the bull's-eyes or aniseed balls. There was no hygienic hand washing between operations then. With the threat of a dose of brimstone and treacle hanging over you no-one's stomach dared to erupt in protest. This once-a-week only, chance to buy groceries certainly kept the memory up to scratch for any forgotten item had to be done without for a long seven days. George Joplin and Son were the grocers travelling from Castleacre which was some six miles away in the opposite direction to the other tradesmen's base. Joplins also delivered the newspaper, a copy of the previous Sunday's News of the World and a bit late to check your pools results but the only source of news before the arrival of the wireless set.

Fresh milk was collected from the small farm dairy at Soigné and usually brought home by the men returning from work. The drinking water came from a pump over a well situated near the bullock yard and had to be carried into the house in metal buckets. Most households had a large clay crock standing in the pantry and this would be kept topped up, providing enough clean water for use during the day. I wonder how much seeping effluent came from the yarded animals and found its way through the chalk subsoil into the drinking water - another job for a dose of brimstone and treacle to keep the bugs at bay. It would have been Grandad's job to fetch the water either after his long day's work or before he set out in the morning. Every drop of water used had to be carried in and all waste water taken out again to be tipped on the muck-hole at the bottom of the garden where all the rubbish came to rest and the smell was least offensive to the

Rats Hall

neighbours.

The only public transport in the early days at Rats Hall was a small bus running to King's Lynn on a Tuesday which was market day. King's Lynn held a large cattle market on that day, and also a busy stall-holders' market for all the many farming folks attending. This bus, owned jointly by Bert Eves and Billy Carter of Marham, picked up in Westacre village, came up past Pretoria cottages, High House, The Buildings and down the Milestone where the Rats Hall residents would be picked up. The bus, usually driven by Billy Carter with Mrs May Eves taking the fares, would go into town about nine forty-five returning from Lynn at a quarter to three in the afternoon. If by chance you had a crate of chickens for the market Billy would climb the ladder at the back of the bus and deposit them on the top in an early form of roof rack. But for many the trip to Lynn was only taken once a year or in a case of dire emergency. Money was so short in those days that my dad, Fred, before he married, would give his mother his board money on Thursday to help her pay for the meat needed for the family prior to Friday pay-day. His natural thrift and keeping his own expenses to the absolute minimum enabled him to carry a small nest egg, one week's wages in hand. Dad cared a lot for his mother as in fact did all the Bumfrey children. With the nearest pub being at Gayton over three miles away there wasn't much temptation to waste money on drink. Pub landlords never grew fat from any of the Bumfrey family - a good cup of tea was very much more in their line I'm glad to record. Nor were they great sportsmen either although Fred and Sos played football for Westacre around 1930. In fact Fred played until his marriage in 1931 when the fear of injury resulting in being unable to work forced his retirement. This was in the days when the legendary Tubby Morton of twenty-two stone frame played full back for Massingham.

One bizarre injury Fred suffered was when the bus engine stalled on the way to a match then kicked back as Freddie cranked the starting handle causing him to bang his jaw on the radiator cap. I'll bet the resulting language would have produced a red card had the referee been on the bus. Tales of referees being ducked in the village pond when the home teams lost were often told, but as to their actual truth I am not prepared to comment. Anyway, they are all part of local folklore now. I do know that when my dad told football stories Tubby Morton was wide enough to block the whole of the Massingham goal, so from that you can draw your own conclusions.

In 1929 Will returned to civilian life and came home to swell the numbers of working men operating Soigné Farm. That same year Marjorie left school at the end of the summer term and presumably went out to service, leaving only Ivy and Stanley trekking the long distance to school, with probably Geoffrey Rye from next door for company. Ivy was twelve and Stanley nine, from August 5th and September 3rd of that year respectively.

Alfred Bumfrey was a firm believer in the maxim of early to bed, early to rise. It certainly made him healthy, not very wealthy in the financial category, but rich in other ways, and very wise in country ways. He would rise at just after 5 a.m. in winter and summer. The first job of the day was to riddle out the dead ashes from the kitchen range carrying them out to use as garden path repair material. A few dry twigs kept in the warm oven overnight would be placed on a sheet from that one weekly newspaper and set alight. Some thicker sticks or seconds as they were known were gradually added, and the tin kettle, half filled for the first pot of tea of the day, was placed on top. A quick swill with cold, soft water drawn in a hand cup from the rain water butt by the back door would soon dash any sleep from his eyes, leaving him with a marvellously fresh complexion which stayed with him throughout his ninety years. Rainwater and yellow washing soap were his secret. His shaving was done with soap lather and cut throat razor, stropped on the leather strap hanging by the fireplace. Breakfast would be prepared and no doubt his wife, Rosa, would be down to join him by this time. Freshwater buckets would have to be filled, and wood and coal carried in from the shed just depending on whether these jobs had been left from the previous evening. Then at about 6 a.m. would begin the ritual of getting his sons out of bed and off to work. The stairs door would open and Alfred would call up the stairs "Will, WILL, Fred, FREDDER, Archer, ARCHER, Scysh, SCYSH" - the final delivery designed to shake Uncle Sos from his bed would echo through the entire hamlet. If you need translation the slumbering bodies upstairs belonged to Will, Fred, John and Cyril. Eventually the first three would appear to have some breakfast but Sos would remain in bed until his father shut the back door dead on 6.30 a.m. as he made his way on foot to the farm in order to be there before the zero hour of 7 a.m. Sos then flew out of bed, dressed, grabbed a cup of tea and ran up the footpath clutching his dinner bag and fastening buttons en route. He knew that one minute late on arrival and his wages would be docked by a quarter of a day's pay. A repetition in the same week could well have meant the sack. Alfred Lewis, as were most farmers at that time, was a stickler for punctuality. I presume that when Sos became the proud owner of a bicycle he could have at least five minutes extra in bed each morning.

I know Fred owned a bicycle before he came to Rats Hall and used it afterwards to cycle over to Briston to see my mother when she returned home from service in London to spend a short holiday with her parents. It was about twenty-five miles each way and he would set off after work

Rats Hall

finished on Saturday and return for work by Monday morning. It was in March 1931 that this long-distance courting finished and they were married in Briston church and came to live at High House in the cottage to be described in the following chapter.

Life at Rats Hall continued in its routine vein; only Uncle Will as best man attended the wedding at Briston. Lack of transport and money made it impossible for the others. The Wall Street crash may have been reported in the old copy of the News of the World, but would have had no effect whatever on their lives or their thinking. The only passing flicker of change on their horizon was the death of Henry Birkbeck, the squire, in 1930. The Estate passed to Major H A Birkbeck, the elder son, who was a leading figure in the world of banking with Barclays in London. At that time the squire would only have been a shadowy figure to the employees of the tenant farmers, although in later years Major Birkbeck became very central in all our lives as he eventually farmed all the Estate throughout the Second World War.

Chapter 2
High House

The first time I appeared on the Westacre Estate was in the winter days early in 1933. My father, Fred Bumfrey, had married my mother, Alice Eke, in 1931 and had come to live in one of the middle cottages situated across a meadow at High House. Mum was the daughter of a railway workshop worker at Melton Constable. My mother's parents lived all their lives in the adjoining village of Briston some twenty-five miles from Westacre. It was in this community that I was born on January 15th 1933.

My parents had first met when the Bumfrey family lived and worked at Baconsthorpe, a small village in North Norfolk about four miles inland from the bracing seaside town of Sheringham. Dad was already into dairy farm work, driving the milk float to Sheringham, and delivering fresh milk to the hotels. Mum was in domestic service at the local rectory. The courtship followed a pattern very familiar to young people of those days: local boy meets and walks out with girl employed at the big house. Things progressed to a more serious stage and both parties saved what little money they could from their very low wages in readiness for marriage in the near, or not so near, future.

The courtship of Fred and Alice wasn't without its stresses, but true love triumphed eventually. In 1927 the Bumfrey family moved en bloc to Westacre as previously recorded. Alice Eke shook the dust of Norfolk off her feet and took up domestic service in London where her two elder sisters were already working. What a change for a country girl who had never left the county before. Fred continued his agricultural employment at Soigné Farm and courted his Alice by letter, very limited I imagine, and annual meetings at Briston, when his beloved returned home for a short holiday each summer. Fred saved his money faithfully, Alice by her own admission spent hers on theatre trips and sightseeing in the big metropolis, but despite the distance, the difference in lifestyles, and the long absences, they were married in March 1931 and took up residence on the Estate at High House in the cottage across the meadow.

What an idyllic setting for two young lovers to begin their lives together, or was it? Let me attempt to set the picture as we try to assess the situation. The cottages were about three miles from the village of Westacre which boasted a post office, and tiny shop. Castleacre, three miles away, had a grocery shop-cum-haberdashery, plus barber's and shoe mender's. Transport consisted of a bicycle for each family member. To get to either of these centres of commerce one pushed one's bicycle across the meadow,

9

High House

through the churned up mud by the farm gate, splashed across the farmyard and took off along the semi-made-up private road and on to the king's highway. The return trip, with the added encumbrance of shopping bags on the handlebars, was even more hazardous.

The bright lights of married life soon began to dim to the London butterfly, Alice. No hopping on a bus and off to the theatre now, just a crackly wireless to keep in touch with the fast-changing outside world. For her it was like stepping back into the Middle Ages. It is very difficult to see the beautiful scenery and appreciate the peace of the countryside when your best shoes are covered in mud and your only pair of stockings has been laddered, and with little money to spare from the income of thirty shillings a week to pay for replacement clothes let alone fripperies such as thin fashionable stockings.

On the other hand Fred was in his element with a house, regular job and a large vegetable garden, and with a wonderful young wife, his world was complete. As I was yet unborn I cannot record how they came to terms with the situation. Years later my mother told me of her unhappiness during this readjustment period. Her summing up was in these words, "If your father hadn't been such a good man I would have gone back to work in London." And I would now add that if she hadn't been such a good woman their marriage would have finished before it had hardly begun.

My parents were good in every sense of the word, both of strong, country stock, straight and honest, through and through. With parents like them I had a marvellous start in life, tucked away in rural Norfolk and far, very far, from the madding crowd.

To be able to enter the Westacre Estate on that auspicious first day I had to travel from my grandparents' home at Briston. Their row of cottages rejoiced under the name of Plums Cottages. They have now been demolished and replaced by modern, sheltered accommodation, so there is no hope of placing a plaque to commemorate my birth upon that spot. My first journey therefore began with a pram ride for one and a half miles to the station at Melton Constable junction. Boarding the train for King's Lynn we puffed in and out of Thursford, Fakenham, Raynham Park, and East Rudham, before disembarking at Massingham. A four mile pram ride along lonely country roads brought me to the turn leading to High House, then through the farmyard mud, across the meadow and I was home. Westacre Estate, be warned, I had arrived. I wonder how many people noticed.

Let us now pause a few minutes and take stock of this place I was to call home. As previously stated it was one of the middle cottages of four. If my memory serves me correctly we had a kitchen, a living-room downstairs

10

and two bedrooms above. The downstairs ceilings were quite low and upstairs the ceilings were non- existent, with only bare rafters to stare at from your bed. In fact I do remember lying at an angle and seeing a star peeping between the pantiles. The ground floors were of brick with no damp course membrane underneath. Sinks and running water were unheard of for labourers' cottages. The toilet was a bucket underneath a wooden seat at the top of the garden housed in a wooden shed. The contents were emptied weekly into a freshly-dug hole up the garden which in turn meant a well-manured crop of vegetables for next year.

A cooking range gave heat in the kitchen and an open fire tried to dispel the damp from the living or front room. Life generated in and around the kitchen range for most of the year. Incidentally there was no form of heating in the bedrooms and it wasn't unknown to wake up with a line of hoar frost down the centre of the bed clothes. Very cold weather meant that every blanket and overcoat was needed to prevent hypothermia taking its toll. The tiny windows with thin glass did little to keep the wind out in winter and seemed to do even less in letting air in on stifling summer days when the swallows and martins swooped around in blue, uncluttered skies and hot days seemed to go on for ever.

At the time of their wedding my father had saved a sum of £100 with which to furnish the home. My mother, whose financial contribution was negligible, had been busy for months filling that bottom drawer with hand-made curtains, covers and linens - well, perhaps it was my maternal grandmother really as she was very good with the treadle machine and Mum was her youngest daughter. The house was sparsely but serviceably furnished with no fancy frills. Life in the countryside in 1931 didn't allow much time for frills. The bedrooms then had bare boards and slip-mats, lino' came later in our future homes. The brick floors downstairs were covered with coarse coconut matting which was in strips, was hard-wearing and allowed the floor beneath to breathe. A thick sack was strategically placed by the back door for boot wiping. The front door didn't need one as it was only used for posh visitors, and we never had any of them.

The highlights in flooring were the piece-mats in front of each of the fireplaces. These were made from sugar-sack backings into which were pegged as many coloured rag strips as was possible. All discarded rag garments were cut up for this purpose. What a joy to wriggle your bare toes in the warm, dusty tassels of an old rag rug. The cat curled up on it, the dog snored there, and the humans drew their chairs up on it. The centre of life at the end of a hard day was the rag rug before the kitchen range, with the aches and pains of heavy, manual work forgotten, the cold and wet dried out of the joints and clothes, the feet dry and warm once more, and no TV to break the peace of family harmony, just the simple joy of a comfortable rest after a day's hard work well done. That is certainly a memory on the plus side and one rarely experienced today.

The buildings themselves were of brick interspersed with flint. These are very common building materials in many parts of Norfolk. The red bricks, fired locally, kept the corners and windows and doorways square, whilst the flint, knapped flat on one side, filled in between. All the materials were held together with lime mortar. The walls were capped with a roof of red pantiles. These were also used very extensively in that area of the county. Each cottage had its own wooden shed out the back, and the wooden lavatory in the distance, with the door usually screened by a big bush of some kind. Shed roofs were either tiled or of corrugated iron sheeting. At the end of each property both front and back was a soft water butt. Water was a precious commodity as all drinking water had to be carried in buckets from the farm. Conversely all waste water from the house was caught in a waste or slop bucket and emptied on the muck-hole which was our equivalent to the modern day compost heap. Soft rainwater was used for all washing purposes, whether for bodies or clothes. Baths were kept to a minimum especially when the water level fell in the butts. Most washes were of the top and tail variety using an enamel bowl and a bar of hard, yellow washing soap. This water scarcity often came to my rescue in later years, as I was like most small boys who were afraid that they would melt if subjected to excess contact with soap and water. I also wished hair-brushing was rationed, but that is another story.

To continue the picture of my first home we turn to the garden. Along the front of the row was a strip of overgrown land full of wild fruit trees and clumps of brambles. This was set inside a very tall hedge bordering the farm meadow. I suppose at one time this strip had been front gardens, but was surplus to requirement and had been allowed to run wild. At the back was a large vegetable plot, with a good loam soil and several well-established fruit trees of the usual useful mix: a large cooking apple tree, russet apples for keeping, early summer apples and plums, blue and victoria. Dad grew all the year's supply of vegetables and potatoes. We had to be self-sufficient as there was neither money nor opportunity to pop out and augment supplies from a greengrocer or farm shop. A big clump of rhubarb helped purge our systems in the spring, and also I remember, brought me up in large, itchy spots in the process. I presume there were a few soft fruit bushes which were adorned with old lace curtains to keep the birds off them at fruiting time. All fruit was either made into jam or bottled for use during the long winter months. A "boughten" tin of fruit was almost as far out of our reach then as caviare is to us today. Nothing grown in the garden or gathered in the wild was wasted. We knew where all the best hedgerow harvests could be found, as later chapters will reveal.

High House

The food that we couldn't produce ourselves was brought to the door by motor van. It was a very big plus. Not only were our basic food supplies delivered, all the local news came as well. Who needed a newspaper when such local characters as Jack the Baker, Charlie Fitt the butcher and Oliver Joplin the grocer and paraffin purveyor called at least twice a week? These tradesmen from villages outside the Estate served us well in all weathers for many years before and during World War 2 - real friends, always ready to help and oblige in any way possible.

Having just referred to the paraffin purveyor reminds me about the lighting system used in the home. The only electricity at High House was confined to the Hall itself where an engine-driven generator supplied the house. Our lighting came from paraffin oil lamps and candles. Each lamp had to be trimmed and filled daily, a very necessary but smelly job undertaken by the lady of the house. The lamp with its sparkling lamp glass or chimney stood on the table casting a very soft light but presenting a very real fire hazard, especially where young children were playing round the table, as it could be so easily upset. I remember our deal table had the corners angled off to prevent pockets catching thus causing the lamp to topple. White candles were set in their brightly-coloured metal candlesticks and used to light the way to bed, again a fire hazard being an open flame just waiting for long hair or flimsy curtains to brush across and ignite. But this was a way of life used for centuries and so people lived with such dangers, because at the time there was no choice or nearby fire engine to save our home from disaster.

I have already spoken about the high hedge at the front separating the cottages from the meadow; we always called it a pasture. This meant that the view was very curtailed in that direction. If one walked to the front gate then the Home Farm with its distinctive high sawmill chimney, complete with lightning conductor, could be seen, and also the rear view of three more cottages, next to the farm itself. Many lovely mature trees were dotted along the hedgerows, giving a pretty rural scene. Looking north over the back gardens we saw the Nurseries, a thirty acre arable field with Mink Belt, a narrow spinney, which made a good windbreak on the far side. To the west was a small wood, and to the east a rutted track leading up into the fields beyond Mink Belt. Running beside our garden path was the linen line on which the pure white sheets and khaki shirts strained to escape their captive pegs every Monday morning. I have no doubt my white towelling nappies were out every day, but Monday was always the traditional washing day, for the main boiled wash. There was a great pride and rivalry over the whiteness of the wash. It is amazing what could be done with a bar of washing soap, a boiling copper and a blue bag in the rinsing water. Also one would think that a special prize was awarded to the first lady to get her washing out. Often a 4 a.m. start was needed to get this much sought after accolade.

Two very important items could have been seen as our eyes looked out over the gardens at the back of that house. Both were essentials and would be present in every garden on that Estate, without exception. One was the hens scratching away in their large wire netting run, under the cooking apple tree, alongside the path leading up into the wood. The netting would be six feet high, staked down to prevent the chickens getting out underneath. The whole structure was held up with wooden stakes which had been cut from a nearby nut-bush, these being as straight as possible. A small, wooden hen house kept the birds safe from the fox at night, giving both warmth and shelter as they dozed on the wooden perches. Along one side were the nest boxes where eggs were laid daily in soft barley straw provided for this purpose. A lid on the outside enabled us to collect the eggs easily without having to undo the gate and risk letting the hens out on to the cultivated garden. It's amazing how much damage an old hen can do when searching for worms on a newly-sown seed bed. Very occasionally one over-adventurous egg machine would fly over the wire and take to free-range lifestyle. This would be very short-lived, and after catching her, Dad would cut the ends of the long feathers on one wing, thus making an unbalanced flying gear and almost complete loss of flight.

Feeding time for these happy egg layers tended to be quite hair-raising at times. Their diet consisted of boiled household scraps or small chicken potatoes mashed up with a small amount of balancer meal, bought from Gayton Mills in small sacks. To distribute this tasty mixture one had to undo the gate, a thick wire hook top and bottom, and get inside without letting out any of the pressing crowd of hungry hens. This in itself was no mean feat as they squabbled and shoved against your legs or tried to leap up and knock the bucket to the ground. Having got inside the run one then tipped the food into wooden troughs where it was gobbled up by the gang of hungry hens. On numerous occasions one of the hens would have managed to escape and would be frantically trying to get back to the food by pushing at the wire and leading everyone a pretty dance as they tried to guide her back to the gate. But as everyone knows, an escaped hen is blind to an open gate and will spend ages trying to get her plump body through the two inch mesh in preference to the short and painless walk to the open gate. This hot mash feed usually came in the morning, with some form of green stuff pulled from the cabbage patch being thrown over the wire around lunch time. Later in the afternoon some cracked maize, to give the egg yolks colour, mixed with tail corn, would also be thrown over into the run causing another mad free-for-all as every last grain was sought out and consumed with very unladylike haste. The only other thing to remember was to top up the handleless saucepan which always served as a water container. This daily routine was never varied and it was considered as important as our own domestic requirements. An additional weekly chore connected with the fowls usually fell to the youngest of the labouring family. This was to remove the droppings from the hen house and spread a layer of fresh barley straw across the floor under the roosting perches and replace any soiled straw in the nesting boxes. This seemingly insignificant yet very important task made its young operator a tiny cog in the wheel of everyday chores that each family member performed to make country life run on well-oiled wheels. This system of distributing jobs to all members of the family gave everyone a responsibility which had to be shouldered however young the member might be. Very few people even thought about shelving their share and this helped to make a very caring community, something which we feel is so lacking today. Yes, the rewards did outdo the pain of labour. A lovely brown egg with golden yolk and bread soldiers was worth all the money in the world when you came in hungry at tea time. It seemed a very ample reward for a few minutes' work even if your head had to be in a smelly hen house for part of the time.

The other essential commodity at the top of the garden was the wood-stack. This would be situated under another one of the fruit trees and consisted of lengths of dead firewood propped up on end to let the rain run off and keep the wood as dry as possible. A wooden structure of crossed timber was set to hold the wood in a horizontal position for sawing into nine inch lengths for the fire. A large log set upright served as a chopping block for splitting the larger sawn logs. All logs were sawn by hand in any spare time after work, and very often by moonlight on a winter's evening. It was laughingly said that we who sawed our own logs had two warms, one with the effort of sawing and the other in front of the log fire. It was true, I can assure you, as I have spent many happy hours warming myself in both cases. One of the perks on the Estate was the permission to gather any fallen timber for our own use and transport to cart it home if needed. The only proviso issued was that no one disturbed the laying pheasants in the spring. The woods were only out of bounds for three months. This unwritten law was adhered to without question except in the case of a very few incomers during the war. Bird-nesting small boys were soon taught the error of their ways by the gamekeeper's hand or boot, whichever was the most convenient to the law enforcer. I can vouch for the accuracy of their blows and wouldn't have dared complain to my parents for fear of another telling-off from them.

I hope that I have been able to set the scene of my first home for you. Sorry if I digressed along the way, but you will understand that in the country, one path soon leads on to another and you are over the hedge

High House

before you realise it. It was very important that I set down the pattern of my earliest memories for all to see and understand, for I am sure the beautiful and peaceful depth of the countryside surroundings had a deep-lasting effect upon the way I have led my life. The stability, anchored firmly in natural and traditional ways of life, has stood me in good stead throughout my 60 years during which time the world about me seems to have progressed to a state of madness beyond the wildest thoughts of any fiction writer. Looking back I can see that my whole life has been built on the firm foundation put down in those early days of a natural and honest way of life, begun with two good parents across that meadow in the deepest Norfolk countryside.

Chapter 3
Life Across the Pasture

After spending the last chapter describing at length my very first home, I now have to move on to tell about my second one. Not so much detail is necessary this time I hasten to add, because it was only next door.

The cottage on the western end of the row became vacant so it was agreed that we move in there as the building was in much better repair. The layout inside was very similar to our first house so there is no need to go into any lengthy descriptions in that field. A few vague memories come back to me through the mists of time - remember, I was only around two then. The first is the discovery of a cupboard which had been papered over, adjacent to the front room fireplace - what mysteries did it contain? One of my uncles, it was either Sos or Stanley, helped my mother remove the paper sealing the door before gently easing it open. Anticipation ran high, speculating on its contents, which might range from a skeleton to treasure trove. The only treasures revealed, apart from the dust of ages, were half a dozen very dry and very wrinkled broad bean seeds. I can't remember if they grew but I am sure that there was no repeat of Jack and the Beanstalk. Everyone laughed about the treasure. "Just our luck", was Uncle's summing up after the dust settled.

The second outstanding memory is the much-patched, wooden coal-house door at the side of the cottage. The reason for this poor old door with its rat-gnawed bottom standing out so plainly is very simple: it seems to have been used as a background on every photograph taken in those early days. Perhaps that position allowed the ardent box camera enthusiasts to have the sun shining over their shoulders, which was so necessary for that type of photography. At any rate that battered old door was well recorded for posterity.

The Home Farm, or High House Farm as we always called it, may have been isolated but nevertheless quite a large number of people resided in its proximity. In those days, around 1936, when I really began to register my fellow human beings, farming still required quite a high density of labour and families tended to be way beyond the 2.4 child average of today. After we moved into our end house the middle two cottages remained empty and their condition deteriorated rapidly until they became condemned for demolition. Sonny Smith with his wife, Beattie, and daughter, Yvonne, lived at the far end. Then across the pasture we go to meet the occupants of the three cottages adjacent to the farm building.

Life Across the Pasture

First was Walter Dack, groom at the Hall, his wife, and son Ted. The middle cottage housed Bert Chase, his wife, and three almost-grown up sons, Basil, Norman and Brian. At the far end came Hubert Watts and Beryl, his wife. Hubert combined his chauffeuring duties with servicing the engines which made electricity and pumped water for the Hall. In the farmhouse itself lived Willie Thaxton, the bailiff for all the Estate farms. He and his wife raised six children, Billy, Bob, Peggy, Geoff, Ted (who was also known as Tich) and last of all June. The youngest daughter, June, was about two years older than me. With them lived Grandfather Thaxton who was semi-retired but looked after the many chickens that roamed the farmyard. At the rear of the house Granny Abel, who was Mrs Thaxton's mother, also lived, caring for two grandsons, Lou and Tom Abel. The last residence was also part of the farmhouse block and was the home of Arthur "Toe" Curl, his wife, and family of Banker, Marjorie, Audrey and Tom. The latter contracted sleeping sickness which left him with a severe type of palsy; he was unable to work and died very soon afterwards. Arthur was the team-man caring for the working horses on the farm. I remember him returning from Massingham station with the corn-wagon loaded with huge lumps of steam coal; this drove the steam engine supplying power for the new saw mill. Some also went out to the steam threshing tackle when it was in the area. The wagon was blue, and lined out with deep pink. The name-plate on the side proudly read, "Major H A Birkbeck, Westacre High House". There was also a little seat which was held by chains on the front board for the wagoner to ride if the vehicle was empty or only lightly-loaded. How those iron shod wheels used to grind over the rough road when he turned round by the huge barn.

This barn gave an enormous amount of storage space, with big wooden double doors giving access right through the centre of the building. The farm itself consisted of a great conglomeration of buildings, open cart-sheds, stables, bullock yards, pigsties and milking sheds; a large nettle-filled stack yard at the rear completed the complex. Sadly parts of it were already starting to fall into disrepair as the land surrounding the farm had been largely combined with the much bigger Soigné Farm, let out to Mr Alfred Lewis, for whom my father had worked. Many of the cart-sheds housed old or broken horse machinery, which made roosting perches for the many chickens clucking and scratching around. How Grandad Thaxton ever found the eggs I don't know. A flock of white geese led by a very fierce gander also wandered around helping to keep the grass down and making a good mess at the same time, both with their large feet and their rear ends.

Their, and every other animal's water supply came from a dark, brooding, scum-edged pit in the corner of the park. A little petrol engine, housed in its tiny black hut with a tank on top, pumped the stagnant water for the stock. I found it very amusing on one occasion when my father, just descending the ladder after checking the water tank level, slipped on a rung and came down at high speed, his worn wellingtons beating a tattoo on the ladder as he came. Needless to say he saw nothing funny at all in the situation, but there, I always had a strange sense of humour. I am still laughing as I look back at the shocked expression on his face as his nose flew past the rungs. At least he didn't lose the tiny piece of hand-rolled cigarette which was almost always in his mouth; the loss of that certainly wouldn't have been a laughing matter as far as he was concerned. Those sparrow-legged cigarettes were supposed to be the only comfort that he had in life and, no matter how much fun we poked at him, he never gave up the habit.

All the people were very friendly. Mr Thaxton was rather stout and quite jolly; he had come to High House originally as cowman and had graduated to bailiff after Major Birkbeck inherited the Estate on the death of his father in 1930. Some people were jealous of Willie Thaxton's position but he was always very good to us. And anyway it couldn't always have been easy trying to run successfully a huge Estate without a thorough training in all the varied things involved, especially with the owner so heavily involved in banking, being on the board of Barclays Bank. The children were all older than me with the exception of Yvonne Smith, but I can't remember having played much in her company. One occasion does stand out and that was when I helped her tear Mrs Smith's wallpaper off the front room wall. The only problem seemed to be that the said Mrs Smith wasn't ready to redecorate at that precise time. That misunderstanding might have been the reason for me not being invited too often.

Ted (Edward) and June Thaxton I remember most, probably because I saw them daily when we fetched our milk from the farm dairy. Mrs Thaxton distributed fresh milk to the cottagers when they brought their metal or enamel cans. Sometimes there was a shortage especially when the Hall needed extra supplies, because the dairy really existed to supply the big House.

Once Ted found out that my second name was Edward he decided that, as we had the same name, we must be twins. On another occasion we were all waiting out on the grass for an ice-cream man to call and playing around a parked horse-rake; somehow my coronation mug, brought to hold my ice-cream, got broken and I was in tears. Away sped Ted to bring a replacement cup from the farmhouse and help dry my flow of tears. I presume the ice-cream must have been pretty runny to require a mug. Also I don't remember if the salesman came on a "stop me and buy one" tricycle or by motor van. On another occasion Ted and I both had red, knitted

Life Across the Pasture

jerseys which doubly cemented in Ted's mind that we must be twins.

There were two other farm buildings I omitted to mention: one was the blacksmith's shop where the horses were shod at intervals when the travelling blacksmith called - the joyous sound of hot metal being struck on the anvil and the roar of the fire was a lovely sound especially on a cold, winter's morning; the second building should have been in the forefront of my mind as it was so unusual - a black, wooden structure with a tiled roof, it was raised up about three feet from the ground on huge staddle-stones. A set of stone steps led up to the door whilst at the other end a door opened up into space. This was designed for the grain- wagons to back up when loading or unloading. It was, or had been in the past, a granary with the staddle-stones to keep rats from climbing in through the floor. I had often fantasised about a big, black cat sitting on the top of the front steps to turn the rats back should they come to the door.

To the right of the farm drive as the vista opened up to show the farm itself was another black-boarded building; there must have been a special offer on black tar wood preservative at the time. This structure was half hidden in the trees and designed as a recreational hall or reading room as they were called locally. I have to admit I know very little about its origin or uses come to that, but a vague memory takes me there for what I believe was a harvest festival celebration on one occasion - other than that I don't remember it being used and it remains at the back of my mind almost as a figment of my imagination. Perhaps it was used for local religious services in earlier days when all employees and families were expected to attend church. With about forty souls housed on the farm and augmented by the servants from the nearby Hall, it would have been quite viable.

I suppose as we are in the farm drive we should go back to the entrance off the main road. There was no farm sign, the only notice on display was a white board with black letters boldly stating, "No thoroughfare, private road". Ignoring this instruction, we could proceed along the post and rail-lined drive, with a lovely row of mature walnut trees inside the pasture to the left. To the right, between dotted thorn bushes and bramble clumps, we could see the back of the Hall across the park. Entering the farm premises, the pond was on the right of the gate leading to the Hall, and the road then divided with the left fork leading around to the cottages and main barn area. By taking the forward direction we would pass the main farmhouse block and meet up with the aforementioned rutted track which passed our cottages and led up into the back fields. Two small pastures lay to the east of the steadings. The pig pasture was well rooted up and often very muddy, being home to a number of large black sows whose ears seemed to cover their eyes, but they were able to see well enough when any food was thrown over the wire fence. My father often took me to watch them rooting around and we stood under a couple of huge horse-chestnut trees at the lane side.

Next door was a small field with a number of chicken houses dotted about. This was Grandfather Thaxton's domain and, I suspect, a fox's paradise if he forgot to shut the chickens away at night. The fowls were kept primarily to supply the Hall with eggs, and poultry should it be required, and I have no doubt that they would need a change from pheasant and partridge sometimes. Remember that in those days chicken was regarded as a special treat in most households and not used or bred as commercially as today. When a hen had hatched her brood of chicks the females, or pullets, were kept for breeding and egg-laying, whilst the cockerels lived only long enough to be fattened up for the table. These chickens were all free-range and spent the day happily scratching and bustling in the dry earth under the large hedgerow-trees or around the farmyard. Some tail corn would be thrown down for them, causing a great scramble between the hens, with latecomers hareing across the yard oblivious to any wheeled traffic that might be around. The cockerel, meanwhile, would keep sedately to the edge of the scrummage trying to attract the attention of his favourite wives by picking up and dropping down an extra-fat kernel of wheat. His comb and wattles were very red and he looked rather pompous and self-important and just a bit intimidating to a small boy, but far more frightening was the flock of white geese that roamed the farm area keeping the grass short and making a mess with their droppings and surplus feathers. The old gander was a fierce fellow who hissed his displeasure at all and sundry whilst his many wives cackled and made a great noise at anything in the least bit strange to them. I always hid on the other side of my mother when we had to pass them on the way to the dairy.

The nicest, feathered residents by far were the ducks that swam on the pond or sat on the grass chattering away to one another in the lovely way that ducks have. Whether they discussed the water temperature or what to have for tea I don't know but they all seemed very interested in the conversation and replied in such an intelligent way. Very occasionally a drake would set up an extra loud quacking but when no one took much notice he would subside and swim away to leave an arrow on the surface of the stagnant pond which would spread right across as he sped on his way. This slight disturbance would gently rock the shed feathers which floated on the pond's edge, and then very slowly the surface would return to its original mirrored reflection showing all the trees and clouds upside down with the latter speeding away without making a ripple. It intrigued me as my mum held my hand tightly to prevent any accidents as she always had a great dread of the still but deep ponds - pits we called them - that were in

Life Across the Pasture

the area and she continually warned us against going too near them.

I realised in writing the last two paragraphs I had been using words like "bustle" and "tail corn" which may not be self-explanatory, so perhaps I'd better translate. When a chicken "bustled" it settled down in a warm, dusty spot and flicked the dust up between its feathers which were all opened out. They set up quite a dust in the air as they enjoyed what was in effect a dust bath which helped rid them of mites and chicken fleas. When you saw your poultry enjoying this exercise you knew they were well fed and happy and would keep up a good egg supply. The "tail corn" was the thinnest and poorest of grains that came through the smallest riddle on the threshing drum and was collected in a sack that was hung on the "tail end" of the grain shoots. This was always used for poultry or pheasant feed being of no use for flour or pig meal.

As I progress I will try to remember to translate any Norfolk expressions, but continue to use them as I attempt to paint a picture with words and transport my readers into that world of my childhood. My one difficulty at the moment is to find the right form of words to describe the quietness. Try to imagine a world with very few artificial or man-made ear-splitting noises. There were no aeroplanes flying overhead, no tractors in the fields and no blaring ghetto-blasters from the neighbours' open windows - just natural noises that didn't jar on the eardrums: the drone of insects, the rustle of leaves, and rattle of chains on the harness of the horses as they shook flies off their skin, the call of the cow for a calf or ewe for her lamb, the birds singing or the rooks cawing as they circled around the rookery, the hiss of a plough turning a furrow on a winter's morning and the hum of the threshing drum through the still, frosty air, the cheerful whistle of the boy enjoying his work and life in general. Westley Morton, a young man from Castleacre, who worked at the farm was renowned for his whistling. His cap was worn at a jaunty angle to accentuate his happy outlook on life and everyone looked forward to meeting him. Incidentally, I tried wearing my little cap at an acute angle but it wouldn't stay on my unruly hair without me tilting my head at a funny angle thus spoiling the effect; neither could I manage to whistle despite blowing my milk teeth out before their time. There was just one discordant sound that spoiled the idyllic peace I am describing. This was Geoffrey Thaxton's attempt at yodelling. My father thought Geoff had a painful tummy causing him to make such a dreadful noise. Poor Geoff was quite rightly offended by my father's lack of understanding regarding the modern trends and Geoffrey's youthful talents. They both laughed over this many times in later years as they were always very good friends betting on the results of various football matches, with a hand-rolled cigarette as the stake. Geoff was an Arsenal man and Dad a true Norwich City canary. Another strange instance, apart from Geoff's yodelling, was the presence of an old, windowless railway carriage in the pasture running past our front gate. It was situated near the spinney with a lovely sunny aspect and, if the thick layer of chicken droppings was anything to go by, it had been used to house fowls for many years. I often wondered how it had been transported from the nearest railway to its final resting place, a journey of at least four and a half miles. Unable to run on its own wheels and too heavy to lift on to horse-drawn transport, how did it arrive? This mystery puzzles me to this day. These railway carriages popped up on the Estate in other very unlikely places such as in the middle of the huge Soigné Wood where one was used as a keeper's grain store and shelter for the guns at a wet shooting party lunch, a railway carriage mystery rivalled only by the modern occurrence of corn circles in Wiltshire.

Another memory from those early days comes back with a picture of four men walking down the path from the spinney one dull, winter's day. The procession was led by Charlie Welham, the local keeper, and he introduced his three companions as itinerant rabbit warreners who would be living next door for a while. During their stay they would dig rabbits with the help of ferrets in order to keep the pest numbers down, and would sell the rabbits to butchers and game dealers. I was quite nervous of the strangers as it was such an unusual event to see anyone apart from the tradesmen around our houses. I know my mother would have greeted Charlie Welham with a very cool grace as she had only recently accused him of shooting our pet cat which mysteriously disappeared. Charlie was an old-fashioned gamekeeper who believed in shooting any animal or bird which might be a possible danger to the game he was paid to protect. This made him very popular with his employers but alienated him from most farm workers who often rewarded his unsociable and unnecessary actions by driving their horses right up into the hedge bottoms, trampling pheasants' nests, destroying the eggs and often a sitting bird - cruel and vindictive perhaps, but there was very little love lost between the keeper and farm workmen at that time. I would hasten to add this all changed in later years when Clem Softley came to live amongst us with a very different attitude to children's pets and boys' escapades of which we shall hear later.

The tradesmen's vans were just as important at High House as they were at Rats Hall. Joplin's van delivered groceries to us, and also bumped across the pasture and parked on the grass outside often to be surrounded by a group of very curious young stock as well as by us human customers. The van was always driven by Billy Harrison, a lovely character, who made a fuss of all the youngsters on the round. In later years he took over the fish and chip shop at Castleacre and Ezra Boldero replaced him. Morris Brothers, butchers, came from Massingham, the van being manned by either the Morris brothers themselves - one was Philip, I know - or the red-faced and always cheerful Charlie Fitt Savage. Our baker was either Gayton Mills with "Jockey" Alcock at the wheel or Jack the Baker who came all the way from Pentney arriving at all times of the day or night. Beeston delivered household coal and Mr Castle came on his bicycle to collect the Prudential insurance once a fortnight.

If underfoot conditions were very bad in the depths of winter we had to trek across to the farm and wait there for the vans to arrive. This allowed for a good, long gossip with either Mrs Thaxton or more often Mrs Curl. The latter lady kept a small stock of cigarettes and sweets she sold from the door. Her son, Tom, used to borrow the odd packet of fruit jelly from the store room and divide it between any workmen at the farm. To their discredit some men encouraged this unfortunate action when they should have known better as Tom suffered from palsy which affected his physical and mental actions. It was very sad to see such a fine man reduced to a shaking wreck by the cruel illness of sleeping sickness. The community was kind to him but the situation put a great strain on his parents and family, especially as there were no supportive organisations to help in cases of health abnormalities. Up to 1938 when he joined the army, my barber was Uncle Sos who came over from Rats Hall to give me a trim when required. On one occasion his scissors just clipped the lobe of my ear causing much blood, some tears, but very little loss of life. Eyes had to be kept tight shut when he cut along my fringe and I still find myself sitting with eyes shut when the barber is working on my hair. Old habits die hard, even after almost 60 years. After Sos went off to fight for King and country I had to go over to the house of Mr Bert Chase who took control of my unruly hair. Grandfather Bumfrey, who wore his hair close-cropped like a convict, thought I must be red-hot with all that "wool" on my head. I was certainly well thatched and in sharp contrast with Dad and my uncles who went very thin on top at quite an early age. Will's barber at King's Lynn sold him all sorts of patent hair restorer which did very little good and raised much derision from my father who never worried about his hair loss. Will used to get quite wound up when this "mickey-taking" started. It was rather ironic that their father, who had a full head of hair, should choose the crew-cut style years before the Yanks brought the fashion over during the war. Rats Hall was apparently a leader in some fashions, hair styles being one, and trousers another, as Sos became the proud owner of a pair of Oxford bags. These very wide and baggy-legged trousers were apparently the "in thing" of the Thirties but again cut little ice with the locals especially my dad who made a great game of Sos's pride and joy. It would seem and it was a fact, that my father put very little faith in so-called modern progress especially in the field of fashion. He never went outside without a cap on his head and never wore a pair of shoes but always working or best boots, an old "stick in the mud" maybe, but his solid, no nonsense commonsense and ultra-basic principles, helped me get my priorities right in a world that has changed beyond recognition during my lifetime. The great thing is they are still relevant and continue to work for me today. What a wonderful rock-solid example he was; nothing ever shook him from his chosen path, however world-shattering. Maybe a slight adjustment here and there but he knew his right path and stuck to it whatever the rest of the world might say or do. It's only as I look back that I realise how right he was and that my post-National Service ideas of "change everything for the better" were far off course. Luckily these ideas were of short duration in my life and I saw some of the errors of my ways before permanent damage was done to my countryman's life- style.

Chapter 4
Out for Tea on Sunday

We had one other pet besides the ill-fated cat mentioned in the previous chapter. This pet came as a small bundle of black and tan tucked inside my father's coat as he rode his bicycle from Castleacre. It was a puppy given away to a good home and brought to High House as company for my mother during the long, lonely days of her early marriage. I think Rip, for that was his name, arrived before I did, but whichever way around it was we grew up together and he was the most faithful, devoted dog you could ever wish for. His pedigree could only be described as belonging to the Heinz 57 variety; he was a mongrel if ever there was one, thin-legged, and medium-sized with a bark far worse than his bite, although his ferocious first approach to any stranger was enough to deter undesirable callers. My pram could be safely parked under the apple tree because Mum knew that no one would dare touch it with the faithful Rip left on guard. My father always trained a dog well and Rip would walk with us anywhere remaining at heel whatever distraction might cross his path - no mad chase after a flushed rabbit unless ordered to do so and the often over-curious cattle made no impression upon him. When Mum was baking I usually made him a pastry delicacy with small offcuts and onion peelings. This offering was always eaten with relish but a sweet would be spat out every time. Perhaps he was practising for sweet rationing which came at the latter end of his life. We did everything together and the dog would sleep with one eye open as I played outside. He was never off guard, always gentle and good natured a lovely companion for an only child which I was for seven years at any rate. Rip was approaching the veteran stage before brothers Michael and Brian appeared on the scene. As he never wandered from the garden we had no need to fear the trigger-happy Charlie Welham but Rip recognised him as public enemy number one when he led the rabbit diggers to the back of our cottage and gave him an extra-aggressive barking reception until called to heel by his mistress.

An event much looked forward to was Sunday tea at Rats Hall. I am sure my grandparents, aunt and uncles were always prepared to welcome me with open arms. Grandchildren were in short supply for them at that time and I was, in somebody's famous words, "heir to the Bumfrey millions". Something special was always bought from Joplin's van on the Saturday prior to Derek coming to tea. All the cigarette cards were kept for me and after-dinner naps quickly taken before our little caravan came over the hill. After Sunday dinner (not lunch, as that meal did not exist for us then, breakfast, dinner and tea being the meals of the day), we would don our Sunday-best clothes for the outing. I would be put in the Tansad, strapped in for safety as the road could be rough, and off we would go with the faithful Rip trotting along behind. Incidentally the Tansad was our equivalent of the modern buggy, the only difference being that it had larger more serviceable wheels for use on the rougher ground. Which route we took depended on the time of year and state of the crops in certain fields which could provide a short cut.

On winter days the only option was to keep to the roads, so after negotiating the churned-up mud in the pasture gateway we would go through the farmyard, down the farm drive and join the Westacre to Massingham road. After about a mile's walk along the reasonably-metalled surface, the T-junction at the edge of Massingham Heath would come into view. We would turn left towards King's Lynn proceeding west with the large expanse of heath-land to our right and rough scrub and dead bracken partially hiding the fields to the left, and on for almost two miles, up one incline, and down the steep Norwich Hill with the isolated house and buildings on the right, as far as the Milestone. We then turned left into the Milestone gateway and along the cart-track to Rats Hall and there would be no wheeled traffic to bother us on the way, and no need to pull up on to the grass verge every three yards to avoid a motor car on the narrow road. Best boots and good walking shoes would soon cover the distance from one end of the farm to the other. Boots were made for walking in those days and nobody thought otherwise. Having traffic-free roads on Sundays made walking far more pleasurable than it is today. The walking also worked up a good appetite for the nice tea waiting in that cosy living-room at Rats Hall.

Dry, summer weather would allow us to travel by a shorter route using cart-track most of the way. At the end of the farm drive we would cross the road into Honeypot Lane which was a rough, often rutted track leading directly into the centre of Soigné Farm land. Tall hedges lined the lane with mature hedgerow-trees interspersed making the lane a shady walkway on a hot, midsummer afternoon. Skirting fields to both right and left the track finally met up with a narrow private road joining Soigné Farm with the Litcham to King's Lynn road at Long Plantation, or "Long Planton" as we pronounced it. After a short distance on this road we would make a left turning into Water Pit Lane and on to Rats Hall, descending the hill from the opposite direction to the bad weather route. You may think these journeys were irksome, dull, soul-destroying and just a foot-slogging effort designed to transport bodies from one home to another in order to eat a meal before repeating the exercise in reverse. Well you couldn't be more wrong. No journey was ever the same as the countryside was always

Out for Tea on Sunday

changing with seasonal field work filling each section with interest to the countryman's eye. From a speeding car window things all look the same, but on foot each small change could be noted and enjoyed for its own special attractions. There was the satisfaction of seeing the results of work well done with signs of hope and promise for the future: the first tiny green shoots showing up in the brown, harrowed earth of Eighteen Acres; the rooks searching out grubs and wireworms and enjoying the peace of the one day of the week with no crow-scaring boy around with a rattle or flag to send them cawing into the air; later in the year the same green shoots advancing into a sea of whispering barley heads gently waving in the breeze; the oats on Big Strawberries neatly cut and shocked to stand in very straight lines for three Sundays before being carted and stacked at the bottom right hand corner of the field. (Why the bottom right hand corner of the field you may ask - the answer is simple: all farming operations had a very definite reason, a method to their madness you might say. The first reason was that the field sloped to that corner so all the full, horse-drawn wagons were pulled with the slope helping the horses on their long harvest day; secondly, the threshed oat straw was on hand to feed cattle housed for fattening in the yards at Elbreck Barn just nearby. All this was worked out without the need for computers - you may gasp! Work was hard enough for man and horse without making it harder due to lack of forethought and common sense.) Walnuts could be picked up along the farm drive, sweet chestnuts from amongst the leaves on the heath corner, and hazel nuts from the bushes on the sunny side of the woods leading down to Grandfather's house.

Three silent, horse-drawn binders, with canvas sails covered, under the hedge in Big Elbreck waiting for Monday morning were another sign of the times. There was no work on Sundays then, with the exception of the men tending stock. All the machines were silent as horses and men enjoyed their one day of rest. After six days of hard slog they were ready for it, I can assure you. Even the cold winter days held their own fascination with the hunched outline of the threshing tackle, sheeted up and drawn in by the wheat-stacks of Little Ashbeck, and the gathering mist making the machines look even more hunched and silent and in such contrast to the vibrant working scene to come the following day with the whirring belts and the puffing steam engine providing unlimited power. A freezing wind from the north-east, perhaps carrying ice needles direct from the North Pole, blew over the heath-land and seemingly straight through the thickest coat and gloves. Huge flocks of finches fed on seeds left by the thresher during the previous week's work. My, were we ready for a warm in front of the kitchen range at both ends of our journey on days like that. Obviously the trip was much more pleasant on a warm summer's day.

Out for Tea on Sunday

One of my very first memories of being at Rats Hall was sitting out on the track leading down from the whin border and playing in the warm, silver sand washed down by the last heavy rain. It was my first experience of sand as the seaside was unknown to me at that time, and sand pits in the garden hadn't come into fashion. Grandad also had a little dog whose name was Gyp; she was a sandy-brown colour. They also had two pigeons, Sam and Lucy who lived in a nest box fixed to the front wall. Unfortunately Sam failed to return one day, probably the victim of a sporting gun. I am loath to lay this disappearance at the door of the much-maligned Charlie Welham as this area was off his beat. Pigeons were always classed as pests so any passing bird was liable to be shot at. Tea was always nice with a tin of red salmon and thin slices of bread and butter, or perhaps tinned pears with Carnation evaporated milk followed by home-made cake and numerous cups of tea. I remember Uncle John had a small, sharp-tined fork with a bone handle. I can still see it as plain as day. I used to have different preferences on each visit, and sometimes I was a salmon king and at other times the pear king. Aunt Ivy used to play along with my game. She loved children then and has always been our favourite aunt throughout all the years.

After tea, whilst it was still light, Grandad would put on his cap and pick up the water buckets. We would then go around the bullock sheds to an underground water tank that collected all the rain-water from the roofs. The buckets would be dropped in on a rope, filled and carried back to the house for washing the next day. First the copper, and then the zinc baths were filled. I enjoyed this job, gazing up at my very tall grandfather in his striped shirt and dark trousers held up with both braces and thick leather belt. We chatted away whilst the two dogs waddled behind taking in all the interesting smells, with Rip cocking his leg at regular intervals even when his bladder had long since run dry. We men had to do our chores even on Sundays and I felt very important doing such a worthwhile job. After this we would go indoors once more and Grandad would reach down his battered trilby hat in readiness for a game of "shake hat". This took in all the male members of the family who sat around the deal table in the kitchen. We would each have a supply of halfpennies, some very black and almost worn smooth, bearing the head of Queen Victoria, some not so worn showing King Edward VII or George V. Each player would place either one or two halfpennies in the hat and then take turns to shake it; after giving the coins a good jingle we turned the whole lot upside down on the table counting the number of heads showing. The player with the most coins showing heads, won the coins, whilst a tie and a second shake between the equal competitors found the winner. I loved this game especially as I was playing with money given to me by others. Towards the end of the session, and if I was winning, Grandad would suddenly pick up his hat and declare the game over despite the howls of protest from the losing participants. "The boy's getting tired", would be the reply and I would gather up my winnings as we prepared to make the journey home. Light or dark I would see very little of the return journey as I would be drowsy after all my excitement. The rabbits along the heath would freeze as we passed or a white barn owl would ghost about his nightly business and a soft sizzle of steam would breathe out of the threshing engine as the fire slowly warmed the boiler in readiness for the morrow.

All too soon Monday morning would wake the sleeping countryside. Mum would be up early to do the weekly wash and Dad would be off to work by seven, but I could slumber on as I still had no school or work to worry me for a few years to come.

One other "going out to tea" occasion I remember was to Mrs Dack after they had moved from High House down into the village. Walter Dack had become tenant of a smallholding and landlord of the Stag public house. This pub only had an outside licence which meant the beer had to be consumed standing out in all winds and weathers. It only opened on week days and in reality did very little trade. The pub didn't belong to any brewery but to the Birkbeck Estate. We took tea in the front room which was quite dark with small windows covered with thick lace curtains as they looked out on to the road. What we had for first course I do not recall but we had mandarin oranges and cream as well as cakes for afters. I know I was very shy and said very little which was to be my hallmark throughout my childhood. My shyness was a great burden to me.

Two great sadnesses were to hit the Bumfrey family around this time but were well-shielded from me. The first was in 1934 when Granny Bumfrey suffered a stroke which left her partly paralysed down one side. I always picture her sitting beside the living-room fire place. All her things were kept on a table tucked in the recess of the chimney. Ivy, who was only 16 at the time, kept the house going and looked after all the family. She had been kept at home to help her mother who was never strong enough to carry the really heavy burden of a large family. When Ivy left school at 14, Mrs Sybil Birkbeck, the Major's wife, decided she needed more help at the Hall and went to Rats Hall with the intention of ordering Alfred's daughter into domestic service, but she met with unheard of opposition to her decree as Grandad stated categorically that Ivy was staying to help her mother. Alfred was always his own man and had suffered for it during his earlier days. The second blow came in June 1935 when Stanley died from rheumatic fever at the age of 14. He had left school at the harvest holidays in 1934 and become keeper's boy under the ageing Grandfather Welham who also lived at Rats Hall. Stanley was fair haired, bright and a lively, likeable lad. This terrible loss must have blighted the lives of all the family but especially Grandad as he and Stanley were very close, and Ivy, who had to care for an invalid mother, a large family and then lose her younger brother - all this grief, miles from anywhere, and nothing but memories to take it off. I can just remember Grandad, or "Bumf" as they called him in the family, taking his candle and following Stanley to bed in what must have been quite early evening. Grandad had white potatoes in the heels of his socks as the feet disappeared upstairs. I could hardly have been two at the time but the pictures stay with me as plain as can be. Stanley was laid to rest in the churchyard at Gayton Thorpe, a tiny village about two miles over the rise towards Gayton. The church was of Saxon origin having a pretty little round tower. Granny Bumfrey was also buried there when she died just before Christmas in December 1940. That left Ivy to keep house for her father and brothers which she did splendidly for so many years at Rats Hall and then after the war at Pretoria Cottages. From leaving school, she gave her life completely for others and should be remembered for the selfless, caring lady she is.

I have just two more quick memories from Rats Hall before we get back to High House. One is a picture of a very old gentleman with white beard and brown suit. This was Geoffrey Warner who was Mrs Lydia Rye's father and lived with them. The other is of Peter the Painter who came to live next door towards the end of the 30s. Whether he painted pictures or doors I don't know, but he was a bit "way out" and must have been one of the first incomers of a more modern breed, very different to the "normal" Norfolk stock. On the lighter side I must tell the story often laughed about afterwards of when Aunt Jane was single. A certain lady nearby had been repeating or starting malicious rumours about her. Grandad, on getting wind of these stories, made sure of the source and marched up to the lady in question and took her to task, ending with the observation that, "You need a tad in your mouth, missus". On the occasion of Aunt Jane bringing her boyfriend Wilby Dye home for the first time she wanted everything to be done properly. To make sure of this she took care to school her mother and father in the pronunciation of his name. The name Wilby was rather unusual although not difficult so there shouldn't have been any trouble with it. But after the practice session nerves must have taken over turning a mole hill into a mountain. Grandad leaped forward with, "How do you do, Rubbah", whilst Granny, trying to cover the gaffe already made, came up with, "Good afternoon, Trilby". Needless to say, Jane was mortified. But it all came right in the end and true love blossomed as they married later and "Rubbah" alias "Trilby" became one of the family.

31

Out for Tea on Sunday

Times were very hard both for master and man in the 30s with the agricultural labourer coming near the bottom of the pile. Admittedly the farm worker had a job even when his manufacturing counterpart had none, but the pay was abysmally poor. Much depended on a good harvest to supply a little extra money. In those days harvest was "taken" by the men. This meant that the whole workforce undertook to get in the entire harvest for a given sum of money to be shared equally amongst them. The senior man or "Lord" oversaw the work and financial distribution. If the weather held good the harvest could be gathered, stacked and thatched in a short time, thus allowing the men to draw their normal 30 shillings per week and retain a good size lump sum at the end. If the weather was wet the operation was extended leaving very little to draw at the finish. One year, 1932 I believe, was very wet causing harvest to drag on into October by which time the men were all working for nothing and very dispirited to say the least. Piece-work was a very two-edged sword but it was used quite extensively for hoeing, harvest and sugar-beeting. Most workers preferred it as the monotonous nature of some operations was livened by the uncertainty of the system. But after the 1932 harvest few people went on Bert Eves' bus to spend their harvest bonus at Lynn. No money for little extras that year.

Around 1936/37 Alfred Lewis decided to move his farming operations to Ashill some miles away beyond Swaffham. The entire Bumfrey family was asked to go with him but they all declined, preferring to stay and work for Major H. A. Birkbeck who was taking over Soigné and High House Farms with Willy Thaxton as bailiff and Charlie Wilson as farm foreman. Charlie had previously been head team-man for Lewis and had a wide knowledge of farm cultivation and crops. I think it was at this changeover time that my father was offered and accepted the cowman's job at High House. It was all hand-milking throughout his time there although he had learned to use an early type of milking machine at Baconsthorpe many years before. Working at the Home Farm meant he'd come home to dinner every day and this helped enormously in the lonely day for my mother. Sometimes Grandfather Bumfrey would call to eat his dinner with us, and then nearly kill us with smoke from his rather foul black pipe. Mum used to open all the windows after he'd departed to rid the house of smelly shag or whatever noxious weed Alfred smoked. Poor Grandad, I remember the deep cracks that seemed to reach right down into his huge hands. These were caused by the metal crowbar he used to crow the holes for net stakes as he moved the sheep daily across the sugar-beet tops or swedes. The frosty metal caused the skin to crack open and stay all through the winter. He wore no gloves or wellington boots. Usually his thick leather boots were sodden wet from standing water in the ruts made

Out for Tea on Sunday

by tumbrils carting beet from the fields. A Protos sack made an apron and another draped his shoulders to keep out the wind and weather. A coloured neckerchief kept the wind and chaff from his neck and his cap crowned the crew cut head. A tough, labouring man, he had a soft heart for his family, and the animals he cared for. They were his first concern whatever the hardship to himself. And this concern was shown by all his sons who had the welfare of animals so often in their hands. By the way, Protos was the trade name for a rolled maize product used for cattle feed, sold in large, light hessian sacks ideal for the uses Grandad put them to. If on the way home the wind blew from behind he would reverse his "seck" to keep his ass warm - what a character, with his very broad Norfolk accent perfected during his youth spent in the area around Bodham and Baconsthorpe, just inland from Sheringham on the north Norfolk coast.

As the dark war clouds began to show over the continent of Europe several of the younger men were persuaded to join the Territorial Army or Terriers as they were known, amongst them Billy and Bob Thaxton, and Tom Abel I know for certain. My dad had been in the Terriers sometime during the 20s manning horse-drawn gun carriages as used by Kitchener's army in World War 1. Matthew Bonass from Castleacre was with him on one occasion and thought he could hitch a ride on the gun carriage but he was spotted by the Sergeant-Major who yelled, "Get off that carriage, Bonacks". He was Mathy Bonacks to his mates for the rest of his army days. Dad went to camp at Arundel and got around a bit. Of course he had long since left the Territorial Army by the time war loomed again. Only Sos was in the armed forces during World War 2 and the horrific experiences came back to haunt him at the end of his life in 1993. I have often wondered what horrors Stanley was spared as he would have been of an age to go to war if he had lived.

By 1937 my mother was thoroughly fed up with living across a pasture and, with my fifth birthday looming early in 1938, she pressed my father to apply for a house at least by the side of a hard road. When the house at number 6 Pretoria Cottages became vacant Mr Thaxton offered it to him and the end of an era was approaching. Both the Bumfreys and the Smiths prepared to leave the cottages, we to go to Pretoria and Sonny Smith to Gayton Thorpe, working as a tractor driver, a new innovation, at the Great Barn Farm, but still on the Birkbeck Estate.

We two families were the last to live across the pasture; soon the row of cottages would be demolished and the rubble used to fill the many deep ruts in cart-tracks over the Estate. The fruit trees ran wild and the only thing left standing, for some strange reason, was the little wooden structure housing the lavatory bucket. Alfred sat and ate his dinner in there one day. My mother, on hearing him mention it, was appalled but Grandad was

Out for Tea on Sunday

unmoved. "If you'd a bin out in the wind all day like me, Alla, you would have set there as well." His bread and cheese washed down with black, cold tea were not affected by his dubious surroundings. Those of my readers who have had the pleasure of reading that fine book, Brother Ox, will understand.

I believe that as we close the gate at High House we also begin to shut the pages on a period of agricultural life stretching back into the Middle Ages with very little change. From now on, change, which started very slowly, soon accelerated to speeds that overtook we players and prevented us stepping off when and if we had wished to do so.

Chapter 5
Pretoria, Here We Come

At last the day of the big move had arrived. After weeks of packing and preparation everything was ready for transportation. The crocks were wrapped in newspaper, blankets and linens tied in bundles and the mats beaten and rolled. Outside, the chickens were shut in their house whilst their run was dismantled. The coal was bagged and linen lines were taken down.

After a very early breakfast I sat by an upstairs window looking out over the pasture in order to catch the first glimpse of the promised transport coming from the farm. At about 7.30 a.m. the far gate swung open allowing two horse-drawn farm wagons with huge iron shod wheels to pass through. Our removal men were on their way in the shape of Herbert Wing and Laddie Richardson, two team-men from Soigné with their Suffolk Punch heavy horses in the shafts.

With the comfortable rattle that wagons had and the jingle of harness chains the two men drew up alongside the front gate and loading began in earnest. Furniture and bedding were carefully lifted over the sides of Herbert's conveyance with the less valuable and outside goods going with Laddie. Last but not least Rip and I were comfortably installed at the front of the first wagon and off we went on my first big step towards civilisation. Over the pasture, through the farmyard, and down the drive we travelled, the iron-shod wheels making a lovely crunching noise on the rough stone surface.

Turning onto the tarred council road the wagons pulled easily down the long slope from High House to Pretoria, first of all under a canopy of trees and then out into the open with a wood on one side and Pretoria Breck on the other. The three-quarter mile journey was soon over and the wagons turned right off the Westacre road and drew alongside the row of six tall cottages, made of yellow brick with red/brown pantile roofs. Our new home was number six at the far end of the row. After being lifted down, Rip and I went inside the single front gate set in neatly trimmed thorn hedges. This was the only hedge that had been kept in order, as the long hedges round the large garden had been allowed to grow tall and wild.

The houses seemed enormously high after the low cottages we had just left. For agricultural houses these were very modern boasting high ceilings upstairs and down, as well as large windows letting plenty of light into good-sized rooms. The front door, with one step up, led into a tiny hall containing three other doors, front room to the right, living- room to the

Pretoria, Here We Come

left and a large cupboard under the stairs directly in front.

The back door, which faced due north, led into a scullery-cum-kitchen. A long walk-in pantry completed the ground floor with three bedrooms leading off a landing up above. The main bedroom faced south, looking out over the road and fields, whilst the two others had windows to the west over the garden.

Two more blocks of houses further up the hill consisted of semi-detached properties making ten houses in all at Pretoria. It seems that the first six cottages were built around the turn of the century hence the name having connections with South Africa and the Boer War. The other four were completed later near the commencement of World War 1. These were constructed in Fletton-type brick, again with red pantile roofs. All in all it was a lovely setting with deep woods rising away from the bottom of the hill, south-facing with a narrow belt of fir trees behind to help break the cold north wind. The road running up past the houses led to Soigné Farm about half a mile further on. A drinking-water pump at the bottom of the row was fed directly from the Hall and a red letter box on a wooden post completed our services. The same tradesmen's vans called on us as before and the weekly bus service to Lynn passed the corner on Tuesdays.

But the big difference was the mere fact of being on the roadside in a much brighter and more open environment. Clean shoes would stay clean for going out and there were neighbours to speak to over the hedge. My mother was thrilled with the new surroundings. My dad, like all the male side of the Bumfrey family, was perfectly happy tucked away in the back woods; both High House and Rats Hall suited them down to the ground.

Our house was very light inside due mainly to the pastel-coloured doors and other paint work. The previous tenant was Reggie Baxter, a painter of doors for certain this time, who worked on the Estate. These pinks, whites and creams were a big contrast to the dark browns usually used for Estate dwellings. The large windows had wide sills ideally suited for potted flowers. But as my mother had no inclination in that direction there was no light restriction there. No need for lace curtains either, for none of the main windows was overlooked. Only the scullery and pantry windows had half lace curtains. Roller blinds were pulled down at night to keep the draught out and retain the heat in rather a large living-room. My Granny Eke was appalled at the lack of geraniums in the window but her daughter was not to be moved on the subject and the light had free access into our indoor lives both from the front and side of the main living-room.

The residents at Pretoria Cottages were all employed in varying capacities on the Estate and farm. Number 1 housed George Wright the head gardener at the Hall, Nelly his wife, along with schoolboy son Georgie. Next door was Jimmy Reynolds, an Estate woodsman, his wife and two working sons; the eldest, Harry, was an apprentice carpenter with a Swaffham firm, and Roger, who had just left school to work on the Estate. At Number 3 lived Mann the butler also at the Hall, his wife and two small daughters, Ann and Gillian. Both he and the head gardener were considered to be higher-class servants and were certainly viewed as "Mr" Wright and "Mr" Mann by us of the so-called lower orders. The fourth house was home to a younger man and his wife; Lawrence was an under-groom at the Hall and had no family at that time.

Next door to us at number 5 were George and Sheila Hall; also in that family was Hazel, a young daughter, and George's elderly parents. George was very tall and energetic being the lord or senior ganger at Soigné, and also stacker, and efficient rough carpenter. He kept rabbits, chickens and bees in his garden and really had ambition to better himself which he eventually did by moving up into Leicestershire at the end of the war. He was blind in one eye, this reputed to have been caused by his brother wielding a table fork during youthful over-exuberance. I always had visions of the fork being thin-tined and sharp like the one used by Uncle John Bumfrey.

Passing us at number 6 we move up the hill to the end of our long garden and the first of the four additional houses, number 7. Here lived a gamekeeper, and surprise, surprise, it was Mum's sparring partner, Charlie Welham, his wife and son George. There was not much neighbourly chat along the top fence I can say for certain.

The eighth cottage was home to Diddie Frost and his wife. Diddie was a jockey-sized groom employed by Colonel Carlyon at Soigné Farm House which was let privately since the exit of Alfred Lewis to Ashill. Another childless couple, Walter Wilson and partner, had possession of number 9. Walter, or Blustrous as he was nicknamed, did the milking and pig feeding at Soigné. He was short in stature and rather short in temper, a man to treat with caution if the wind happened to blow the wrong way. He was, I believe, Charlie Wilson's Uncle.

The top house, which was number 10, was home to Frank Clarke along with his wife who suffered badly from asthma which eventually claimed her life at quite an early age, and one son, Bob. Frank was the first mechanic on the Estate working with the early tractors which were appearing on the farms for the first time. He travelled on his bicycle with a box of tools strapped to the carrier and it was a few years before he became equipped with a little van.

From these very insignificant beginnings Frank was to become the most crucial tradesman on the farm as mechanisation quickly took over from horse power, especially when the Second World War demanded a big increase in home food production. The first tractors I can recall were all designed to work in the fields without travelling on the road at all. They had large metal wheels at the back equipped with metal spuds which sank into the earth giving increased grip and pulling power. The front wheels were smaller and solid metal in construction. The engine started on petrol by means of a handle in the front, switching to tractor vaporising oil, or TVO, when the engine warmed up. The driver's seat was of metal on a primitive spring system and was made slightly more comfortable by lining it with a couple of thick corn sacks. The operator was exposed to all winds and weather as well as all the dust and mud thrown up by the spud wheels, especially when wartime shortages meant the tractors were manufactured without a full rear mudguard.

Mum and I went for a walk one day up towards Soigné, with the north wind turning our pallid cheeks to fire within a few minutes. Peeping through the gappy hedge of Middle Thirty Acres I saw my first working tractors ploughing the old stubble. Bob Thaxton and Artie Keeley were driving a couple of blue Case tractors and Geoff Thaxton, of yodelling fame, had one of the tubby Standard Fordsons painted in a bright orange. Their trailer ploughs turned two furrows at a time working up and down the field, keeping a very straight furrow, which was very important to the critical eye of the foreman and fellow workers. The ground was ploughed in lands which meant that a strip of some thirty yards would be set out and then ploughed around to allow ample turning room on the ends. This system was continued until the field was almost complete. The headlands, about ten yards all around, were ploughed last. The air above the ploughmen was white with seagulls, screaming in their search for worms and grubs, turned up by the shiny plough shares and mould boards. In lesser numbers the black-feathered rooks also worked away, but with much less noise.

To my amazement the machine drivers were walking alongside their charges swinging their arms and stamping their frozen feet. This was all made possible because one pair of the tractor wheels ran in the furrow made on the previous trip and so after being steered into it, at the end, the steering front wheel was held in a straight line. Just before the machine reached the other end the driver would jump on and prepare to lift the plough out of work by pulling a rope tied from the plough to the tractor seat. Then, as the implement lifted itself clear of the ground, the tractor was guided along to a return furrow and off they would go again slowly back and away into the distance. This jumping on and off routine was only carried out when the weather was so very cold and would have been frowned upon by the Health and Safety Officer had there been such a person in those far-off days.

There was always a shout and a cheery wave for the shy little boy peeping through the hedge. The heavy tractors worked very well in the cold, dry weather, just as long as the frost didn't harden the ground too much. In wet conditions they often got stuck, especially the little Fordson whose very fat body gave little clearance underneath, and only needed a sudden wet patch to become grounded. These problems meant that the horse still remained the main source of power on the farm. The three or four team-men would still be employed in ploughing much of the land with their single- furrow horse ploughs, and on occasions they were called upon to finish off land where the more cumbersome tractors couldn't turn. Not one of the men so used to horses would even consider the possibility of tractors completely replacing their beloved animals. Every breakdown, which heralded the coming of Frank Clarke on his bike, would bring that slow shake of the head, and helped them keep their job secure in their minds. But within a decade those same stables would be empty apart from one, and used to store artificial manure brought in from the factory at Lynn. No one, not even the enlightened Frank Clarke, could foresee the biggest change agriculture had ever experienced as the tractor replaced the horse on the Soigné Farm.

Looking back, one can compare it with the replacement of the steam railway engine by diesel locomotives. Tractors were more effective, but the beauty, companionship and peace had left the countryside forever. And those of us who are fortunate enough to remember the before and after, still treasure the memories of those wonderful, faithful creatures, our friends the heavy horses. If my memory serves me correctly, Herbert Wing, John Bumfrey and Laddie Richardson were team-men at the time, with Uncle Will taking over a team when Herbert Wing moved up into the Shires. Incidentally "the Shires" was a Norfolkman's expression for any county outside Norfolk and Suffolk. At Herbert's departure Uncle John Bumfrey became head team-man for the war years until he too became a tractor driver when most of the horses were sold off about 1947.

What lovely names those horses had - Gypsy, Violet, Punch and Prince, Todd and poor old Stumpy whose tail had been cruelly docked, thus preventing him from swishing the flies off his body during the summer. A great variety of colours, sizes and characters made up the teams, some were very skittish, whilst others, like Stumpy, had only a one speed plod although most of them could up at least an extra gear when travelling homewards at leaving off time.

Returning to number 6 Pretoria Cottages we will take a look outside. This house had a brick-built shed with a bucket-toilet attached, all with a pantiled roof and concrete floors. This was a definite upgrade from the usual dirt floor found in most rural sheds. There was a stable-type door on the shed, and believe it or not the lavatory had a porch where the martins flew in to nest each year.

A large lilac tree in front of the shed added class to the building and partially hid the bunches of shallots and dried rabbit skins that usually adorned the front of our sheds. Behind the shed block rose up a huge Malabella plum tree known locally to us as a dilberry tree. Three types of this very sweet early plum grew from the one inter-grown trunk. First came a very dark red one almost like a black cherry, then a brighter red one of slightly larger size and finally a yellow, very juicy fruit but in much less quantity. We ate all we could and gave bags of them away every year as it cropped heavily without fail. The hens in their run underneath ran after any fallers pecking them to pieces. Not so lucky with the Bramley Seedling cooking apple which overhung their run on the other side. These big apples would often fall with a dull thump landing on the back of some unsuspecting hen sending her flapping across the run complaining profusely. This kind of situation could have inspired the story of the world falling down on poor Chicken Licken in the fairy story often read to me in my younger days.

The remaining fruit trees consisted of a Doctor Harvey apple, which gave a dry cotton-woolly kind of fruit, three damson trees, and a Victoria plum. In addition, there were four summer apples which gave some welcome shade and the wasps a feed, but which were of very little use otherwise.

The large garden provided plenty of room for vegetable growing and long paths for boys to play on. Sometimes I imagined I was Bert Pitcher, the roadman, with wheelbarrow and broom. I remember one occasion when Bert was proceeding at a regimental Norfolk County Council pace up the garden pushing his barrow with broom handle stuck up in the air. A roar of anguish from behind increased my speed one hundred fold as I realised my dirty broom handle had trailed all along my mother's hand-washed, white bed linen on the washing line. Bert Pitcher never sped so fast in his life to take cover at the top of the garden until the storm had subsided. It was always safe to return after a given time though as corporal punishment was only administered at the time of the crime when tempers were hot, and then only by my mother. We got more shouts than hits. On one occasion my dad unwisely observed that Mrs Wright, down at the bottom, would be able to hear my mother shouting. This effort to pour oil on troubled water only fuelled the fire and Dad received a verbal ear-bashing for his pains and hastily withdrew into his shed, keeping any further advice to himself.

We were taught to treat all neighbours with respect. All the men were addressed as Mr, and all the wives as Mrs. Only our contemporaries were spoken to by Christian name alone. Blood relations or relations by marriage were the only Aunts and Uncles. Both my dad's father and my mum's father were grandads, their respective wives were grannies. These kind of courtesies were so instilled into my thinking that I always addressed the head gardener as Mr Wright and the bailiff as Mr Thaxton until I left the Estate at the age of 26. My mother also used this form of address to all her neighbours and never, as far as I can remember, used their Christian name.

The man next door, George Hall, was a bee-keeper having a row of hives raised along the sunny side of the belt of trees on the garden's north side. These bees certainly helped to pollinate our fruit trees, as well as peas and beans. My father was not a bee lover and didn't particularly enjoy their presence, especially in summer when they decided to follow a young queen from the hive and set off in a swarm. I remember Granny Hall following one swarm, banging a large door key on a metal shovel. This was reputed to make the queen bee settle, and then the whole swarm of bees would gather on top, to form a football-sized mass of live bees on a tree branch. The last I saw of the bees was a black cloud rising up over the wood and disappearing, with the key and shovel still ringing out to no avail. When the bees settled near at hand Mr Hall would come home, don his hat with veil, gloves and thick jacket, calm the seething ball of bees with his smoking blow lamp, and ease them into a box ready for transfer into another hive. All the time my dad would be muttering under his breath about those blasted bees. None of us ever got stung, as far as I can remember, so why he was so anti-bee-keeping I have no idea. Maybe he just didn't like honey.

Not long after our arrival at Pretoria, Charlie Welham moved away. He had become very disgruntled when Fred Welham succeeded to the head keeper's position on the death of Grandfather Welham from Rats Hall. Fred lived in the village and I believe he had been landlord at the Stag before returning to gamekeeping. This seems to have caused friction in the Welham family which never seemed to heal. Presumably Walter Dack from High House took over the licence of the Stag when Fred Welham became head keeper.

The new keeper at Pretoria was Clem Softley. Clem was a good keeper and felt he could carry out his duties without alienating his neighbours. It must be remembered that most gamekeepers lived in very isolated houses and had no one living nearby. Mrs Softley was a nice, homely person but with a very unusual name, Wilhelmina. Us local boys called her Minitonk between ourselves, but without any malice. She was Clem's second wife and had helped him raise a family of children after the death of their own mother. This family was by then grown up and married so the Softleys were just Darby and Joan. Mum and Mrs Softley had a gap in the tall hedge at the top of the garden where they could exchange all the news, until the chill wind, so often with us in Norfolk, forced them to return to their respective warm kitchens. We note here that none of our neighbours was ever invited inside the house to gossip, or we to enter theirs. All exchange of news was done over or through the garden fence. A saying I've often heard my Grandfather Eke repeat was, "Good fences make good neighbours".

Once again my dad grew all his own vegetables on the garden. Great store was made of being self-sufficient. It was always a very special Sunday tea when Dad brought in the first radishes, lettuce and spring onions. He would cut the lettuce so fine with a very thin, sharp knife that he always used. The first pea pods were popped secretly, and after the sweet, green contents were eaten, the shells would be hidden under the potato tops. I am sure my dad knew I had been to the pea row for a taster because I expect he had been through all this when he was a boy. How delicious were those first Aran Pilot potatoes, their skins just rubbed off and gently boiled, those runner beans picked fresh from their hiding places between the large leaves, and those ripe, juicy plums right at the top of the tree which were jerked off with the help of the long clothes prop - and we could never catch them as they bounced from branch to branch on the way down. The dust and grit added when they bounced on the garden seemed to enhance the taste. Even when the ripest side had been attacked by a wasp it was still very edible. The bitten section was just spat out before the rest of the plum disappeared down red lane. Too many plums consumed at the start of the season often meant an upset tummy or acid spots on the skin, but the risk was always worth taking.

One last farming memory from those early Pretoria days was formulated in the harvest field. Mum, Rip and I had walked along the green lane leading eventually to the village of East Walton some three miles on. The Twenty Four Acres alongside the track was being cut by three horse-drawn binders. They made a lovely picture with their neat little sails gently pushing the barley back on to the canvas from where it was carried up to the tying mechanism. When the sheaf had been tied, a fork-like hand turned over and flung the sheaf on to the floor. Each binder had a four-foot cut and was pulled by two horses. As the standing corn was receding towards the centre of the field, rabbits trapped in its cover began to appear and run towards the safety of the hedge. Some were caught and killed by the men working in the field, but most escaped. Rip would be shaking with anticipation but was held back for fear of him getting injured by the machines. Finally, the last narrow strip was cut and the three machines drawn by the sweating horses came slowly back to rest in the shade of some huge trees in the corner of the field. Several dead rabbits were stretched out on the now still canvas waiting to be shared amongst the men involved in other aspects of harvest. A rabbit for the pot was a very welcome bonus at that time.

A gang of men was already working steadily around the outside of the field setting up the sheaves into shocks in order to keep them dry should rain come before carting. That was the last time I remember seeing horse-drawn binders working on Soigné Farm. At the time I wasn't to know the occasion was the end of another era, the end of horse power in its original sense. Larger machines pulled by tractors and taking a six- or eight-foot cut now came into use, speeding the operation. Though not so picturesque, perhaps this change saved the horses from very heavy work. The power to work all moving parts on a binder came from the slow turning of a large land wheel set in the centre of the machine. This drag, plus the weight of a man and machine, made a workload almost too much for the horses, which had to be changed at regular intervals during the long day.

When the tractor became the workhorse, a new power system came into use. This consisted of a turning shaft from the engine which fairly rattled the mechanism round whether stationary or moving. The wider cuts taken and the faster speeds travelled enabled more corn to be cut with much less effort. The only minus count for the farmer was the fact that two men were needed for the operation as opposed to one originally but this did not stop the rapid rise of that early mechanisation.

This peaceful rural picture was soon to be shattered not just by the increased noise of the internal combustion engine but by the effects of two outside events which were looming like dark clouds on my horizon. The first which affected me to a lesser degree than my older companions was the war. The second event was much more frightening and gave me a sick feeling of acute apprehension. That event was entering into the village school scheduled to take place after the Easter holidays in 1938.

Chapter 6
Off to School

One of the first jobs undertaken by my dad after we moved to Pretoria was to attack the unsightly hedges surrounding most of the main garden. Reggie Baxter may have left the inside of the house in good condition but what marks he gained as a decorator he most certainly lost as a gardener. As my father detested any form of DIY perhaps he wasn't too displeased with the way things had worked out. The large overgrown hedge saplings were soon cut down with the help of a long-handled hedging hook, known as his "slasher". Once the rough stuff and long trailing brambles had been cleared away he could train and lay a substantial hedge, a fence of the correct height and width to be kept tidy with garden shears and provide a sturdy barrier between himself and his neighbours, keeping our animals in and their stock out, be it two or four-legged varieties.

Remember once again the aforementioned maxim about good fences making good neighbours; I can't remember Dad falling out with any of his. Only the bees, which had no respect for fences, caused slight friction.

What lovely bonfires we had in the centre of the garden. I loved watching the sparks and smoke flying up into the sky. The only thing we had to be careful of was the wireless line which ran from a very high pole tied to an apple tree across the garden and down the wall to connect up with our large battery-powered wireless set. This line gave us a good reception picking up the BBC and Radio Luxembourg. One extra-high flaming bonfire had to be doused with water to prevent the line being burnt through. My mother thought him mad for trying to put out his fire after working so hard to get it going. In those days we could have bonfires with garden rubbish as long as the smoke didn't go towards any of the other houses. Sometimes they were banked up for days in order to get rid of green matter of which there was no shortage as we worked to clear the garden of the ravages of nature, caused by a few years' neglect. Rip and I were always actively involved in all these operations and I can vividly remember working away with my rake and wheelbarrow on the Sunday evening before I had to go to school on the morrow. "If only I could go on with this tomorrow", I thought, but that was my last day of complete freedom in term time at any rate.

The only thing I can remember about my first day at school was returning home with a bilious-type headache. I suffered these attacks on the first day of every term throughout my early school days and on some of the later ones as well. My nerves were so knotted up and tense every

44

Off to School

time. Mr Thaxton picked us youngsters up in his car on the way to take Ted and June to school. This was very kind of him and helped us little ones until we were old enough to cycle. I can still recall the registration number, CBY 22, but the make escapes me. It had very saggy seats and I believed it once belonged to Major Birkbeck. Rip may not have known the make or number, but as soon as that car rounded the bend near Shortrow Pit he would rush from his vantage point, barking loudly, and get to the gate to greet me home. No other vehicle, with the exception of the butcher's van, had this galvanising effect upon him. My, was I glad to see him as I certainly didn't like school.

The headmistress was Mrs Ayres, and the infant-teacher Miss Wiskerd. The latter had spent a great many years teaching there, cycling from the neighbouring village of Castleacre, where she lived with and cared for her elderly mother. She had taught Aunt Ivy when she went to school and was even reputed to have taught Mr Wright, the head gardener, when he was there. On this evidence she must have been well past retiring age and it couldn't have been much fun teaching young children all day on top of her cycling and domestic commitments.

At any rate, being shut up in a small room with high windows all day was like prison to me, and I learned nothing from her. I am sure she thought I was in some way mentally retarded. My nerves wouldn't even let me tie my shoe laces properly and Miss Everard, the school cleaner, used to help me with them sometimes. We played with dirty old plasticine, beads on wire, and could only use pencils and not ink. On cold days Minnie Wiskerd would stand with her back to the big metal fireguard and warm her behind with dress lifted up at the back. How we wished a spark would fly out and send her hopping round the room. Any lack of understanding would result in a few hard raps across the fingers with a pencil or ruler. Sometimes the head would become a makeshift drum kit and a rapid rat-tat-tat would be played on it. My friend, Gerald Andrews from Soigné, took a lot of stick like this. I know we were a bit thick but really it was fear that prevented us from learning.

Soon after my schooling began Mrs Ayres left the school house and Mrs Clark took over the reins. She had four children of her own and was a much more progressive person. Small in stature, but large in character and discipline, she ran a school which I came to enjoy when I eventually moved up to her class.

Whilst still with the infants we played in a small gravel-surfaced playground, divided from the seniors by a six-foot high wall. The girls' toilet was in our playground, and the boys' lavatory on the other side of the wall. All the food we had was brought from home and was of course cold. I believe on very cold days some of the senior girls were detailed to

45

make Horlicks for us. Otherwise we had little bottles of cold, fresh milk, sealed by cardboard seals, with a push-through section in the middle for our straws. Free Horlicks tablets were distributed as part of an advertising idea, I presume. Sometimes our balls would roll on to Mrs Ayres' vegetable garden and we would have to creep up to retrieve them before Mr Ayres, who was a semi-invalid, looked out and shouted at us to get off, but Mrs Clark was more understanding.

One morning Miss Wiskerd had not arrived, so we infants were left in the charge of two senior girls, with the door left open so that Mrs Clark could detect any horseplay that might begin. News filtered through later on in the morning to the effect that Miss Wiskerd had fallen from her bike whilst crossing the wooden bridge over the River Nar, ending up in the water. Severely shaken but otherwise uninjured, she had been taken home. A silent cheer went up from twenty silent throats and prayers were offered up in the hope that she would never be brave enough to mount her cycle again. But unfortunately for us Minnie was made of sterner stuff and she returned after a few days' rest, though we enjoyed our little holiday and felt we had learned something - it is an ill wind which blows nobody any good.

1938 soon slid into 1939, and the news coming out of our wireless set became more grave by the day. Of course I knew nothing about Neville Chamberlain's visit to Munich to bring back "peace in our time". The lovely, hot, harvest days of 1939 were there to be enjoyed. Grandad Eke, now retired from the hot railway workshop and on ten shillings per week pension, came over for a month's holiday. He took me and Rip up into the harvest fields, armed with a stick and picnic tea. I don't think the stick ever hit the back of a rabbit, but we used to try. Grandad would run behind, sometimes losing his panama hat in the process. If a rabbit took cover under a sheaf he would fall on it and catch it that way. After such violent contact with the ground he would carefully brush himself down in a most fastidious manner for Walter Eke was always most particular about his appearance. We had to take a bottle of water and a container for Rip as his tongue would be hanging out with excitement before we had hardly entered the field. Grandad was very deaf and always called Rip, Nip, and Mr Thaxton, Mr Claxton, but nevertheless we had lots of fun that summer.

Sunday, September 3rd was another warm day, with a clear blue sky. We had been digging up potatoes and throwing them in rows to dry. My father and Grandad Eke stood outside the open window listening to the fateful words that we were at war with Germany. Having experienced the previous World War to end all wars, their faces told me that something very serious was about to happen. Uncle Sos was already in the Tank Corps, and Uncle Alfie, my mother's youngest brother, was soon to follow suit. They both fought through the North African desert and Italy surviving many battles and returning to us at the end of the war, their bodies intact, but their minds irretrievably scarred from what they had seen.

Changes soon took place around us; by the time we returned to school the next week all our window panes were crossed with brown, sticky paper to prevent glass flying to injure us should a bomb drop nearby. We were soon to be taught how to use gas masks and had to carry them in their little cardboard containers wherever we went. A couple of years later this little cardboard container was to prove my downfall when it caught between my leg and bicycle handlebar, throwing me unceremoniously on to the road. Landing face first, my two rather-protruding front teeth were considerably loosened, with much blood flowing down the front of me. Was I the first civilian casualty of the war in Westacre? At any rate, the incident caused one of those two teeth to die always remaining a dull, off-white colour. Those two large, front teeth were a continuous embarrassing burden to me throughout my early life and did little to help me in overcoming my shyness at school and elsewhere.

While on the subject of teeth, I am reminded of the annual visit by the school dentist. This dreaded person arrived with a white, mobile surgery, which parked on the grass just below the school. By most of the pupils it was viewed with the same horror as a mobile gas chamber might be in occupied Europe; it certainly wasn't regarded as a giant step forward in the health of young children, as it was designed to be. The examination was a trauma in itself, with the probing hook and tiny mirror causing me to attempt to shrink right back into myself. All defects in the molar system were duly noted and a report sent home to our parents seeking permission to carry out all sorts of imagined torture.

The dreaded call came next day when each tiny victim left the classroom with leaden steps to walk down to the van. As each body returned ashen-faced and clutching a blood-stained handkerchief, the tension grew amongst the remaining classmates. The few lucky people with no fillings or extractions lived on cloud nine for the whole day. But for we others, who neither watched our sweet intake or bothered to clean our teeth regularly, this was judgement day. When my turn came my legs would hardly carry me to the van. Stiff with tension all the way through, it's a wonder my heart kept going. Faint and groggy, I would stagger up the path and into school once more to be tended by my seconds as if I had been wounded in a duel. Why was it that my teeth were bigger than everyone else's, and always bled more profusely and for longer?

After these early experiences with a dentist, using the word loosely, I have always been terrified of the dreaded chair and allowed my teeth to fall into awful decay before seeking treatment. The fear of this annual torture added yet another burden of worry to my early school days, giving my head an easy excuse to develop a sick headache as all of my small molehills turned into mountains of worry.

But some relief was on the way, as the dark, overriding figure of Miss Wiskerd was replaced by a much brighter picture in the form of Mrs Clark, the new headmistress. I am sure it wasn't my academic excellence that gained me an escape from the dreaded infants' room. Perhaps Mrs Clark took pity on me, or Minnie Wiskerd despaired of ever teaching me anything, but on one never-to-be-forgotten day I was given a desk at the lower end of the big room. This was in every way different from the little room. The sun shone in through the tall windows on three sides; the ceiling was high, with light-coloured beams and electric lights on long chains hanging down. A large, open fire in the centre of one wall was surrounded by a heavy, metal fireguard; Mrs Clark's desk stood to the left of it, with the door to the infants' room on the right. Front and back doors flanked these in the far corners, but by far the greatest difference for me was the teacher with whom I jelled straight away and began to blossom at last. She soon convinced me I could learn things and wasn't as dim as I had convinced myself. Learning became a pleasure, though never easy, but once I could read, things opened up and that door has never closed, although nervousness over new things has remained to this day and always held me back.

The very first thing I remember my new teacher showing me was how to make a perfect figure 2; I can see it now, a wonderful row of Zs right across my book. Gently, my stiff wrist was persuaded to form a nice curly 2, and from then on a team was formed and I set off on the road to become the first boy from the village school to win a place at a grammar school. I often think what a beneficial effect her choosing to live and work in Westacre had on my future life. Mrs Clark was a born teacher and did the job, not for the monetary reward, but for the joy of seeing youngsters achieve their full potential in life. On the girls' side, Eileen Softley also went to grammar school in the same year as I did, so the local educational standard became very good during the war years, but we mustn't rush on too quickly or we will miss many enjoyable and some not so enjoyable experiences of school days at Westacre.

Returning just for a moment to the subject of teeth, but this time to the cleaning thereof, the makers of Gibbs toothpaste sponsored a competition to encourage we children to clean our teeth regularly. I've no idea what the reward was, but we all entered the fray. Each entrant received a card covering the seven days of the week, extending to twelve weeks in all. Our parents were asked to tick twice a day if the cleaning operation took place morning and night. The card had to be checked at school each Monday, and, if the required fourteen ticks had been registered, a red sticker would be placed at the bottom. Gibbs toothpaste came in a round, flat tin and was pink in colour and quite hard in texture. The toothbrush had to be wetted, rubbed over the paste surface until some paste came on to the bristles, and then cleaning began. Twice every day my brush worked away until the Saturday and Sunday of the tenth week when it suddenly went on strike and the cleaning stopped. My mother refused to tick my card, so I did it myself. After a severe lecture about cheating had been administered to my eardrums, she put in four crosses with a thick pencil. I protested loudly that every other parent in the school had allowed their offspring to cheat; perhaps that was a bit more than a slight exaggeration, but my plea fell on deaf ears. I diligently cleaned my teeth for the last two weeks, but at the end I received no prize. That lesson was well learned by yours truly and has kept the Englishman's sense of fair play in the forefront of my life. That learning has been far more valuable to me than any of Gibbs' prizes would have been.

As I have previously mentioned, very few people in Westacre owned a car, with the exception of those who lived in the big houses. Mr Thaxton, the bailiff, was one, the other being the Reverend Ainsworth, the rector. A third vehicle was a maroon-coloured Austin 7, with a soft hood, known by all as "the flying flea". This was at first driven by Hubert Watts, I believe, but I know Dick "Fluffy-cat" Welham owned it for years afterwards. The rest of the community either walked or rode their bicycles. The majority fell into the second category, the Bumfrey family at number 6 included.

At the age of six, it was high time I mastered the art of cycling. A little black machine was purchased for me and on the traffic-free road I went. My dad ran up and down, holding the seat and helping me to balance, but I didn't improve. My concentration wandered to anything except the art of balance. As I pedalled back towards Pretoria, I noticed and remarked upon the chimney on Mrs Wright's wash-house. At this, my puffing parent gave vent to a string of harsh words, promptly gave up my tuition, and left me pushing the bike home. On reporting back, a very red-faced dad was told by his spouse that he had no patience for teaching children. This was grossly unfair, but as Dad had no breath left to retaliate, my rather shorter-tempered mother won the day on a technical knockout. Left to my own devices, I just sat on the carrier with feet dangling and soon learned to balance round the garden path, and so it was that I was ready to join the group of older children who cycled to school.

By this time Mr Thaxton was ready to relinquish his taxi job, although we were eternally grateful for his help in those early days. Rip still continued to bark at his car, even though there were no children to greet from school. June and Ted Thaxton came down from High House,

Off to School

accompanied for a time by Brian Chase who left school soon afterwards; Gerald Andrews and Mavis Welham came from Soigné to join up with Bob Clarke, Georgie Wright, Hazel Hall, Ann Mann and myself. The elder children were quite good, taking care of us tiddlers. The only danger really was the steep Tumbler Hill leading down into the village. Motor traffic, even at the beginning of the war, was almost non-existent on that road. If a vehicle did appear then there was ample time to stop by the bank until it had passed. As we became braver, great speeds were achieved down the hill and competition was fierce as to who would freewheel the farthest from a given point at the crown of the hill. Pedalling beyond this point was banned but twisting of the front wheel in the last vital feet was allowed. How much precious tread was worn off doing this I dread to think. But there, many a trusty bike tyre showed its canvas lining in these times of wartime shortages. We leaned down low over the handlebars to make better streamlining and kept our noses just clear of the front wheel; caps were pulled well down and scarves tucked in. On wet days our legs were well-splashed and sometimes a missing rear mudguard resulted in a muddy line up the middle of someone's coat, especially if sugar-beet carting had brought half the field on to the road as liquid mud. That was all part of the joy of cycling and being able to cut through the air at speeds approaching Mach 2 at least.

Once you owned a bike you never walked anywhere. I rode from the shed to the gate, with Rip hastily backing into the potatoes to avoid serious injury to his spindly legs. My dad was once heard to remark that it was a wonder we didn't bike up to bed. At school our machines were all stored in a long, dark shed, named appropriately the bike shed. They were parked any-old-how with pedals through spokes, no-one worried about scratched paint as many had more rust than paint. Coddie Eagle and Charlie Lop Andrews used to cycle into Swaffham market on Saturdays to sell or exchange one machine and ride home on the new and sometimes better model. On one occasion this theory came to grief when Gerald's new machine broke in half on his way to school first day out. We laughed but Dilbury, as he was nicknamed, was not amused, and his dad's bike-buying prowess was placed in severe doubt. My father never went in for this pastime but bought good bikes and kept them in good repair at all times. We enjoyed waiting to see what kind of machine Dilbury would arrive on after each weekend.

Just one last story of my good friend Dilbury and his bikes. One morning we stood outside waiting for the Soigné contingent of Gerald, Mavis and Bob to ride with us, They hove into sight, rounding the bend at the top of Pretoria Hill, and rode down quite fast to our cottages. Bob and Mavis pulled up beside us, but Dilbury continued past at high speed,

Off to School

yelling out that his brakes had failed. He shot over the bottom road, and careered over the grass verge to brake sharply (excuse the pun) in the middle of a thick holly bush. We raced down to discover the extent of the damage and help drag a badly-scratched mate from the dense bushes. After inspecting himself for missing limbs and kicking the offending machine a few times he set off with us to school, vowing never to allow his old man the chance to buy and sell a bike at Swaffham again. On hearing the tale, his dad shook with laughter as any mishap with a bike in those days was always treated as a huge joke. No one ever saw any danger, and somehow our heads survived without the protection of helmets. Perhaps we were naturally thicker in the skull.

Arriving at school with scratched knees and oily hands from broken cycle chains was par for the course. While this went unnoticed, Ma Clark threw a wobbly at the sight of any fingers stained brown from walnut skins, and even resorted to caning the offending digits on one occasion. What strange creatures schoolmistresses were; didn't anyone tell them at College that boys will be boys and walnuts were an essential part of a schoolboy's diet, especially in war time. Nuts and sour apples had to be scrumped whatever the penalty incurred. The cane used was a thin, hazel stick and Mrs Clark could wield it very efficiently for such a small lady.

As a small boy I had an aversion to hair brushes. If I could possibly avoid contact with one I did. Whilst waiting for our Soigné colleagues to join us in the cycle convoy outside the front gate my mother would suddenly fire the question, "Have you brushed your hair?" I would tentatively nod to the affirmative, but I was never a very good liar. Off would come my cap and a thick mop of unbrushed hair would be revealed. Back indoors I had to go, under the grinning gaze of my contemporaries, in order to rectify my lapse in personal grooming. If the second inspection didn't come up to standard my parent would seize the brush and almost take my ears off in a vain attempt to bring a semblance of order to those unruly locks. On would go the cap and off we would go amid the sympathetic mutterings of other anti-hair-brushing members of my gang. Looking back I realise that our dress sense was non-existent; in fact the desire to look as scruffy as possible was a dominant feature of our young lives. The Just William look was our fashion model and the threat of clothes rationing was yet another boon to our cause. It wasn't that we really copied William Brown, but the fact that William was us, a typical small boy of the early forties portrayed so well by his author.

Chapter 7
Westacre - the Village

Having written six chapters I feel it is high time I took you down into Westacre village. We have beaten the parish bounds by visiting Rats Hall and High House which are on the northern boundaries. The nearest we got to the village proper was the school on the northern edge of the community and separated from its neighbours by the Castleacre to King's Lynn road.

Westacre is one of three villages in the Nar valley bearing the suffix "acre", namely Castleacre, Westacre and Southacre. I have listed them in order of size with the first being much the larger. The first two still boast ruins of religious buildings in the form of Castleacre Priory, and Westacre Abbey. A well-preserved arch stands alongside Westacre church, straddling the road down to the Abbey farmhouse. The pretty little Norman church has an unusual clock in that the hour numbers have been replaced by the twelve letters in the words "watch and pray". The clock chimed out its hours over the houses clustered round the green and could be heard plainly by all who lived in the village as its layout was very compact, being almost square and contained within three roads and the river.

The Nar was a quiet, meandering stream with water-meadows on either side before the ground rose away quite steeply after about a mile to the north and to the south. This gave any traveller a wonderful view of the settlement nestling below with the silver thread of the river glistening through the trees. The narrow roads through the village were rather sunken, almost like those of north Norfolk, and quite unusual in our part of the county. Most of the houses which made up the tied homes of agricultural workers were of brick, or flint and brick, with red pantile roofs. A very few were thatched.

The one building which stood out was the "wooden hut". This quaint wooden house stood adjacent to the central T-junction right in the village centre. The second storey jutted out over the ground floor making a wonderful nesting site for house-martins who had stuck their mud structures to the boards for countless generations. Various elderly people had lived there. The last I remember was Horrie Everard who said he wouldn't move out, and that it was handy for him to be carried to the church when he passed away.

The Stag was the only public house and that had only an outside licence. Horrie Everard and little Davey Howard used to stand under the shelter of Walter Dack's cart-shed to consume their pints even in the coldest weather - no fear of warm beer being served on these freezing winter nights. At times, Davey's teeth were reputed to have chattered on the edge of the glass while consuming his drink.

The church, already mentioned, stood on slightly-raised ground, with steps up to the front path and yew trees on either side. The churchyard spread round three sides and sheep fed off the grass during the summer. The other place of worship was the Methodist chapel on the western side of the village, opposite the cricket pitch, near to the river. There were some very strong Methodist people in the village, the Wilsons and the Blys to the fore and the Misses Everard sisters also I believe. Westacre village was part of the Westacre High House Estate, lock, stock and barrel. The land, houses, pub and church came under the jurisdiction of the squire, who was then Major H.A. Birkbeck. It was he who chose the rector as he provided the living. The school was Church of England and the cricket pitch was on the Abbey Farm land.

The Estate itself took in the villages of East Walton and Gayton Thorpe as well as all the land around and between. We didn't think this at all strange or irksome in any way - I was born to it and was part of it. Not until many years later did the tied house or the lack of choice in work become like a chain that rubbed my neck. Then it was no fault of the Estate, only my itchy feet that sought greener grass and pastures new after National Service.

There were some interesting characters in our community as well as unusual nicknames. Davey Howard was only about five feet tall, if that even. He lived by himself and worked on the farm at Soigné cycling up with Horrie Everard. At harvest time he would be loading the wagons with sheaves. One dinner time Davey decided to slide down the front of the wagon. Well before his short legs landed on the shafts, the seat of his trousers caught on two hooks designed to hold chains for a driver's seat. The unfortunate Davey was left suspended between heaven and earth until two of his laughing workmates hauled him up and off the offending hooks. The thick trousers worn then were plenty strong enough to hold the tiny man without tearing.

Another man of interest was Stumpy Baxter, or Miller, the mole catcher -we were never quite sure what his surname was. He had lost a leg in the Great War and made do with a straight wooden leg. Somehow he bent down to set the mole traps by pushing the wooden leg out behind him. I can see him now swinging along. I believe he also rode a bike with a fixed wheel mechanism to keep the pedals turning in order to bring his own leg up to the top.

Nicknames were rife and stuck like glue. As well as Charlie "Lop" Andrews and Dick "Fluffy" Welham, already mentioned, there were

Westacre – the Village

"Bigun" Sculpher the postman, "Stacks Battersby", John "Pont" Softley the foreman at Abbey Farm, Old and Young "Laddie" Richardson, as well as "Coddie" Eagle and "Diddie" Frost. Some of these names were used in place of Christian names, whilst others were only used outside the owner's hearing.

One of the latter type was the one referring to the rather large nasal organ belonging to our postman. My mate, Gerald Andrews, could be quite cheeky at times, but on one occasion he quickly got back as good as he gave. Cycling to school one morning we met Freddie Sculpher the postman. Up piped Gerald, "Good morning, Mr Big Nose". The reply came faster than a rapier thrust, "Good morning to you Gerald Loplugs". On receiving such a slapping rejoinder, the lugs in question turned bright red and we taunted him with Gerald Loplugs for the rest of the journey.

Freddy Sculpher was the village barrack-room lawyer. Being the only independent worker on the Estate, he kept an eagle eye on the public rights of way and on all actions the Estate might take which could be considered by him to be detrimental to the villagers. This didn't make him over-popular with the Estate hierarchy as there were some who loved to curry favour in the eyes of the squire. Not that I think Major Birkbeck cared much for them as he always seemed to be a very fair man. But I do believe that lone voices like Fred's helped to keep a reasonable balance in local affairs. In later years my mother's voice often joined, and eventually replaced, that of Fred Sculpher, taking up causes such as school transport and local bus service needs. She was a lady who cared nothing for Estate etiquette or the cap-touching mentality of many tied cottage dwellers. Born into a much freer environment at Briston, where everyone tended to live and think as an independent person, she never failed to say what she thought. This early form of free spirit rubbed off on me and caused me some grief in my life, as I sought to defend a principle against overwhelming odds, refusing to be beaten down whatever the cost.

The post office and tiny shop sat opposite the wooden hut and was an essential part of village life. Sally Sculpher, Fred's wife, ran it with the help of her daughter, Stella. A big, red 'phone box sat outside with the post box in the wall. What a funny smell the 'phone box always had when we heaved open the heavy door to peep at the instrument that we had no idea how to use.

On the other side of the green lived Nurse Battersby, a district nurse of strong Irish descent. Although not appearing to be in the top drawer where hygiene was concerned, she travelled the dark roads to deliver babies in all weathers, sometimes wading through snow drifts feet deep. Later she had a little car, her white terrier travelling everywhere with her. She became quite well-known in our house as she came in April 1940 and April

1941 to attend to my mother when brothers Michael and Brian were born. Granny Eke came to stay on both occasions, so we were well cared for.

The only occasion when I needed the nurse personally was after a stone fight at school when fighting ceased abruptly as I fell almost mortally wounded. A flint stone smashed into my chin, cutting it badly and felling me like a stunned ox. The nurse cleaned the wound, stemmed the bleeding and made a marvellous job of bandaging me. My mother nearly had a fit when I came home with the snow-white bandage round my very painful jaw. I believe it was the last big stone fight in that playground. I realise how lucky I was not to have lost an eye instead of just suffering a sore chin. Incidentally, I still carry the scar to this day.

Billy Plummer deserves a mention as he had a special tie with the past. By the time I knew him he was an elderly man, rather bent, with no apparent attributes towards sporting prowess. But even then he was a pillar of strength in the bowls club which was well-supported for such a small village. But Billy's real claim to fame was that he was the last surviving ex-cricketer who had bowled under-arm and was reputed to have been very successful during his long career, shades of W.G. Grace, but without the stature or the beard.

Bob Oxborough lived with his wife and daughter, Blanche, in a bungalow near the river bridge on the exit road to Swaffham. Bob was a bullock feeder in the winter months, spending his days at Tumbler Hill sheds alongside the path trod by the Rats Hall children as they walked to school in years gone by. Bob worked on the Abbey Farm and was very slow of gait and had the complexion of a man who died yesterday, he was so pale, a man who kept himself to himself. His home looked to be no more than a row of garden sheds, it was so low and so narrow, but I suppose the Oxborough family was comfortable there.

One day Bob was returning home, down past the house of Fred Welham, the head keeper, with his dinner bag on his shoulder. Coming up behind in the car, Mr Thaxton, the bailiff, noticed the tail feathers of a cock pheasant sticking out of a hole in the dinner bag. Fearing the loss of a good bullock feeder should Fred Welham spot the feathers, Willie Thaxton hastily stopped and suggested to Bob that if he must risk his job by poaching pheasants, then perhaps he could remove the long, tail feathers before concealing one in his bag. With this advice, the bailiff drove away leaving Bob open-mouthed with shock after hastily jamming the offending feathers out of sight. There is no doubt that had the head keeper spotted Bob with the pheasant he would have lost his job immediately and with it his tied cottage. There was no bigger crime on the Estate than taking a pheasant. I imagine the murder of a fellow worker would have been viewed more leniently than poaching, but nothing more was said, thanks to the quick thinking and kind heart of Mr Thaxton; the shock of discovery would have been enough to put Bob back on the road to obey the strict Estate code of conduct regarding game birds. So it would appear, the deathly-pale complexion of all the Oxborough family was not due to lack of good food, although many laughingly said that the eating of too many pheasants caused deafness. Pardon, I didn't quite hear what you said.

That story is told exactly as it was passed on to me and I have no need to doubt its authenticity as it fits the characters so well. It helps to show the family feeling within the farming community, where any failings were corrected with words, and dismissal, or sacking as it was called, became a very rare occurrence anywhere on the Estate. Employment was there for life as the army of part-time pensioners proved even in the post-war years. All school leavers were found places in the pattern of things if they wished to apply. Most boys joined the work forces of Abbey Farm, Warren Farm or Soigné. Very few took outside jobs until after the war, when change began to accelerate and personal transport became more common. The Hall, Abbey House, Warren and Soigné Farm houses still employed domestic help, taken up mainly by village girls, whilst the Land Army offered an alternative to this in the form of farm work. Quite a few healthy young women joined the ranks on local farms, much to the embarrassment of the foremen who had never experienced female labour before. The younger male workers enjoyed this new order, and at least one mixed horse-hoeing crew found life on a haystack preferable to hoeing sugar-beet rows. When Charlie Wilson dismounted from his bike to find the horse tied to the hedge and the two young people missing, he lifted his trilby hat, scratched his bald head, kicked up the dust with a size 12 boot and yelled, "Let's be having you, my fellahs". A very red-faced youth leapt up from the hay, to be quickly followed by a partially-dressed female. With a gruff, "Get on with your work", Charles remounted his bike feeling even more embarrassed than the two ardent lovebirds.

Charles was a local Methodist preacher and unused to this kind of wanton behaviour amongst his staff. When relaying this report to Willie Thaxton, his superior, he was very uncomfortable, but Willie, with a broader mind and a family of six, took it in his stride as a sign of the times. Needless to say, Charlie made sure that those two employees never worked alone together again. He wanted to avoid any smell of scandal on his patch and, happily for all concerned, none arose from this incident, although the young man, who shall remain nameless, became the local Casanova from that moment on as the tale swept round the farm, losing nothing with successive telling.

Another problem that arose from this new era of unisex labour was the question of toilet facilities. The custom adopted by men working in the

Westacre – the Village

fields miles from any proper toilet was to turn towards the hedge and urinate there, making sure not to face into the wind which would result in wet boots and legs. If one's bowels needed relieving, a walk into the woods with a handful of dock leaves as toilet-paper would suffice. Crude perhaps, but that was the way every workman managed away from home in those days. It seems only the foreman himself was worried about the situation, as men and women soon forgot any embarrassment and took their toilet strolls in opposite directions, and no one abused the other's limited privacy. So Charlie Wilson's worst nightmares were never realised and the farms became brighter and more cheerful places as the new, mixed workforce strove to grow more food, so vital to the war effort.

And so back to the village in wartime. The church bell was silent, and no longer did the five minute-bell call the laggards to church. Spencer Bly and his brother, Jack, were regular attenders; they were the Church of England half of the Bly family. Their sister, Edith, and younger brother, Joe, were staunch Methodists. How this split came about I don't know but would dearly love to find out. Another church regular was Edgar Coe, who sang in a very deep, bass voice, whilst Spencer rang out as a tenor I think - anyway, you could always hear him above all else. Edgar's sons had pumped the organ for a while, but my friend, Dilbury, took over the wooden handle and pumped the bellows from the side of the organ, whilst Jean Plummer sat on the stool and played as loudly as Dilbury's pumping would allow. If the organ boy should by chance nod off in the sermon, no sound would come out for the closing hymn. This could very well happen as the heat and fumes coming up from the fire beneath the open gratings down the middle of the church could have a brain-dulling effect. Whether Jean kept a long prodder at hand to wake him up I do not know. A brilliant cartoon picture springs to mind of yelling organ boy being jabbed into frantic action by a very irate lady organist.

Talking of Edgar Coe brings to mind his near-tragic accident of a few years before. Edgar and his wife lived in a row of cottages opposite the church and had a family of boys. Whilst they were engaged in a rowdy game one dark evening, a jacket pocket caught the corner of the table, overturning the lamp. Paraffin and flames spread everywhere and Edgar was badly burned in preventing the house catching fire. A long period of treatment was required before he could return to normal life. An even more tragic accident happened around the middle of the war when one of our school girls, Margaret Eagle, set fire to her nightdress with a candle. Although her father bravely put the flames out, the little girl died later from the resulting burns and shock. These pre-electric light tragedies were all too frequent, and danger stalked every time a candle or lamp was lit.

My contact with the village was very limited, except for school, and

Westacre – the Village

later my paper delivery service at Pretoria. The papers had to be collected from the post office daily. This was quite easy on school days, but more of a bind on Saturdays and in the holidays when a special three-mile round trip had to be made. My delivery charge was two old pennies per house, making a weekly total of one shilling and sixpence as I had to deliver my own paper free. The two houses I approached with fear and trembling were number 10, where the Clarkes had a big, brown dog that barked fiercely, and number 3, where a much sharper, white terrier belonging to Mrs. Mann made me scamper back into Mrs Reynolds' garden until the coast was clear. I felt like claiming danger money from these two. I don't think Prince, the brown dog, was dangerous to pedestrians, but he had a nasty habit of pursuing cyclists down the hill and snapping at their legs. My mate, Dilbury, tried to beat him off with his bicycle pump on one occasion, but only succeeded in bending the pump beyond repair, not one of his better ideas, but as will have been gathered by now, Gerald had no luck with bikes or anything remotely connected with them. Old Prince led a charmed life when pursuing wheeled vehicles down that hill. On one occasion, he was run over by one wheel of Charlie Wilson's horse-drawn trap but suffered no ill effects, and had several narrow escapes while chasing motor cars, which began to increase slightly in number despite severe petrol rationing for non-essential vehicles.

One Boxing Day morning a football match was arranged on the pasture in front of Pont Softley's house at Abbey Farm. No one had proper boots or kit, but wore long trousers and hob-nailed boots. Freddie Sculpher, by then well into his fifties, was giving us his version of a Stanley Matthews wing-play exhibition when Coddie Eagle came across as a defender and cut Freddie down so that he hit the floor with earth-shattering force and almost cut a furrow with his nose as he slid along the grass. By the time "Bigun" had recovered his feet and breath Coddie had adjourned to the far side of the field, well clear of our postman's strong language and clenched fist. We boys thought the incident highly amusing as we surveyed the mighty fallen. That fall took all the shine out of Freddie's performance as he tried to relive past glory when Westacre won a soccer cup in the halcyon days of the mid-thirties. Sadly, the football club was never resurrected after the war, whereas the cricket club only missed one post-war season and was always very popular with team members and spectators. Maybe it was because the football pitch had been ploughed up as part of the war effort and kept in arable cropping after the hostilities ceased. Another Westacre stalwart was Mr Wilson senior, father of Charles, Eva, Bertie and Jack. This man, though well into his eighties, had never slept outside the village and was very proud of the fact. How ironic that at the end of his long life he should be taken into Swaffham Cottage Hospital where he died the next day.

The village hall, or reading room, was a wooden construction, black of course, put up after the First World War, and used for all social functions, of which there were many, especially fund-raising war efforts. A games room with billiard table was at one end; the kitchen facility was in a small building separated from the hall by the front path. Many a rousing concert or dance was compèred by Walter Williamson or Joe Bly, drawing both young and old to join in the family fun. My parents very rarely attended, but I went down with my mates and we enjoyed ourselves fooling around both inside and outside the hall. The dust raised from the foot-stamping dances was quite considerable, whilst the coke stove sent out a good heat on most occasions.

The major event of the year was the church fête. This was held in turn at Abbey house, Warren Farm house, and High House Hall. The gardens were lovely, with neatly-cut box hedges, and I can smell the scent of the huge cedar tree at the Hall even now as I write, over fifty years on. Mark the treasure, highest darts' score, bowling for a pig, skittles, to name but a few, were games on which to use your money. Bowling for the pig was always the favourite attraction, with the prize penned away in the corner, wondering where his fellow piglets had gone to. I once scored a modest thirteen to take the lead early on and had to watch for at least three hours as the whole of Westacre tried to beat me, but no one did, and I became the proud owner of a little pig, although I had no idea what to do with it. As we had no pigsty, Joe Bly suggested to my mother that we auction it off; this was agreed and I finished up with cash instead of a little squeaking, pink pig. So I had been the centre of attraction for an afternoon and enjoyed it very much, although all the tension caused me to have, you guessed it, a sick headache.

Billy Plummer always sold the threepenny entrance tickets sitting at a folding card table by the side gate. Only certain ladies took charge of the tea urn. These were jealously-guarded positions and no one dared to usurp them for fear of upsetting the delicate balance of the local fête hierarchy. On one occasion at the Warren Farm, Mrs Gooch had requested her chauffeur, Ellis, to help with the aforementioned tea urn in some way. For some reason an argument broke out and Mr Ellis burst out of the kitchen muttering words not fit to print. Anyway, even after Mrs Gooch, the lady of the house, attempted to pour oil on troubled waters, the irate Ellis could not be persuaded to re-enter the kitchen and the "damned" women were left to struggle with their even more "damned" tea urn. I thought the whole scene hilarious, but after a short interlude the whole thing simmered down and cups of tea were produced. Just a storm in a teacup you might say, but a storm whose memory has far outlived those involved in it. Poor

Westacre – the Village

Mrs Gooch had no idea of the hornets' nest she was stirring up when she sent the unsuspecting man into such a closed order as the tea-makers' union. We didn't need paid popular figures to help draw the crowds when so much excitement was forthcoming free of charge.

Chapter 8
Work - at Home and Away

I was born into a world of work. It was the word that dominated our lives because we were workers, born and bred for it, kept and paid for it, and no good if we couldn't carry it out. In pre-war days there was no place for poorer people if they couldn't work. That had been the pattern of life for hundreds of years and it had hardly changed by 1939. The only place for the majority of spent, workforce material was the local workhouse where somehow or another the very last ounces of work were squeezed out of tired and worn bodies. It is not of Dickens' times that I write, but of the world into which I was born. But I don't write this of the Westacre Estate. Certainly pensioners were expected to do some useful work, but no one lost their home when too old or too ill to work. Somehow a roof was kept over their heads, though not always up to modern standards. The Estate offered a rough kind of safety-net for the weak in the days when social security was only a dream in the minds of progressive socialists.

Both husband and wife rose in the morning early to start work, and only stopped when it was too dark or they were too tired to do any more. It was inbred, and to be called a good worker was the highest accolade one could be given by one's fellow men. Each family member had specific chores to do and no one thought otherwise, and woe betide the slacker, for scorn was poured upon his head and corporal punishment applied to the other end, helping the workshy to conform quite rapidly.

Before the cut-off date of 1939, most work-practice kept to a set pattern whether on the farm or in the home. One such pattern was the chalk line between men's and women's work. Wage-earning for the married couple was the man's job, coupled with all duties outside the house, with the one exception of caring for the domestic fowls. The complete range of household chores, coupled with the care of the children, was handled by the wife and any older children if they existed. No self-respecting man ever lifted a teapot or laid a table, or if he did no one would be told about it. My dad worked from 7 o'clock in the morning until midday, then, after one hour for lunch, worked on to finish at 4 o'clock. This he did for six days, but on Sunday he managed to knock off an hour earlier in the morning. He was a cowman at High House and the job was continuous for seven days a week. One week's holiday a year was his only break. In the lighter summer months he went back at 6 p.m. to do three hours' overtime, either hoeing root crops, or nettle- or thistle-cutting in the rough pastures. As soon as he came home in the afternoon he would drink a cup of tea before collecting his spade from the shed in order to dig the vegetable garden whilst the daylight lasted in the spring. Only the gathering dusk would drive him in to tea. Quite often on moonlight nights he would saw wood for the fire before settling in his upright armchair to listen to radio programmes such as "Monday Night at Eight" or "In Town Tonight". After so many hours outside carrying out heavy manual work most of the time, his head would soon nod and the wireless would continue to play to itself, as Mum would be snoring on the other side of the fire. In fact, even in later years she often had to have a little nap to gain enough strength to get up to bed. This became a standing joke between us, but as Mum always rose first this was quite understandable. If my mother hadn't yelled up the stairs half a dozen times every morning it is very doubtful if Fred Bumfrey would have ever made the 7 a.m. deadline. To see and hear him coughing his heart up over an eighth of an inch of hand-rolled fag every morning was enough to put me off smoking forever. And it did, as I have never tasted a cigarette in my whole life. That is something I can thank my dad for. Neither did my brother Michael take up the habit, which was very unusual in an age when every male smoked and it was thought that no man was complete without a cigarette stuck in the corner of his mouth. Despite almost dying every morning, my father stuck to the habit and always insisted that smoking was his only tiny piece of joy in life. I never attempted to discover this joy and never felt deprived in any way by not having joined in. But despite his claim of not having much enjoyment in his life, he was the most contented man I have ever met and never complained of his lot, in my hearing at least.

As already stated, my mother's day started first, and also took in the seven full days of the week. In the days before I started school, her week's work was carried out in a very strict pattern which was followed by all the wives on the Estate - Monday was wash day, and very early the fire had to be lit under the copper which was bricked into the corner of the scullery. The fire-box was long and low with an open ash-pit at floor level. The cast-iron copper was covered by a round, wooden lid with a handle on the top. Once the rain water, which had been poured in overnight, started to boil, washing of linen began in earnest - hot and cold water were mixed in a zinc bath on the pine table top and, with the aid of a bar of yellow washing soap, the white sheets and pillowcases were rubbed and scrubbed until clean. Then vests, pants and all underclothes went through the same water, with the shirts and other coloureds coming last. The whites were then transferred into the boiling copper and pushed down with a wooden copper stick, which in some households doubled up during the rest of the week as an instrument of corporal punishment. The air quickly filled with a steamy, soapy smell as the suds bubbled out of the sides of the loose-fitting lid. After a considerable boiling time, the steaming sheets were lifted from the cauldron by means of the said copper stick and dropped into a bath of cold, usually hard, water to rinse. This rinsing was followed by a second one, with the water containing a few squeezes from the blue bag to enhance the already snow-white colour, the blue squares made by Messrs Reckitts being placed in a muslin bag prior to squeezing in the final rinsing water. The underclothes, shirts and coloureds followed the precious white linen through the rinsing process to be followed, last of all, by Dad's milk- and dung-splashed overalls. Note - there were no water changes, but in each stage the precious liquid was used as economically as possible.

The complete wash was now ready for the mangle. This machine squeezed as much water as possible from the clothes to assist with drying. The sheets were first of all passed between the two large, wooden rollers - great care being taken to hold the sheet clear of any dirty objects during its passage from front to back. This operation often needed a contortionist to operate the mangle as one hand turned the handle attached to a large wheel and cogs, a second hand kept the dripping sheet straight at the front, and somehow a third needed to catch it at the back. This was where an extra pair of small hands came in handy! The surplus water gushed out into a tray on the front and then down a spout into the zinc bath beneath. Great care had to be exercised over the fingers as very energetic cranking, coupled with over-zealous concentration at the back, could result in the guiding hand at the front finishing up between the rollers. This happened to my Aunt Ivy at Rats Hall, and she nursed badly-blackened fingernails for weeks afterwards. This mangling job was one I enjoyed, especially when I became old enough to operate the wheel.

Off then to the clothes-line, taking care to dry the hands for fear of chapping from the cold, north-east wind that often tore through the shelter belt at the back, making the fir trees roar and bend alarmingly. First wipe the line, then hang the sheets like huge, billowing sails, attaching them to the line with gipsy-type, handmade, wooden pegs. These pegs were bought at the door from travelling gipsy ladies who called from time to time. I still have some in my peg bag that came to me via my mother and I value them greatly. In with the clothes prop, and up with the line as high as possible. How those clothes jumped and flapped up there in the wind! Very occasionally one garment broke free to land on the muddy garden, and had to go back for a re-wash. Even more rarely, complete disaster struck with either the line breaking, or the linen post snapping off. On occasions like this, the master of the house spent a very uncomfortable dinner time as the secure state of washing lines and posts came down very firmly on the side of the man's responsibility - a complete wash in the mud could cause a spouse to remain in a mood for days on end.

Work – at Home and Away

Back inside the house again to finish off the job by soaking the baking tins in the warm copper water, some of which was used to scrub down the brick floor. The waste water all had to be carried out in buckets and shot on the muck-hole - note the reference to water conservation during the operations - not only had all the water to be carried in, but afterwards there was a job to get it all out again. No taps, sinks or drains then! Mangle rollers were dried by passing a dry towel through them a few times and the bath wiped out and hung on the wall outside. By the time the dry washing had been folded into the wickerwork linen- basket, meals prepared and cleared, Monday's time had been well and truly taken care of. Monday was probably the hardest day for the lady of the house, but the following ones were certainly no half-day holidays, I can tell you - I feel quite worn out writing my way through all the hand-washing, let alone actually doing it!

The large sheets had to be folded neatly in readiness for Tuesday, which was ironing day. Sometimes I was called upon to hold one end of the sheet, with Mum on the other. One fold, then a second, and finally a good strong pull to get some of the creases out . Often the sharp tug on the other end would jerk my slight frame forward or whip the ends out of my semi-feeble grasp. The ironing was done with a thick cloth on the large, pine-topped, living-room table. The two flat-irons had previously been placed on the range top to heat, then these triangular shaped pieces of heavy metal were used alternately in a shiny metal shield keeping any black particles away from the clothes. If the linen had over-dried, Mum would lightly sprinkle it with clean water, which would help to get the creases out. I was highly amused at this apparent lunatic of a parent who spent one day drying washing only to wet it again the next. Actions of adults were very difficult to understand at times! The smell of hot iron on clothes was very homely, especially when the weather was foul outside. Granny Eke used an ironing-box instead of flat-irons. This consisted of a heavy, metal box with a handle on the top. Even heavier, metal triangular blocks were heated in the fire until they were red hot, then transferred by means of tongs to the box through a sliding door at the back. Granny's ham-like arms propelled this hot box over her clothes with a clank every time her iron changed direction. I doubt if my mother's stick-like arms of those days would have been strong enough to push the ironing-box around. After ironing, the clothes were hung on a wooden frame, known as a clothes-horse, to finish airing round the fire. If the sun was hot, then outside the horse would go. When not in use the frame folded flat, being designed with hessian hinges which enabled the three wings to fold in any direction. Often, when not in use for airing, the frame was used to make a tent for any number of varied games.

Wednesday was reserved for bedrooms when the slip-mats were taken down to the garden to be shaken vigorously. A soft brush and dustpan collected the white blanket-dust from under the beds. A stiff hand-brush sent dust flying from the stair carpet, as a brightly-coloured, apron-covered posterior worked slowly backwards down the stairs. Much settled dust had to be taken up from the furniture by a duster, which was then shaken from the upstairs windows at regular intervals. Of course, in springtime the curtains had to come down and the lines were full of washing on Wednesday as well.

Every day the slops were emptied from the bedrooms - this entailed emptying the chamber-pots from under each bed, rinsing them with clean water and returning them in readiness for any weak bladder on the next night. These chamber-pots were very necessary as the only toilet available was half-way up the garden - not a trip to be taken in the middle of a wet or frosty night! The white, slop pail, with an enamel lid, was a standard utensil in all country cottages, certainly in Westacre.

Thursday saw the living-room get the full treatment. If I wasn't at school I stayed in bed until most of the hard work was done. After cleaning and blackleading the grate, Mum would take up the strips of coconut matting, hauling them out on to the line, and proceed to beat the dust out of them with a stick - thwack, thwack I could hear as the long nut stick did its work. What a way to get rid of all the impurities from one's system - I wonder who those matting strips were in Mum's mind as she belaboured them (I bet Charlie Welham flinched if he passed by!). Then came the sound of scrubbing as the brick floor was cleaned. This took place after all the dry dust had been swept up. This dust slowly sifted through the open matting during the week. I always covered up my head during the scrubbing as the sound of coarse bristles on brick made my flesh creep. The mat that held the most dust was the large, home-made hearth-rug pegged with cloth pieces into a hessian back. Clouds of dust flew as this wonderful, warm friend was put through its paces in the yard. The front room would only need a light dust round, because front rooms were never lived in and were used more for laying out cooking apples on sheets of newspaper than entertaining guests. The only other downstairs room was the scullery, but this was left until the week's work had been completed and was then scrubbed out on Saturday, as its Monday scrub would have been by then lost.

Friday was traditionally baking day. First the fire had to be lit under the wall-oven, sited on the opposite corner to the copper in the scullery. These wall-ovens, especially when the metal became thin, were very temperamental, and much depended on the direction of the wind - an easterly gale could give you burnt offerings, whilst a breeze from the south left your fruit cake white on one side and black on the other! Right!

Work – at Home and Away

Fingers crossed, and away we go, with the oven well-heated and ready for pastry, which would consist of sausage rolls, apple tart and man-sized shortcakes, with next week's dinner bags in mind - then some small buns and a fruit cake, as the oven cooled slowly. Mum produced some good, home-made baking, despite the vagaries of the old oven. The cakes, when cooled, were stored in deep tins which still displayed assorted biscuits on the few patches of paper left on the sides. The containers were then placed in the cool of the brick-floored pantry where they kept the food fresh, just so long as the lids were replaced tightly. Our own eggs were always used for cooking, although in winter, when the hens laid fewer eggs, they would be taken from the large crock in the larder where they were stored in water-glass - this special liquid sealed the shells and kept the eggs edible for months. The crock was filled with any surplus eggs in the summer months of plenty for use in leaner days of winter.

Saturday was odd-job day when often the pantry and scullery floors were scrubbed, as well as the long strip of concrete by the back door. Windows, of course, were cleaned with their individual rooms. Deal-topped tables also saw and felt the scrubbing brush and were pure white as a result. In later days we had a wipe-down, oil cloth on them which saved some work. The fender in the living-room was of stainless steel - an emery cloth was used to clean that, along with Brasso. A tin of Zebo blackened the stove. Ashes, cleaned from the stoves daily, were either sprinkled on the path or in the hens' run in a vain attempt to dry up the mud. As frost came out of the paths, great lumps of ash adhered to our boots, and much scraping on the metal bar provided by the back door was needed before attempting to wipe the rest off on the strategically placed sack on the step. It's no wonder there was always plenty of dust under that coconut matting, as dropped mud from boots dried out.

My allocated tasks early in my school days were as follows: to chop enough sticks for the week using dead twigs and thin sticks collected in faggots by my father - on one occasion a rough-ended piece flew up from my hook and hit me clean in my eye. Fast reflexes must have caused me to close my eye before the missile struck, so no damage, except for a black eye, was sustained. The second job was to clean out the chickens and lay fresh straw - the golden, barley straw was always there in a sack for me to use. The soiled straw and droppings went on to the muck-hole. A third task was to remove and replace the wheat-straw in Rip's bed in the corner of the shed. He slept in a wooden, box-like structure to keep his straw in place and help warm him on cold winter nights. Our dogs always slept in there, never in the house. Of course, their coats thicken up as the nights get colder and they take no harm as long as they're kept dry and draught-free. When Waggs, Rip's replacement, came on the scene, she would hide away when bed-changing time came and you would know her straw had been soiled. It did smell sometimes, and the reason for this periodic bed-wetting was never discovered. Rip would never let his bed be soiled as he was scrupulously clean in all departments - a yearly bath was all he needed, and this took place in the summer when we could take him up to the park where a good run in the sun soon dried his short coat.

Slightly later I had a big, white, pet rabbit which lived in a wire-fronted hutch situated on the sunny end of the shed. He was always placed on the flat top of his house whilst his soiled straw was removed - at first I feared that he would jump down and run away, but I soon learned that a rabbit won't jump downwards, so there was no danger there. A large sack, secured at the top with two bricks, could be dropped down over the wire when the weather was cold. There was always plenty of green stuff in the garden to feed him, and this was augmented by hogweed and clover pulled from the road sides in summer. A special treat came in the form of a sugar-beet in the autumn, when odd beet could be found by the roadside, having escaped from under the net of a lorry transporting them to the factory in King's Lynn. These red lorries belonged to Somerfeld & Thomas, and came daily, carting the farm crop to be processed into sugar, so vital in our fight for survival in those desperate days of war.

I was allocated a small piece of garden away at the top under the cooking apple tree, and here I attempted to grow my vegetables. Quite why my efforts had to be hidden so far away on such an unproductive patch, I'm not sure; in a large garden it does seem strange, but perhaps it sums up my lowly position in the important world of vegetable production! At any rate, very few vegetable seeds grew into anything remotely edible, but I kept trying until one year my reward came in the form of a larger plot, which got more sunshine, though was still partially under a tree.

A self-imposed Saturday task sprang from my gardening efforts when, in the late autumn, I took my barrow into the Hall drive to rake up and collect wet, fallen leaves from the roadside - these leaves were then composted in a vain attempt to provide manure for my next year's crop. Even with my compost dug into each trench, the effect of the tree drawing goodness from surrounding soil was too great for my tiny plants, and the result was no better. Perhaps the apple crop was enhanced. I don't know, but at any rate I enjoyed my leaf-carting, so all wasn't lost!

My most exciting and enjoyable time was when I worked with my dad. Often in September we would go off into the wood to collect up a load of fallen branches and small, dead trees in readiness for carting home to replenish the wood-stack, and subsequently for winter fuel. It would take us about three evenings to amass sufficient timber to fill the wagon that

Work – at Home and Away

Dad borrowed from the farm. We would beaver away, using saw and axe to render the fallen timber into liftable lengths for transportation. All these lengths would be carried or dragged to the wood edge, where the wagon could pull up alongside. Next evening would see us riding our bikes to Soigné to collect the horse-wagon. Uncle John would have kept one, quiet mare back from being turned out at leaving-off time and have her hitched up ready. Parking our bikes under the cart-shed, we would mount the wagon and set off for Pretoria, with Dad driving, using long reins from the wagon-front. Into the Squires field gate we would rattle and up the side of the wood with the westering sun lighting up the changing colours of early autumn and turning the barley stubble to gold. We were lucky in having the double-summertime, extra daylight after tea, which we made full use of. Pulling the wagon alongside our timber-stack, Dad would tie the horse to a handy nut-bush and loading would begin. While the mare pulled and ate all the leaves within reach, we heaved and struggled to get all our wood on board. Then, turning our heads towards home, Dad would lead on back to Pretoria. On arrival, the wagon would be pulled as close to the road fence as possible, and the wood thrown over to be stood on end round an apple tree the following evening. Mum would make us a drink before we set off once more up in the wagon to return our charge to the farm.

The old mare would almost trip over her big feet as she headed homewards, and begin to neigh loudly as she came within earshot of her fellow workers enjoying their after-work freedom in the pasture. After parking the wagon, we would unharness the horse and turn her out to graze in the pasture next to Charlie Andrews' house. Off she would go to the middle of the field, and there get down to roll on her back, with dinner-plate sized feet flying in the air with the last rays of the evening sunshine sparkling on her shining, metal shoes. How those horses loved to get rid of their harness and run free on the grass! After a few cheery words with Charlie Andrews, we would re-mount our bikes and speed home for a quick wash and then bed.

Those wonderful times with my dad lit up my life like beacons, and taught me the enjoyment to be gleaned from simple country ways and, even if they were work, could be themselves a very enjoyable form of leisure. I've often thought how awful life must be for those who don't enjoy work - neither of my parents were afraid of work, and had a wonderful knack of turning many tedious tasks into a form of game which was enjoyable to both them and me.

The hour my dad gained by finishing early at the farm on Sunday mornings was never wasted by sitting around. Mostly it was spent at his wood-stack, sawing his lengths of wood into logs for the fire. His sawing-horse was set up and the chosen length laid across it. Now this is where I came into the picture from quite an early age - using a long, two-handled cross-cut saw, we would commence, with him on the main handle end and me on the other . Each pulled the saw in their direction allowing the arm to rest on the return draw. The logs had to be roughly nine inches long - shorter was okay, but longer lengths were out, owing to the limited space in the range grate. After a short time my thin arm would begin to ache and a second hand was needed to take up the strain - I didn't give up though and managed to stick it out for the full hour. Oak, ash, beech, and sometimes elm were our main types of firewood. Sycamore was very light, soon cutting through, but with no lasting power on the fire. Elm was very tough, making the saw jump out of the groove, and was very hard to split. Sweet chestnut and pine were never carried home as both these crackled and spat on the fire, sending glowing pieces flying into the room - a fire hazard like this could well be done without! Ash would burn whether green or dead, as would white thorn. Most hedges were of thorn, and some good firewood came from tall, overgrown fences when they were cut and thinned out. This work was carried out during the winter months with the thicker wood, or thorn bulls as they were called, being shared out amongst the men whether involved in the cutting or not. These green logs used to lay on the fire with white sap sizzling out of the end, but they always gave a good, constant heat once the fire was established. Dead hazelnut sticks, or thin beech branch ends, were favourite fire-lighters and were jealously kept dry, for the first cup of tea in the day depended on the fire going first time. No electric kettles or tea-makers to help you to that first cuppa! The saying went to the effect that a fire that was sluggish put the man of the house in a bad mood all day - I can see why if he set off for a day on the land with no warming drink inside him.

Another source of fuel we collected from the wood was in the form of wood-chips - these were quite large flakes of wood that flew from the axe during the felling operations. Horace Shackcloth and his brother came from East Walton and did all the tree-felling for the Estate. Many woods needed to be thinned, so certain, straight trees were marked for felling. After the operations had been completed, we would set off, armed with sacks in our old pram. Everyone had an old pram to use as a form of transportation, mainly in the wood line. We were no exception and spent hours collecting and carrying lengths of wood to help augment the main load brought on the wagon. Mum and Michael used to go with me, with the faithful Rip trotting along behind. On one occasion we had been to Mink Belt for chips and were returning, with the pram piled high with filled sacks - suddenly the wheels hit an extra deep pothole and the whole load went up on its nose. My feet left the ground, and I was left hanging on the handle, well clear of the ground. As I slid down I grazed my poor

Work – at Home and Away

shins on the back axle, whilst the bags all fell into the road, spilling out in all directions. Nothing for it, but to pick them all up and re-load the pram, cursing loudly the lack of care given to our highway by Norfolk County Council!

The road-repair gang did come our way periodically - three men, namely Tommy Clark, Willie Spooner and Bert Pitcher attempted to repair the potholes. A large tar-pot on wheels, with the firebox underneath, had a barrel of tar suspended above the cauldron. This slowly dripped its contents into the hot interior, and was run off in turn into a large watering-type can. The potholes were swept clean first of all over a certain stretch of road, then Tommy poured the hot tar around the hole, Willie Spooner spread it with a long-handled brush, and Bert spread some stones from his roadman's barrow. The tar barrels were dropped off at regular intervals along the bank, and gravel was also heaped nearby by Council lorries. The tarring operation took quite some time as the crew only worked at the regulation, County Council pace of very slow or stop! The Council workmen were the butt of many a joke, sometimes unfairly, but compared with most land work, they were considered to have a "downhill" load.

Motorists were warned of these frenetic road repairs by two large, Norfolk County Council boards on metal poles driven into left-hand banks in both directions - perhaps they read "Danger, Men at Work". The smell of tar was wonderful and was always with us somewhere on our roads during the summer months. During the rest of the year, Bert Pitcher worked his lonely length by himself, cutting back road edges and clearing rainwater ditches. Icy weather saw him spreading coarse sand from his barrow on treacherous surfaces. When Bert eventually reached the High House road, we would know that a thaw was imminent. Looking back, I can see that the much-maligned Bert and company kept our roads in a much better state of repair than the mechanised Council operations of today. Oh, for the return of a lengthman to our roads, with that lovely tarry smell an extra bonus!

Chapter 9
Westacre at War

The fingers of war were slowly spreading themselves over the whole country. At first the effects were very slight, coming only through the wireless and reports in our newspaper, The Daily Herald. Early bombing scares sent several evacuee families fleeing to Norfolk, but after suffering a few weeks of deathly quiet (their words, not mine!) they returned to London until bombing began in earnest.

One family that did stay with us throughout the war was the Jones family from Plymouth. Mrs Jones was an elder sister of Mrs Lawrence at No 4. Both sisters' husbands were by now in the army , so they were company for one another. Dulcie, Cyril and Terry Jones came to swell our youthful ranks. Later also came David Bunker, their cousin, whose father was a naval man. Cyril was about my age and we became friends, spending hours together roaming the countryside with David, who was younger, tagging along behind. So, from being almost a lone child over the pasture at High House, by 1941 there were about eighteen children under the age of fourteen at Pretoria for company.

There had always been some aerodromes around us during my short lifetime, but with the increasing emphasis on aerial warfare, things hotted up. Airfields seemed to spring up like mushrooms and our previously empty skies began to show more activity. Marham was the nearest base to us, being only seven or eight miles away as the crow flies. Heavier lorries began to roar along the main road at Westacre as gravel and other building materials were transported to extend runways for bigger aircraft. These came in the form of two-engined Wellington bombers and Mosquitos in the fighter-bomber range. On our northern side, West Raynham and Bircham Newton housed fighter aircraft, so we could watch practice dogfights, as well as the heavies taking off and landing. Hedge-hopping was often carried out by young pilots, and they would wave as they flew along almost at ground level. We youngsters thought this was wonderful, but it didn't go down too well with the men in the fields as horses became very frightened of this noisy, unknown invader of their normally quiet environment. As the war progressed, this game, as we viewed it, became more serious - a few real dogfights were seen as the Battle of Britain came and went. I remember standing on the old piece-mat one morning listening to the news as I dressed, with the announcer proudly giving figures of the German aircraft casualties: 184 aircraft destroyed in one day. Soon the grinding tones of Mr Churchill came through the airwaves, encouraging us

71

Westacre at War

all to greater efforts in the deadly fight to halt the Nazi aggressors. How everyone hung on his pugnacious words as the skies overhead became metaphorically darker by the day. Post-war cleverdicks have criticised Winston Churchill's leadership and highlighted his mistakes, but those speeches encouraged all of us to shake a fist in the face of Hitler when all seemed lost.

A few army convoys were seen in the area, complete with camouflage nets. A contingent would conceal its vehicles on the side of the Hall drive under a canopy of trees which hid them very well from any aircraft taking part in the operations. On one occasion, French Canadians were among the troops, and it was the first time I ever encountered people who spoke another language as they jabbered away at high speed in French. We boys wandered between the lorries, having no fear of molestation or danger of any kind - how different from today, when children have to be constantly watched in a supposedly civilised country, at peace with the world. Perhaps all the know-alls and do-gooders who criticise our actions in the desperate days of war could explain where their theories of the flower-power sixties went wrong - if their idea of heaven is these sick days of the nineties, then give me some of the simple, but strict discipline of my schooldays!

By degrees the young men of the village were sucked into the war machine. The volunteer members of the Territorial Army were the first to go, being actively involved in France. Billy and Bob Thaxton were taken prisoner during the Dunkirk evacuation, spending the rest of the war as prisoners in Germany. As already mentioned, my Uncle Sos fought as a member of the Tank Corps; Billy Smith, whose family lived at The Buildings, had just joined the R.A.F. as ground crew. Tom Abel, Young Laddie, Barnie, Gordon and Oscar Coe, Reggie Wright, Harold Plummer, Mann the butler, and Cyril Goose were some of the men to go. Others were drawn in by degrees as conscription took its toll on the fast-depleting workforce. Geoffrey Rye, a neighbour of Ivy's at Rats Hall, went as well.

Girls, including Gracie Williamson, Jean Plummer, Peggy Thaxton, Barbara Dickerson and Pat Cale (the latter being an evacuee) came in as land-girls to help fill the gaps. Major Birkbeck's three sons, Harry, John and Bill, served their country. Mr John was in the R.A.F., whilst his brothers served in the army. We would note here that the squire was always addressed by his retired service rank of Major and his sons as Master or Mister as they grew up. At the end of the war, on demobilisation, they would assume their service rank and be addressed by such. This was the pattern followed in those days, and still adhered to as far as I can ascertain - certainly Captain Harry Birkbeck still heads the Westacre High House Estate.

Westacre at War

Of the men and women who served their country from Westacre, three made the supreme sacrifice and never returned to their families: Reggie Wright, Gordon Coe and John Birkbeck are remembered on the war memorial placed at the top of the green. I well recall the day when we entered the post office to collect our newspapers and were told the sad news that Reggie had died of wounds. This hit us boys especially hard, as Brian Wright, Reggie's younger brother, was at school with us. Gordon Coe, I can picture now sitting up in horse-drawn trap outside Charlie Welham's house (I presume he was delivering some keeper's needs or collecting rabbits to take down to the head keeper); I believe Gordon died in a Canadian port from a disease picked up while serving his country. John Birkbeck was a pilot in the R.A.F., and lost his life when the 'plane he was piloting crashed somewhere in Britain - he was the only one whose body could be brought home, and he was buried on the south side of Westacre church.

Willie Thaxton and his wife spent the war worrying about the fate of their two eldest sons, held prisoner by the Germans. All sorts of stories circulated as to the fate of prisoners of war - some indicated that the men were being used as forced labour in factories, thus being sitting targets for allied bombers; others said prisoner of war camps were lit up at night to attract bombers away from the military sites. Leslie Richardson was taken prisoner by the Japanese, and held in atrocious conditions. His parents kept their faith in his safe return, despite the horror stories feeding back from the Far East. It was very unfortunate that some fellow workmen had to discuss the gory details of these atrocities in the company and hearing of Old Laddie, forcing him to sit alone on occasions. This was both cruel and thoughtless, and can only be put down to utter ignorance. Leslie did return, and was nursed back to pretty good health, but only he knows the mental scars still to be carried even today. I do know that the least form of exertion caused rivers of sweat to run down his face, but he never lost his sense of humour, and we had many a good laugh with him - I hope to be spared to record some of them in a future book!

Agriculture became a vitally important industry, as imports were strangled by the German U-boats operating in the Atlantic. A large percentage of old pasture land was forcibly put under arable crops. Land which had never seen the plough was soon growing lush crops of oats as Britain struggled to become self-sufficient in food production. The run-down state of many farms had to be rectified, and huge grants were suddenly available to help implement this. For the agricultural workers, this in turn meant unlimited overtime and a slightly better wage scale. As the Government was footing the bill, farmers on the whole loosened their traditional, tight-fisted hold on the purse-strings, allowing just a little more cash into the labourers' pockets. Don't run away with the idea that we became rich overnight, but for the first time, the counting of every penny could be listed as an age-old habit, and not a life or death necessity.

All brightly-coloured tractors were painted battleship grey to render them less conspicuous should prowling enemy aircraft come around. The Twenty Five Acres, Horse Pasture and tiny Cow Pasture were ploughed up at Soigné. Codlings, the Brooms and the Chicken Pasture at High House were deemed the best for arable work. Three sections of the park also became arable, although it meant circumnavigating clumps of trees or large single oaks in order to preserve the beauty of the land when normality returned. Oats were always the first crop sown on this type of land, presumably as it was deemed to be most resistant to pests, such as wireworm, which had spent centuries undisturbed under the ancient sward. Here was a job for the rooks, who came into their own as the plough turned up millions of their favourite titbits. After centuries of persecution, the poor old rook became the farmer's friend overnight, thanks to the ravings and insane actions of one Austrian ex-corporal far away in Germany.

Meanwhile, about 600 extra acres were being added to the Soigné land as Massingham Heath was reclaimed. This rabbit-riddled, gorse-covered area had been the home to wild life and tramps for hundreds of years. Apart from some rough game-shooting, it had produced nothing through the centuries until the War Ag set about reclaiming it in 1939. Huge steam engines pulled out stunted trees with steel hawsers, bulldozers pushed out gorse and whin bushes, whilst huge, impenetrable bramble areas were torched before the roots could be torn up. Bonfires burned for days on end until at last the land, which was very light and susceptible to being blown around, grew its first crops. Laced liberally with the new artificial fertilisers, good results were obtained, even if their gathering was always left to last, as this additional land really proved too much for the Soigné resources and help was often needed from other Estate farms as a last resort. On the down side for the farmers in war time was the overall presence of the Man from the Ministry. Although mainly manned and advised by leading agriculturists, there were times when the farmer's local knowledge of his land was overridden by officialdom, and the wrong crops grown despite the farmer's objections. I remember potato crops on the very light land of Ten Acres and Fourteen Acres on the edge of Soigné wood. Here the resultant crop turned out to be the size of marbles, ravished by rabbits and rooks (the latter forgetting their new image as helpers in the war effort), and never even harvested. Potatoes need good land, with plenty of farmyard manure, and this was to be found in and around the bullock yards, and not miles from any steadings. So you see, much of the agricultural war effort was lost in the early 1940s by treating the farmer as a bucolic half-wit.

We boys received full feedback as we spent long hours roaming freely in the fields and listening to the men giving vent to their feelings of frustration as they set about tasks destined to produce nothing tangible, except grant money to the farm coffers and nothing to the country in the form of good food. But the battle went on, despite the shortage of replacement machinery, spare parts and sufficient labour. Horse and tractor worked side by side, as both the new and the old fought its war on home ground - for the tractor it was the beginning of life, but for the heavy horse it was the last desperate throw before mechanisation took over completely leaving the horse-age fit only as a museum piece for us horse-lovers and admirers.

Posters depicting various butterfly or anti-personnel bombs were displayed in public places, especially schools. These explosive devices were being dropped into the countryside from German aircraft and were specifically designed by depraved scientists to kill or maim innocent civilians, especially children. Shaped as pens, butterflies and other interesting things, they exploded on touch, blowing off hands or blinding the unsuspecting person. The posters implored us not to touch anything suspicious, but to inform someone in authority to deal with it. Everyone was repeatedly reminded that "dangerous talk costs lives", and that "walls have ears". "Do not talk to strangers", was another official directive we children received on our walls at school. On the humorous side, Mr Chad was cartooned looking over the wall with his long, fat nose saying, "Wot, no bananas?", or whatever foodstuff had gone on ration or disappeared altogether from the shelves. As the war progressed and shortages increased, Mr Chad could very well have said, "Wot, no anything?" Large newspaper cartoons showed the German Jackboot striding across Europe with Winston Churchill depicted as the British Bulldog showing his teeth on the top of the White Cliffs of Dover. Winston, in his siren suit, large cigar in mouth, and victory sign given with two fingers, cropped up everywhere as efforts were made to bolster the British morale.

As the air-force strength was gradually built up, more and more bombers went out in the evening, bound for German targets. Circling slowly, they gained height before setting off with their heavy loads to attempt to knock out key munitions factories. Some came back at normal speed, whilst others limped home on one engine or with great holes shot in the wings and fuselage. Very occasionally an enemy 'plane would creep in behind to drop a stick of bombs across the airfield before running for home at low level. Some damaged 'planes fell short of their home runway, finishing as a crumpled heap in a field, or a fireball in a wooded area. R.A.F. Police stood guard over the wreckage until the long, R.A.F. Queen

Westacre at War

Mary lorries arrived to carry it away. We boys got as close to the aircraft as possible, searching for pieces of Perspex from which we could cut rings by burning out the centre with a red-hot poker. The sickening smell of black engine-oil tainted the air, coupled sometimes with decomposing flesh if the crash had proved fatal to the crew. Any gory trophy was searched out and taken home after the crash site had been cleared by the authorities, but this passion cooled somewhat after one ghoul discovered a crewman's boot, complete with decomposing foot, in a nearby hedge! All this dangerous poking about was done without our parents' knowledge, whilst paying scant heed to all the posters issued for our protection. It seems as if our limited intelligence, or self-induced wooden heads, prevented us from understanding even the simplest warnings given for our own good - poor Mrs Clark, the schoolmistress, must have despaired of her task to ever teach us load of idiots anything. Was it any wonder Miss Wiskerd had long ago reverted to beating knowledge in with a ruler?

Gas masks soon became our constant companions, everyone had them, carrying the little brown container box everywhere. My brother, Michael, had one with a Disney-character face, while baby Brian lay inside his and we peeped through the Perspex top, fully expecting him to expire at any time. This was during the practice sessions we undertook - thank goodness we were never called upon to use them for real.

The stirrup pump was another innovation - each little community was issued with one, as the fear of the incendiary bomb increased. Walter Williamson, or Wibby as he was known, came to demonstrate how to deal with a fire bomb. After sending my dad for a couple of buckets of water, he set George Hall pumping. Wibby himself lay in the road and proceeded to spray a large stone, keeping his head well down for fear of an explosion. We boys doubled up with laughter as the water dribbled and spat from the end of his pipe - for the life of us we couldn't see why the bucket wasn't emptied over the missile in the first place! Our demonstrator grew quite puce in the face as the pump repeatedly malfunctioned. His discomfort wasn't helped by the alternating jeers and groans from us boys as the water either gushed or dribbled from the hose-pipe. The operation was finally abandoned, and the stone, now well washed, hurled into the hedge by an exasperated Wibby. Luckily for us, no incendiary devices fell on Pretoria, so the clapped-out, old pump was never called into action.

A great source of fun for us came from the Home Guard. All able-bodied men still left at home were called into the local brigade. The retired officers took the lead, namely Major Birkbeck and Colonel Carlyon. I believe Willy Thaxton was a sergeant. At first no-one had uniforms or rifles, and drill was conducted on the park using shotguns and walking sticks as firearms. Every Sunday morning the troops gathered to drill, just inside the park gates, and later, when that was ploughed up, the Mowing Ground next door became the parade ground. As the gentry were present, we boys had to hide under the box bushes just inside the wood. Every time I watch Dads Army the hilarious pictures come back to me; we had no idea just how serious the whole business was, thank goodness. If Hitler could have seen our last line of defence on parade, he would have fallen out of his bunker laughing! As my dad worked on Sunday, he was excused morning parade, as was Gerald's father, Charlie Andrews (he being a shepherd).

The biggest laugh of all came one morning when the troops marched with gas masks on . As the small, Perspex aperture provided for vision steamed over, the ranks began to waver - the problem came to a head when one guardsman, I believe it was Geoffrey Thaxton, tripped over a molehill and went flying, mowing down comrades to the left and right with his lethal walking-stick rifle. As luck would have it, the ensuing noise drowned our laughter as we hastily stuffed handkerchiefs in our mouths and mopped streaming eyes. Well, they say laughing is catching - by strange coincidence, I did the same thing on an icy surface whilst doing National Service many years later, but my rifle was real, complete with fixed bayonet, and I cut down the first six ranks of A.C.2s. I wonder if Geoffrey spent a week on jankers as I did - not much of a laugh, but a great many tears as my job was to peel onions in the cookhouse!

Mid-week Home Guard parade was a highlight in our house. We could all help Dad to get into his uniform prior to cycling to the Westacre reading room. We would try on his gaiters, making a great game of it, with our skinny legs sticking out of them, then try to get his side-cap on at the most rakish angle imaginable. When the games had finished, Dad would set off resplendent in khaki uniform with side-cap stretched as far as possible to cover his very wide hair parting. Mr Wright, the World War 1 veteran taken prisoner by the Turks, wore his little cap straight down the middle of his head, which also caused us much merriment. It was reported that Colonel Carlyon was in such a flap when called out on an emergency, that he couldn't find his braces. The problem was eventually solved by his wife who pointed out that they were dangling from the trousers that he had on!

Anyway, enough of this hilarity as it is bordering on a theme for a theatrical farce. Back down to earth, and proceed with our weekly salvage collection. Those were the days when recycling was for real. All paper, cardboard, bottles, tins, etc, had to be saved to help the war effort. Every Saturday morning I would cycle to Soigné where Gerald would be waiting at the stable. A nice, quiet horse would be put into the shafts of the tumbril and off we would go to Pretoria, collecting salvage before returning to finish off our round at the Soigné Farm cottages. The result of our labours was then separated and stored in a couple of empty bullock boxes given over to this purpose. Periodically a lorry collected the salvage for recycling. I really enjoyed this job as it gave us a ride behind a horse, and Gerald was always good company and very good at handling animals. Although only a few months older than me, he was much wiser in worldly matters, being able to harness horses and understand simple farm implements, whilst I just followed on behind, never attempting to gain experience at all. My natural shyness put up a shutter against trying anything new, or taking the lead. Perhaps it was Grandfather Andrews, foreman at the Warren Farm, who helped to educate his grandson in agricultural ways from an early age, but at any rate, my friend was always dependable and able to tackle any job that came along, so perhaps I tended to remain in the back seat too long using him as a prop.

A small army camp had a permanent base in corrugated iron huts hidden alongside the Abbey ruins at the village. The soldiers didn't make much of an impact on our lives. Occasionally, convoys would pass by, but the only vehicles to cause any real interest were the little bren-gun carriers whirring along on their caterpillar tracks - we all wanted to be drivers of bren-gun carriers when we went to war with our home-made carts and wooden rifles!

Food rationing came into operation with ration books and coupons for most essentials. We were very fortunate as a family to be able to produce plenty of fresh vegetables which helped to fill a big gap in the diet. This, along with as much fresh milk as we could drink, thanks to Dad's job as cowman at High House. A spin-off from this post came in the form of rabbit meat. Dad was an expert rabbit catcher, with only a nut stick to help him. As he walked around pastures daily checking stock as part of the job, he would often spot a rabbit sitting under a grass tussock or in a bunch of nettles. Noting its position, he would walk on, before turning slowly in a circle and work his way closer to the quarry. The animal would hunch closer to the ground, believing itself undetected under the camouflage, until suddenly the stick would descend and one rabbit became meat for a rabbit stew. As rabbit was considered vermin on the Estate, this gave a double helping to the war effort. Incidentally, the nut stick was also lethal when thrown at a fleeing rabbit and it would almost always cut the animal over, winding it sufficiently to allow Dad to grab it before a safe haven was reached. The Thaxton boys often stood at the gate and watched him circling his quarry as a hawk would circle in the sky. They marvelled at his expertise as they often tried the trick themselves, but without the same success. The tendency was always there to lose patience and strike too soon, with the rabbit shooting off a split second in front of the descending stick. Charlie Andrews, or Charlie Lop as we all knew him, was another expert in rabbit-catching, the only difference being was that he used a small, round stone and a catapult. Every man had a very large pocket inside the lining of a working jacket, known as a hare pocket or a poacher's pocket, and into this went the rabbit before it had time to finish its death twitches.

As the rations became smaller, Mum and Dad made sure we boys had the butter and sugar, making do with margarine and a dust of sweeteners occasionally. Petrol rationing forced grocers from the same town to share vans for deliveries. Hannant and Mallets of Swaffham came to Pretoria on a sharing basis, and I believe coal merchants shared their customers around to save lorry fuel. Charlie Fitt still drove for Morris Brothers, the butchers from Massingham, but on a limited delivery basis. Somehow he found a piece of beef for us, as Dad didn't like pork or mutton, but those little slips of ration paper didn't produce much butcher's meat each week. Charlie used to tear out the ration coupons with his blood-stained fingers as he had no washing facilities on the van. I can visualise brass-coloured scales hanging from hooks on the inside roof of the van. Mum used to laugh and say he swept her morsel of meat up before the needle on the dial had settled. Charlie's very red face would break into a huge grin and a wheezy laugh would come forth as the scales were whipped down, the door slammed, and off to Soigné he would speed.

A very unusual war effort was the destruction of cabbage white butterflies. In the height of the season they would descend on our cabbage patch to lay eggs which hatched into ravenously hungry caterpillars. A handful of these could reduce a cabbage to a skeleton in hours. To stem the tide of these pests, which in our eyes were a form of German secret weapon, we armed ourselves with a leafy ash branch, and belaboured the fluttering enemy, leaving them broken and useless on the floor. We totted up our score in the same manner as Battle of Britain pilots as we patrolled the roadside banks, now white with hedge parsley, or hemlock as we knew it. The heady smell of hemlock and May-blossom made us almost drunk with power as our branches flailed the air. We weren't able to contribute much financially to Wings for Victory Week, but we did our bit for King and Country.

My Aunt Gladys and three girls came down from London when the V1s, or doodlebugs, caused havoc there. One night, the sound of a low-flying aircraft broke the silence. I noticed my Aunt's face went sheet-white and the children dived under the table. They had detected the strange sound of a German aircraft engine. It passed over as we all held our breath, but moments later a loud explosion came from a bomb dropped in open country near Soigné wood. How thankful we were for our blackout blinds and curtains. Mum used to push towels in along the top and edges of the blind to prevent even the tiniest chink of light from showing for fear of enemy bombers. Mr Wright had the job of checking the row for any breaks in the blackout regulations and also to ring a handbell if a gas attack was imminent. Quite how we would know this, I'm not sure, as Pretoria had no telephone contact with the outside world, but thankfully, like the stirrup pump, the bell was never called into use.

One last memory of the war comes with the fighter plane which crash-landed on the Nursery field, just below Mink Belt. The pilot skimmed the Eighteen Acres hedge across the road to belly-flop and slide across the ploughed land. No injury was sustained and we had a good look at the 'plane before it was reclaimed by the R.A.F. To retrieve their property they had to cut away the bank and hedge half-way along the roadside, and from thenceforth the Nursery boasted a middle gateway, thanks to the young pilot who had to walk home!

Aunt Ivy often caught the King's Lynn bus at the Milestone in order to attempt to buy some off-ration food to supplement the men's meagre diet. After queueing at length outside Stan Riches' fish shop, she would reach the head of the line and be rewarded with some herring. Imagine her horror on one occasion as she reached inside her bag for the obligatory wrapping paper, only to find it had been left on the table at Rats Hall. Visions of her brothers' stricken faces at tea-time flashed across her mind as the pompous Stan proclaimed, in a very loud voice, "No paper, no fish, madam". A saviour further down the queue held up some surplus newspaper and saved the day. I'm sure that Ivy felt like telling Stan where to put his fish in later years of more plentiful supplies, but, in fairness to the tradesman, wrapping paper was like gold-dust and almost more valuable than the very small amounts of food wrapped up in it.

Chapter 10
Spring has Sprung

The anticipation of spring usually started very early in the year for me as, with the onset of school, came the annual curse of winter colds. If any one of the Westacre pupils developed a sniffle then yours truly could turn it into a streaming, full-blown cold for himself overnight. The virility of my strain of common cold almost defies description. After a couple of days it would develop into bronchitis without fail, and that would mean a visit from Dr Thorpe or Dr Barker and a prescribed lengthy stay in bed, where I would wheeze, croak and blow my way through copious supplies of white, linen cloths obtained by my resourceful mother from old bed-sheets. The washing-line would fly these flags daily for about three weeks at a time before the affliction finally blew itself to a standstill.

I wasn't the only member of the family thus afflicted as brother Michael suffered a worse time than me when he started mixing with other children in the confined space of the school room. During these frequent illnesses my poor mother would almost worry herself to death. As there were no antibiotics available to reduce the chest infection, the body had to combat the severe problem itself, and only a bottle of cough medicine was supplied by the doctor. This had to be collected from the surgery at Swaffham, seven miles away. Dad would set off on his bike immediately after work to reach the surgery before closing time. His very dim light, due to black out restrictions, would only direct a glimmer just in front of his wheel. On one occasion, a very dark, foggy night, he missed the Westacre turning on the return journey and found himself a good mile down the Narborough road before realising his mistake. Turning his bike, he groped his way back to Swaffham, before making the correct diversion into the narrow Westacre road. Meanwhile, my mother would be rubbing me with either Vick or warm, camphorated oil to assist my breathing. A steaming tin kettle would purr away on the long chimney of an oil stove keeping the bedroom warm, but not drying the air. This slightly steamy air helped to make breathing easier. Without the constant ministrations of such dedicated parents I wouldn't have survived those tricky early years. A later physician, the tough ex-Navy Dr Townend, assured my mother that if she could nurse us through to school leaving age we would be okay. His diagnosis was so very accurate that I reached the age of 58 before having a one-off serious chest problem after leaving school at 16.

My bedroom window faced due west and I spent long hours of immobility just watching the cloud formations move across the sky

Spring has Sprung

majestically, and in my mind's eye, turned them from icebergs into mountains and on to funny faces. Angry clouds rushed and chased one another from one side of the window to the other. Then peaceful, graceful clouds quietly sailed across a blue sea. A large oak tree half-way up the hill helped to add beauty to my window pictures, as the wind made its arms wave at me in sympathy for my weak, temporarily bedridden state. I can see now the pattern on the ceiling made by the oil stove, resembling a round, paper doily. The label on the white blanket depicted sheep grazing and declared the product to be a genuine Witney blanket. Little did I realise then the fact that I would eventually spend the greater part of my life in a village only four miles from Witney itself. What would I have done without the pink-painted, sloping boards by my bedside over the stairs? They were my link with people downstairs and a knock on them would summon a trusty parent to attend to my every need.

After all this talk of wintery illness, you may have wondered when a connection with spring would appear. Well, the connecting thread came through six very heavy volumes bound in green covers. These were my bird books, purchased from a second-hand bookshop situated near the back of the Cattle Market at King's Lynn. I first spotted them through the window of the little shop and tentatively drew my mother's attention to them. We went in and examined a volume, and I was hooked there and then. I wanted to possess them more than anything else in the world. I believe the price was £2.10s. How the money was raised, I don't know, but somehow the price was paid and they were mine. The bookseller produced a thick piece of string and used it to tie them together, and away we went to the bus. Mum did the donkey work with the books, whilst I muscled-in under the shopping bags which were much lighter owing to the war shortages. Our fellow bus passengers silently condemned us for being mad, because book purchases came very low on the average villager's list of essentials, but to me they represented an insight into a wonderful world of nature, and must have turned out one of the best investments Mum ever made as they gave me endless hours of joyful occupation and learning.

Just as soon as I felt strong enough to sit up in bed, one of the large volumes would be propped up, using my skinny legs as a makeshift book-rest. The six volumes covered in depth all species of birds recorded as having been seen in the wild over the British Isles. Each illustration was covered by a thin sheet of tissue paper. As I read, my mind collated what kind of nest the bird built, the egg colour and where it might be found on the Estate. It wasn't just seeing and recognising the bird that mattered, it was owning just one of its eggs in a collection that gripped my imagination. In those days schoolboys and egg collecting were synonymous, and as most species of bird came in large numbers, very little harm was caused by

Spring has Sprung

this hobby. Obviously, the thought of damage never entered our heads as we took up a hobby handed down from our fathers who had spent part of their boyhood engaged in this age-old custom of the countryside.

The other important springtime job was to obtain a large, flat, cardboard box, preferably with a lid. This could then be layered with cotton-wool. Having babies in the house was quite a boon in this field, as cotton-wool usually came with babies and was therefore very welcome. The prepared box was to hold the precious egg collection that was always kept on the shelf, well above the exploring hands that also came with babies as they grew bigger.

The sign of spring was always recorded by the tiny bunch of blue and white wild violets picked by Dad for Mum, and placed in a yellow egg- cup shaped like an elephant. Although the most undemonstrative of men, my dad would always pick a small bunch of snowdrops from the Ice-house Plantation, the first violets from just inside Anmer gate, and primroses from the wood nearby. Every year, without fail, the very first harbingers of spring would be drawn from the pocket of his faded, off- purple overcoat. What a faithful, dedicated countryman, husband and father he was, slow to accept change, maybe, but as stable and reliable as the land beneath our feet, of which he was undoubtedly a part - the Rock of Gibraltar on which our little world was founded.

The first birds to prepare for nesting were the rooks which would be seen as early as February carrying sticks to repair their nests in the Ice-house Plantation. This rookery was well-established and used year after year as the white-splashed laurel bushes beneath could show. This was the nearest rookery to Pretoria, being about half a mile up the High House road and backing on to the large, wall-enclosed kitchen gardens of the Hall. There were two other large rookeries on our part of the Estate, one being at Long Plantation and the other in a tree-filled pit hole beyond Field Barn. Rooks do not make very pleasant neighbours, as their constant cawing and smelly toilet habits are not to everyone's taste. As the stick-built nests were about sixty feet from the ground, it was obvious to me that no eggs could be obtained directly from the nests, so I hoped to find one on the ground. Ducking through the bent, iron railings along the roadside, I searched around the edges for the dark, foreboding laurel bushes for sight of an egg. Skirting the dark entrance of the old ice-house itself, my search was partially rewarded when I spotted an egg lying on soft, mossy earth. Unfortunately, the impact of its fall had cracked the shell underneath, but by careful camouflage I was able to conceal the defect in the cotton-wool. So, after all my careful planning, the egg collection had begun.

Having mentioned the ice-house, I had better explain its function. In the days before refrigeration as we know it, there was obviously great

Spring has Sprung

difficulty in storing fresh meat for any length of time. It would appear that when a freeze-up occurred, blocks of ice were cut and placed inside this subterranean cavern, where they would remain in a solid state for some considerable amount of time. Meat stored there was then collected for the Hall by the servants, as required. As all this happened well before my egg-searching days, I must pass on this explanation as it was passed on to me. At any rate, we boys were strictly forbidden to go near the brick-lined hole, for fear that it would collapse on us. It was only on rare occasions that we visited this dark, dreary, north-facing wood as one was never quite sure if the tall, formidable figure of Mr Wright, the head gardener resplendent in green baize apron, would appear at the back gate of the gardens to send us on our way. He didn't encourage small boys to go anywhere near his domain, and we had a certain respect for those in authority, as bad news had a distinct habit of sifting back to our parents. They seemed to know more about our movements than we did ourselves sometimes!

Earlier in this book I mentioned that we had the run of the Estate woods for most of the year, but at pheasant-nesting time, they were strictly out of bounds. As most of the wild birds nested in hedgerows and on the edge of thick woodland, we were able to keep to the rules whilst doing much of our birds' nesting, that is under the keepering of Clem Softley who allowed us some leeway, so long as we kept our exploits within bounds. On one occasion, he was moved to kick my behind when we engaged in a silly, noisy game at the chalk pit, disturbing wildlife for miles around, but in the main he turned a blind eye, as we crept about thinking we were invisible to the adult law-enforcers. Clem must have smiled to himself on many occasions as he stood very still as keepers do and watched us creeping past, oblivious to all except the exciting adventure we were engaged in.

One of the first places to visit in search of nests was the corner of the wood adjacent to the park gates, just off the Hall drive. This corner contained the thick box bushes from which we watched the antics of the Home Guard parade. Blackbirds and thrushes flocked there for nest-building, as the evergreen bushes, with their small leaves, provided instant cover well before the rest of the bushes and undergrowth burst into leaf. One egg would be carefully removed from a nest, then moving on to a thorn bush we would pierce top and bottom with a sharp thorn. Making sure to break the yoke first, the contents were blown out of the bottom by means of wind from the mouth. Once clear, the shell would be carefully placed in a small box lined with cotton-wool. Some boys popped the eggs under their caps, either blown or not - this could be disastrous if one accidentally came up under a low bough - also mates have been known to

Spring has Sprung

give you a friendly tap on the cap, just to watch you trying to wipe yoke from your matted hair! So, being slightly worldly-wise, I always carried my small box with me.

Cyril Jones couldn't understand why we didn't take an egg from every nest found, but we country boys soon explained that the object of the exercise was to own just one egg of as many different species as possible, not a huge mass of blown eggs. We needed no explanation for this, but evacuees weren't bred to the country ways of thinking, but they soon caught our drift. The one big trouble with Cyril was his apparent lack of stamina. If the weather was cold he would complain bitterly about being "starved". At first I thought he lacked food, but learned later that a Devonian being starved meant feeling the cold. If on a long trek, his legs would ache long before we reached our destination, and we would turn back in order to stop him complaining. But, all in all, we got along fairly well, completing most of our missions successfully.

Several types of egg could be obtained in and around gardens - the blackbird, song thrush, and hedge-sparrow all nested in our fences. A chaffinch made a wonderful, mossy-cupped nest either in the hedge, or secreted in the fork of an apple tree where the lichen-covered bark made it almost invisible. "Bob robin" used a discarded kettle tipped on its side in the hedge bottom. It was rumoured that taking a robin's egg meant running the risk of a broken leg. We went about in fear and trembling for a few days after adding one of their eggs to our collection, but as far as I was concerned the rumour was unfounded, as I reached my middle thirties before breaking my first bone. A few years later, brother Michael wasn't so lucky when he broke an arm on two separate occasions. I never thought to ask whether a robin's egg had been involved anywhere!

The swallows' and house-martins' were easy to obtain as they nested in and around the farm buildings. Also, the untidy nests of house-sparrows and starlings hung out of the eaves in all the cart-sheds. Some sparrows built in a line of tall thorn trees adjacent to the Soigné pigsties. We classed these as tree-sparrows, but I fear we were wrong and only added the egg of another house-sparrow who decided to live on the fringe.

There seemed to be an unwritten law that automatically entitled me to the egg from the first nest of each new species discovered. Poor Cyril would have to wait until we found a second nest before he could add to his collection. This was grossly unfair, but as he wasn't so mad keen on the hobby as I, it didn't seem to matter neither did he harbour any ill-feeling. David Bunker, trailing behind, only really came for the company, so his feelings weren't seriously considered by the two senior partners.

The eggs of members of the crow family were very difficult to obtain. As mentioned, the rook built in tree tops, as did the carrion crow, although they were so persecuted by gamekeepers that one very rarely saw, let alone discovered, a nest at any obtainable level. Jays and magpies also lived in constant fear of the keeper's gun, and were so secretive in nesting that one had to travel miles in search of them. The jay would secrete his nest in thick evergreen, hidden in mainly deciduous wood. I managed to find one near the Mowing Ground, but the branches were so thick and impenetrable, I gave it best and never had an egg. We trudged for miles across fields to visit isolated pit holes where magpies, according to my book, built their large, stick-nesting structures complete with roof. Only once were we successful in finding a nest, but after painfully climbing through the thick, thorn branches, I discovered a cartridge of lead shot had been fired through the bottom of it by a keeper, leaving only fragments of egg-shell in the badly-torn nest. Yes, the magpie was public enemy number one on game shooting estates. Alongside our black and white friend were ranged the birds of prey, which were also shot on sight for fear they took pheasant or partridge chicks as part of their diet.

At this point I must clarify the mention I made of pit holes in the previous paragraph. Many years previously, marl or clay subsoil was dug for spreading on light land to give it more body and water-retaining powers. In most fields this hole, or mini-quarry, was too deep to keep in cultivation, so it was left open for nature to take its course. Usually the hole had three steep sides, and the fourth was a gentle slope where the horses and carts had driven out of the pit with the loads of marl. Scrubby bushes and trees grew up the sides, bramble thickets hid rabbit warrens, and to all kinds of natural species it was a very comfortable home. Most pit holes were dry-bottomed, owing to the fact that by digging away the clay, underlying, very porous chalk had been exposed, thus allowing quick drainage. In the one or two water-filled varieties we tried to find water-hens' nests. These were usually situated at the far end of a fallen tree, well out on the dark, brooding water. Fear of drowning added caution to our efforts to obtain eggs, but, by means of a spoon tied to a long stick, we were at last successful.

To some of our schoolmates, these water-hens' eggs were edible, but I never tried them, the main reason being the emphatic warning given by Mother to stay away from water in pits. Quite a few tragedies were reported in local papers as over-enthusiastic boys fell into stagnant water and were trapped and drowned in the thick mud and weed. The annual fall of dead leaves from overhanging trees made a very thick, muddy slime beneath the water. The deep water of Short Row Pit was out of bounds to most of us, and the water-hens and few wild ducks were safe on the roadside pit which boasted a terrifying reputation, though I know of no specific tragedies occurring there.

Spring has Sprung

One member of the crow family, with easier access to its eggs, was the jackdaw. This bright-eyed, blue-headed, little crow nested in large numbers in very twisted, ancient elm trees on the Park and Mowing Ground. These trees were hollow in branch and trunk and the jackdaws made good use of all the holes to make untidy nests of sticks lined with sheep's wool collected from the pastures. Off we would go, either up the Hall drive or along the side of the Squires field. Once out on the grass, we would cut across to the middle gate where a horse-chestnut and two elm trees grew. With the help of a mate's back, and then holes in the trunk, one of us would shin up the tree to investigate the holes from which stuck nesting material. The parent birds would fly round, uttering sharp little "jacks" in characteristic manner. Even when we possessed a jackdaw egg, we still had to spend a session pushing our arm down dark holes to feel the clutch of eggs. Needless damage was inflicted on shoes and clothes as the rough bark was scrabbled over with no thought of clothing coupons or long hours spent with needle and thread to repair the snags and tears.

On one occasion, when examining a tree at the top of the Mowing Ground, my arm flew back out of a hole as a hissing beak and flapping wing hit my hand. Tumbling back to earth, I hastily examined my hand to see the extent of the damage. As none was evident, my fear subsided slightly, and on reflection, I decided the hole must be occupied by an owl. How to get this boy-eating bird off its eggs was the big problem. No one volunteered to climb the tree again, so it was agreed to frighten the bird out. We belaboured the tree trunk and howled like banshees, but no white apparition came forth, so eventually we had to give it best and retire from the field of action without the dirty white egg of the barn owl. Still, I'm sure the chick that eventually hatched from the egg did far more good than the shell in cotton-wool would have done!

About four or so weeks after our jackdaw trek, we would make the same journey again, but this time it was the young jackdaws we were seeking. If we could catch a well-fledged youngster, or "full flopper" as we called a bird just leaving a nest, it would be carried home as a pet. These pathetic bundles of feathers were fed on soaked bread and kept in a disused rabbit hutch with a dish of water for company. The ones that survived the initial shock of being taken, made nice pets and would follow us around "jacking" away for more food. After learning to fly, they would stay around for a time, before one day leaving us for a life in the wild. No doubt we met up with them again on our annual jackdaw-nesting pilgrimage, but no one felt able to offer introductions, so we just passed each other by like ships in the night.

Wood-pigeons seemed to nest for most months of the year. Every other bush seemed to produce a clap of wings as the pigeon, or "old dow"

Spring has Sprung

as Dad called them, flew off the two white eggs precariously balanced on a very few crossed twigs. The smaller, more gentle turtle-dove was also to be found with similar nesting arrangements, but for a much shorter season. The end of April brought the cuckoo, with its strange habit of using foster-parents to hatch its egg and rear the resulting young. I was never able to find a cuckoo's egg, which was deemed to be the pinnacle of egg-collecting achievement.

Early May brought the overseas visitors, in the form of warblers. These all nested in hedges or in brambles at the base of hedges. This meant our attention was drawn to roadside fences and banks. I marvel at the sharpness of our eyes as invisible nests were discovered by young vision that could seemingly see through jungles! Whitethroats and lesser whitethroats, chiff-chaffs and yellowhammers nested in abundance. Strangely, the latter always left a tell-tale piece of dead grass protruding from the nest, as if the parent needed a marker to find its own home again. Great care had to be taken when looking at a roadside nest. No nettles or grass must be trampled or disturbed, for fear rival collectors would find the nest. When working on others' territory, we were always on the look-out for a giveaway track to lead us to a fresh find. As we classed the huge tract of land covering both Soigné and High House Farms as our territory, it was very rare that we went over the border. In fact, it was only in search of the linnet that we went down to the village, where it was known to nest in the furze bushes on Westacre Common. This was a small piece of rough land running from Fullers Bridge and Ford to the Mill and on the one excursion we made, a successful result was achieved, so no further trips were needed.

"Jenny" Wren often caused would-be egg collectors trouble. After finding an unlined, dome-shaped nest of dead leaves and moss, we would wait for the lining to be added and the eggs laid. After a few days, no progress would be apparent, and we suckers would realise we were watching one of the tiny bird's dummy nests, and that the real one was hidden a distance away. The beautiful, domed, mossy nest of the long-tailed tit was always suspended from green brambles in the centre of a dense clump, just out of reach. Scratches and three-cornered tears to our skin and clothes were suffered in our vain attempts to gain entry to this tiny, feather-lined fortress. Success was more readily achieved with the great and blue tits, who nested inside a rotten tree. With the help of one skilfully-bent teaspoon, the tiny egg could be gently withdrawn, if the nest wasn't too deeply situated. Of course, none of these various acrobatic feats could be achieved without first climbing into trees and tall bushes - at this we became expert, but very often our clothes came off second-best, and our escapades played havoc with Mum's clothing coupons and housekeeping

Spring has Sprung

money! Most of the time our play-clothes bore a good resemblance to the boys' attire in a Charles Dickens' play, but we were happy and could enjoy ourselves without any restrictions either from dress or private landlords.

Now the onset of early spring didn't bring with it all play and no work. A large vegetable garden meant much hand-digging, before planting could take place. During the long, winter months I was given a free run of the cultivated part of the garden, and spent many hours with made-up implements, pretending to carry out field operations. One of these was an old bicycle frame, with the rear wheel removed and a garden fork tied straight down at the back. This scraped the earth in the manner of a crude cultivator when pulled along, and I spent hours pretending to be a tractor as it was pushed up and down. The operation only marked the surface, whilst my feet compacted the earth with each trip, making the eventual digging very much harder, but Dad undertook the extra physical effort without complaint and took heart from the fact I had been able to enjoy myself in a pretend-world of farming. I can never remember being bored or howling for something to do - my hardest task was to enthuse Cyril in all the things I wanted to do! He suffered spells of being "starved" and generally whining around, until his mother lost patience and drove him forth, with dire threats of considerable injury if he didn't shut up.

Anyway, back to the digging job in hand. Every autumn Dad would bring home a tumbril-load of farmyard manure, or muck as we knew it. This was piled just inside the road hedge and allowed to rot down throughout the winter months. When the great dig commenced, my job was to barrow this well-rotted muck on to the un-dug garden and then spread a thin layer into every other trench with a small, four-tined fork. Dad would dig slowly across, bending every so often to pull up and throw out any bindweed roots or twitch grass he came across. Blackbirds would seek out worms and use the dry roots lying on the top as very useful nest-building material. Cock robin would flit around us, looking for all the world like the foreman overseeing operations - and woe betide any other male robin who was silly enough to poke his beak into bob's affairs! The interloper would be seen off the property with no mercy shown by the incumbent bird.

This digging ritual commenced as soon after 4 o'clock leaving-off time as possible, making full use of precious daylight. Every fine evening was used until all the garden had been turned over and mucked. The contents of our own muck-hole would be used, as well as the farmyard manure, so nothing was wasted. Of course, I did get fed up with the job well before completion, but only a case of illness allowed me to escape. Nor would I have thought of asking to be excused, for unwritten, country codes of practice were plainer to us than if inscribed on tablets of stone - "parents expected children to do their duty at all times".

Another task undertaken without questions was the cleaning-up of brush after Father had cut the hedges. No games were contemplated if the hedge-shears came out of their sacking cover. Good Friday meant potato planting. Irrespective of the date on which it fell, and the fact that there could be a month's differential, potatoes were always planted on Good Friday. The early variety had been set up in boxes to encourage shoots, housed in the frost-free front room. These went in first, with Dad dibbling holes, and son dropping seed potatoes behind. A boot slid along the row to finalise the operation, and the row was marked with a stick at each end. The late crop followed the same pattern, the only difference being the potatoes had no developed shoots, and would therefore take longer to appear above ground level, and not until all late frost had passed by. The earlies would be carefully covered by earthing-up, and sacks, should frost threaten in May. We had a special marker for potato sowing, which consisted of two wooden struts fixed to a frame and handle, spaced at 24 inches. After setting the first row by means of a garden line, the frame was then drawn across the garden, keeping one leg of the marker on the first row and marking accurately the second. This process was repeated until the job was complete. All vegetables had to be planted in dead straight lines to uphold the honour of the gardener in the eyes of his neighbours. As in the fields, all plant rows or furrows must be straight, for a "dog's hind leg", seen from the road, came in for constant derision, which continued until the crop had been harvested and the damning evidence destroyed.

Spring was the season so full of hope and expectation, with the dark-green cereal crop shooting up to develop ears of grain; the sugar-beet and other root crops spread from the thin, pencil-lines of green, into touching seas of green, and then their dark-green leaves wilted under the warm sun of early summer; there was eager anticipation of fresh vegetables and salads from the garden, all of which has been stolen from our present day lives by the advent of the deep-freeze and the all-year-round muted taste of forced vegetables and foreign imports - all these so-called improvements made in the name of progress.

It is very difficult to record on paper the wonderful feeling of well-being engendered by rapid and lush growth of spring vegetation. The smell of flowers on banks and hedges, combined with so many shades of fresh green seemed to lift the senses to new heights of sensitivity known only to humans when in complete harmony with nature. These are the precious things lost to our present generation, things and feelings so valuable, and yet so difficult to explain to people who have never been fortunate enough to experience and enjoy them. I will count this book as being an

Spring has Sprung

unqualified success if its only achievement is to move its readers to seek to restore some of the age-old values to our farms and countryside.

Chapter 11
Haytime and Harvest

As springtime gradually slipped into early summer, our thoughts turned from bird-nesting to interesting developments on the agricultural scene. Hayfield grass had grown well, as had its red clover companion. These two species made up a mixture known as one-year-ley. Sown together in the bottom of a barley crop the previous year, this type of ley made up almost all the Soigné hay crop, as meadow hay, so popular in more western counties, was very rarely used in Norfolk. Occasional crops of pink sainfoin made an appearance, as did the coarse cock's-foot grass, but one-year-ley was the main crop for us.

We would often sprawl out on the edge of the field and squint up into the clear blue sky in an effort to pick out the dot of a skylark singing away many hundreds of feet above his sitting mate. The smell of the bruised grass lulled us into a state of near stupor as we chewed sweet, sappy grass stems and wished we could summon up enough energy to search for the skylark's nest. This was the beginning of the real dog days of summer, when we were glad to be too young to be actively involved in all the hard work of hay and harvest.

The rattle of the grass cutter would signal the beginning of crop-gathering for animal feed needed in the coming winter season. Horses, sheep, cows and yarded bullocks all needed hay in copious amounts as cake and other bought-in animal feeds were both expensive and difficult to obtain. The chattering cutter laid the grass in neat rows as it fell over the back of the cutter bar. Artie Keeley would drive the dark blue, spud-wheeled Case tractor round the field in ever-decreasing circles working towards the centre. Under a large, shady tree just inside the gate would be forty-gallon drums of TVO and various oil cans belonging to the tractor, as well as Artie's bike. Here also would be old Dick Everard, leaning over his wooden sharpening stool as he applied the file to replacement cutter blades. These blades consisted of a 3'6" bar with triangular-shaped teeth sharpened on two sides and riveted along its length. If one tooth broke, it was knocked off by removing its rivets and a new one fitted. A blade needed to be changed quite often on grass, so Dick was kept busy - although it was a nice job for a man advancing in years, being able to enjoy the open air whilst working under a cool canopy of green. Dick Everard was father to Mrs Richardson and lived in the Laddie household at Soigné. I suppose he would be aged about 70 at the time.

As work continued for at least half a day on Saturdays, we were able to get involved in the action, although rabbits were very difficult to catch in the hay field, as they were able to sneak out from the standing crop and hide under the cover of the cut hay. It was in the hayfields that partridges and their young were at their most vulnerable. Many hen birds were still sitting, and were decapitated by the murderous knives. Usually the local gamekeeper walked the grass in an effort to move them on to safer ground. As both partridges and pheasants were bred as game birds, a keeper's job depended on providing large numbers of both types of birds for the guns later in the year. We spent as much of the day as possible in the field, enjoying our bottles of drink and jam sandwiches, sitting with the men at break times. They always made us welcome as long as we behaved ourselves, as did Mr Wilson, the foreman, on his frequent visits.

After a few days of sunshine the hay was turned by a tedder. This machine fluffed up the hay to allow the sun to dry its underside. Then came horse-rakes which pulled the hay into long rows in readiness for another horse-drawn implement to push those thick rows into heaps. This was a wooden sweep with about eight long teeth and a pair of handles at the back. The horse pulled it along the row by means of two chains with a man holding it down by the handles. When the weight of hay became almost too heavy to pull, the operator would lift the handles slightly forcing the teeth into the ground, and causing its load to tip off and be left behind as the sweep rolled over the top for a repeat performance to begin on the other side. Several men with hay-forks would round up the heap into a very neat, domed structure known to all as a haycock. This miniature stack could then be left to dry further and would be weatherproof should rain come before stacking could take place. These haycocks made splendid, sweet-smelling resting places as we boys burrowed into the soft sides, covering our hair and clothes with dust and hay seeds. My thatch was so thick in those days that a half hundredweight of hay seed could hide in there quite easily - we certainly made a good mess on the bedroom floor when we undressed at night.

After a couple of weeks in the cock the hay was carted to the stack, which was always built at the roadside-corner of the field itself. Many farms carted all their crops to a central stack-yard, adjacent to the farm, but as Soigné had no specific area for this, all crops of hay and corn were stacked in the field. The hay was then pitched from the cock by two men and loaded on to wagons by two loaders. One of the team-men brought an empty wagon out and, with the aid of a trace horse in the front, took the large load of hay to the foot of an elevator which conveyed forkfuls of hay to the stackers. All stacks were of a uniform size, being measured out by the foreman at twelve yards by six. A load of dry straw was spread over the whole area to form a bottom, thus preventing any precious stock feed from spoiling on damp earth. George Hall was chief stacker, with Blackie Wright his backer or deputy. The stacks were gabled in the shape of a house and were thatched with long rye-straw to keep out the weather. Very great care had to be taken to ensure that the hay was fully dry before stacking, as moist hay would heat and catch fire. On the other hand, over-dry hay lost its feed value - so you can see where experience was of the utmost importance in yesteryear farming. Good, wholesome hay was essential to the overwintering of stock, especially in the severe weather conditions often experienced in Norfolk.

One special concession made by the farmer to his men at hay time, was in the form of a stone, gallon bottle of mild ale delivered by Willie Thaxton who brought it daily from The Stag. This was shared amongst the nine men who usually made up a gang carting the crop. The haystack was built to the maximum height reached by the elevator, but soon settled down as hay compacts more readily than corn when stacked. Incidentally, the elevator was still driven by horsepower, and the animal walked in a circle underneath drawing a bar to turn the mechanism as it went. By the end of the war a small petrol engine had replaced the horse, which meant the machine could be lower at the bottom end, allowing the unloaders to pitch downwards or on a level, instead of upwards for most of the time - so the little engine made a saving of work for a horse and less work for the man.

At the height of the haymaking season, Dad would spend his three hours' overtime making haycocks. This meant a romp in the field for myself and Rip. If the field was near at hand we would walk to it, but take our bikes if further away. In either case Rip would run behind, stopping at intervals to investigate some interesting smell, then accelerating in order to catch up - his spindly legs going nineteen to the dozen! At six in the evening the sun would still be quite warm and reasonably high in the sky due to the use of double summertime. This system meant that we were two hours ahead of the sun in summer and one in winter. The only drawback for us boys under this system was the fact that bedtime came with sunshine still pouring through our windows.

Dad would set to with his pitchfork, pulling the hay out of the muddled heap and then building a well-rounded cock, using all the hay in that particular heap, and finishing with a rake round to ensure that no precious hay was wasted. After an initial burst of energy, boy and dog would flop down in the shade of the sweet-smelling haycock to enjoy a cool drink from our bottle (Rip had a small basin to lap the water from and his long, pink tongue slopped it down as fast as possible). By about 7.30 the novelty of rolling in hay began to wear off and I would prepare to go home with Rip as my guard and companion. Dad would, of course, continue with his work until nine o'clock when he would also turn for home and leave the

Haytime and Harvest

silent haycocks with their lengthening shadows to creatures of the night. As the cool evening air descended, rabbits and pheasants would quietly creep out from the hedges and feed in peace. The white barn-owl would soon ghost across the open spaces, seeking out mice whose world had been so rudely shattered by man and his machines. All too soon the sun would rise again, and men would return to spend the day in sweat, dust and companionable work, culminating in that special joy of seeing a job well done, and a good crop gathered and stored for the betterment of man and the animals in his charge. Great satisfaction was drawn by a stockman when he could feed his charges with sweet-smelling clover hay on a cold, frosty winter's day. The wonderful smell of summer that came from the fodder seemed in itself to put new life into both tender and tended - man and animal were part of the team that made farming more than just a job. It was life itself with everyone, young and old alike, a tiny cog in a very large wheel.

As a final, bleached hay field was horse-raked to gather every last wisp of hay, thoughts began to turn towards the biggest and most important event of the year - harvest. This meant long hours of heavy labour for everyone in the parish. Men worked for six days a week from dawn to dusk, alongside horses, boys and pensioners. The women formed a back-up team supplying meals and drinks to the field workers and filling in with the outside jobs around the home. Every positive thought and action was directed towards the successful gathering of the harvest. Not until the last sheaf had been carted and stacked could anyone relax or unbend from that special task.

As July entered its second half, an unsettling apprehension took hold of all we schoolchildren. How soon would the onset of harvest be? How soon would our five weeks' harvest holiday start? You see, the date for the summer holiday commencement didn't come by directive from the Norfolk Education Committee, oh no! This vitally important date would be set by the headmistress after close consultation with Mr Thaxton, the Estate bailiff. The average duration of the harvest was five weeks, as was also the length of our holiday from school. As most older pupils worked on the farms, there was great need to synchronise dates at the outset in order that they finish work before resumption of lessons. This being the position, we all thought that the best person to influence our case for an early start was June, Mr Thaxton's younger daughter and our school-mate. After the first, faint ripening of a crop, we would implore her to inform her dad of the imminent onset of the harvest. She must have been sick and tired of our stupid arguments put forward in the hope that she could influence her father. All our tricks for an early break-up bore no fruit - it was always the cutting of the first oat field that signalled a week's notice for

Haytime and Harvest

an end to summer term.

We were one of the few families to take a summer holiday. Granny Eke always welcomed us for a fortnight's break, and this was usually taken between haymaking and harvest, so that my dad could have his one week's paid holiday in the short lull between both operations. The normal procedure was for him to accompany us on the first week, and then lodge with Aunt Ivy at Rats Hall whilst we remained at Briston for a second week. Great preparations were made for the exodus, with Mum doing all the packing and Dad arranging for Uncle Will to feed the chickens and collect the eggs. Rip took up lodgings at Rats Hall, while in later days Waggs went in the train with us.

Finally the great day came and Mum, myself and two toddlers were packed into Frank Clarke's car. Prior to this innovation the large pram was pushed to Massingham station. Dad always took his bike in readiness for the return trip, leaving it with the landlord of the pub adjacent to the station. We so enjoyed these holidays, that I feel that they deserve a chapter to themselves if not, indeed, a book to tell the wonderful stories of Briston and its railway-orientated families. I have always felt part of the Briston community, mainly through our holidays spent there, but also from the stories of her childhood told by my mother who never really integrated into Westacre, but remained a Bristonion living in a strange land.

The return from Briston usually coincided with the final decision made by joint negotiation between school and farm for the breaking-up date. As already mentioned, it was normal practice for some oats to be cut before that date, which meant we were stuck in school, champing at the bit, as our thoughts were in that field. The very thought of rabbits escaping from the corn with no one there attempting to catch them was almost too much to bear. As soon as the school day finished, we would mount our bikes and be away to the field in question, to ascertain just how much more work was needed to finish the job. We knew that as the square of standing grain diminished, the rabbits trapped there would be forced to flee towards the hedge. After bolting down tea, the populace of boys would head for the action, armed with a stout nut or ash stick apiece. Bikes would be cast down just inside the field, and off to the standing corn we would go. If a terrified rabbit peeped out of the corn, a great shout would go up and the whole pack of yelling boys would chase the unfortunate creature as it ran towards the hedge, frantically dodging sheaves as it went. Some pursuers would trip and fall on the sharp stubble, others would fail in the chase through lack of breath, but the main pack would close in on the utterly bewildered creature and thrash at it with sticks (often striking a fellow hunter in the mad mêlée to be first in with the fatal blow). Finally the squealing animal would be knocked senseless, and the victor claiming the body would quickly despatch it with a blow to the back of the head, using the hard side of his hand. How proud we were if we could claim to have caught the first rabbit of the harvest!

Taking an ever-present "shut" knife from the pocket, one hind leg of our trophy was slit allowing the other to slip through the aperture and forming a handy carrying handle; at the end of the evening's entertainment it could either be slipped over our handle bar, or the stick pushed through to carry over the shoulder in true hunting tradition. For every kill a notch could be put on the stick. The long row of notches pronounced to everyone your hunting prowess, which was all important in our boyhood days. On reaching home the rabbit would be proudly handed over to Dad for inspection and to be gutted - a rather smelly job I declined to take on, although fellow hunters such as my mate Dilbury would have carried out this job at the field. He really was efficient in all practical things of the countryside - the only place I could hope to outstrip him was in the classroom (and then not by much). After gutting and being passed healthy enough to eat, the now stiff body of the rabbit would be hung on a nail under the shelf in the cool pantry for a couple of days. Mum then undertook the skinning and jointing, whilst we all undertook the eating of the delicious rabbit stew - with my special reward for providing it being two kidneys and the heart, for these were special delicacies and reserved for the hero of the day.

Returning to school next morning was terribly hard to bear, especially when bright sunshine beamed through the windows showing all the dust particles dancing as if in a spotlight. The hum of bees round the open front door drove yet another nail through our captive hearts as every free spirit sought escape from this prison to the wonderful freedom of a warm, sweet-smelling harvest field. Often we could hear the roar of a tractor and chattering of binder mechanism as the field was gradually cut and bound on Abbey Farm land nearby. Oh how we longed for Friday afternoon to come, giving us all five weeks' complete freedom! (I've no doubt that Mrs Clark also craved for a long rest from us inattentive numbskulls, who failed to learn anything in the last two weeks of summer term!)

At last we were free, grabbing our bikes to pedal as fast as possible down the rough drive, along the main road, up Tumbler Hill and home! No more pencils, no more books, no more teacher's dirty looks! School clothes were put away for what seemed like ever, and comfortable, well-worn play-clothes donned for the duration. Brown arms and legs, already scratched from abrasive contact with sharp stubble, became a deeper brown and even more scratched. Meals indoors had to be eaten at great speed, so as not to miss even one minute, or one rabbit, in that field. Don't go away with the idea that the odds were stacked against the poor, defenceless rabbit, because this wasn't so - I would suggest odds of about one hundred to one on the rabbit being caught by our sticks, but in perseverance and dedication to duty we lacked nothing. We patrolled every wood-side and every pit hole as it appeared from the uncut corn, yelling like banshees at supposed sightings. The dark, hunched object often turned out to be a distant molehill or a dark-brown, dead thistle, but these misunderstandings and false alarms just added to the fun.

I remember being on the High House Fifteen Acres, when Ted Thaxton suddenly leapt off the binder to run yelling out into the field. I set off behind also giving voice, only for Ted to pull up after a couple of hundred yards and collapse with laughter. The silly fool had been playing a game with me to see if I would run after fresh air! I was most put out and stomped off, very red-faced, and remained in a bit of a temper all afternoon. My erstwhile twin should never have pulled a trick like that - it just wasn't cricket! Still, the Thaxton sons were always game and ready for a laugh. I did consider returning the trick, but just couldn't bring myself to stoop so low as to joke on such a serious matter as rabbit-catching!

Grandad Eke usually accompanied us when we returned from our holiday in order to stay for a month. His advancing age now prevented him from chasing rabbits, as he used to do in earlier holidays. Often Mum would walk with him to the field being cut, pushing the big pram with Brian lying at the hood end and Michael facing him at the handle end. The ageing Rip would bring up the rear, taking great care to water every thistle along the route with meticulous precision. Great care had to be taken with the pram, as Michael's extra weight at the back would cause it to tip, unless the handle was held tightly. On one occasion I tried to be helpful by getting the loaded pram on to the road, but only succeeded in tipping my two small brothers out into the dust whilst attempting to negotiate the steep slope at our front gate. Needless to say, my efforts were not appreciated by Mother or babies as much time was wasted in soothing and cleaning the latter severely-frightened parties. No one cared about the awful shock I suffered as the whole caboodle turned upside-down on the path.

Anyway, no such calamity had occurred on the sunny afternoon I visualise. As the picnic party arrived, we would gather some sheaves under the shade of a large oak tree, one of many dotted along most field hedges. The sheaves, or shoofs as they were known to us, made comfortable seats. Grandad would sink down and mop his brow with a large handkerchief before replacing his panama hat. Rip would lay and puff away, with his long, pink tongue falling out the side of his mouth. Home-made lemonade or milky tea from a bottle would be shared round, as well as home-made jam sandwiches and cake. Stern, care warnings were issued for fear wasps

Haytime and Harvest

might settle on our jam or drop in the lemonade. A small cloud of flies would always hover above our heads, no matter how often we swiped at them with hands or leafy elder branches pulled from the hedge. Rip would make occasional snaps at his annoyers when they came too close to his nose.

Out in the shimmering sun the tractor and binder would chatter their way round the standing corn, throwing out shoofs with monotonous regularity, stopping only if the binder string broke or the knotter ceased to function correctly. When this did occur, the person on the binder seat would belabour, with a stick, the metal cover on their machine in an effort to attract the attention of the driver in front. As soon as the fault had been rectified, they would gather up the loose corn and place it back on the canvas for re-tying, hop up on their respective seats and away they would go in a slight haze of fine dust always sent up around them by the spud wheels of the tractor.

Just before four o'clock Dick Everard would consult his pocket-watch held by a chain and housed in his waistcoat pocket. In the side bag would go his file as he prepared to leave off for the day. A supply of newly-sharpened cutter blades would be propped in the hedge for use later in the evening, as binding would continue on until darkness and rising damp forced the operation to cease. Hopefully, the field would be completed that day, thus enabling the rabbits to be caught by the many stick carriers who would gather for the finish. If the work had to be left uncompleted, the rabbits would creep away to safety after dark and the small square of standing corn would be left empty the next day.

As Dick turned his bike from the peaceful scene of an English harvest field, his mind must have gone out to the other side of the world where his grandson, Leslie Richardson, had vanished into Japanese hands after the fall of Singapore. Alive or dead, sick or wounded, no-one knew. What an awful shadow of fear and worry was cast across their tea table in that small farm cottage at Soigné.

Turning our thoughts away from the war, we can once more taste the joys of a tea in the cornfield. Charlie Wilson, the Soigné foreman, rolled up in his horse and trap to check on progress and throw down a paper sack containing balls of binder twine. After passing the time of day with Mum he also set his sights for Soigné, following the slow figure of Dick down the dusty road. By this time Grandad would have settled his back to the tree-trunk and gradually dropped off to sleep, his gentle snoring getting deeper as he went. Michael and Brian would enjoy their daily ration of Ministry of Food diluted orange juice. We bigger boys would drift off towards the standing corn just in case a rabbit ventured out when all seemed quiet. Willie Thaxton usually looked in on the action as he made his way home from some part of the Estate - he would also stop for a few words with Mum, exchanging news of their respective families. Maybe he delivered a bottle of tea or some "fourses" for son and daughter, Geoff and Peggy, who manned one of the machines. Artie Keeley and Daisy Frost made up the other team; Artie drove the Case tractor, with an eight-foot Massey Harris binder. Geoffrey drove a Standard Fordson pulling a six-foot-cut binder. As Artie Keeley lived at Low Narford on the far side of Westacre village, he was glad of a cup of tea from Geoff's fresh bottle. It was a long day starting at 7 a.m. and not finishing until 8.30 or 9 p.m. Enough food and drink had to be brought to last that time, and continuous picnics in the harvest field seemed to dull slightly when the hot sun turned up the edges of your stale sandwiches. Daisy Frost, whose husband Diddie was in the RAF, lived at Pretoria, and so had the opportunity of returning home at lunchtime to renew her supplies. Even so, it was a long, often tedious, and always dusty working day, but to me it was the most glorious and wonderful job anyone could wish for. Artie and Geoff were my heroes, and when I didn't want to be an engine driver, then I would visualise myself astride a powerful tractor swathing down corn for the rest of my life.

At about 5 o'clock Mum would gather the things together and the little caravan would return home in order to get Dad's tea before he too set off to work for an extra three hours somewhere in the harvest set-up. Sometimes he would come into our field, along with Charlie Andrews, the shepherd, and begin to set up the shoofs in shocks - stooks to the rest of the country. They would start on the outside rows of shoofs and work as a pair. Taking two rows each, they set off in the opposite direction to the binder, picking up a shoof under each arm, walking to the centre and setting them up on their bottoms, making sure to set them down firmly and banging their heads together at the top, thus ensuring a firm stand. Eight or ten shoofs to the shock was normal, but never less than six. This shocking-up kept the grain fairly dry in wet weather, and also allowed any water to run down the stalks. The process was used mainly on rye, wheat and oats - in fact the latter was required to stand on the shock for a length of time equal to having the church bells rung three times over them. This allowed an extra ripening period for its very leafy, well-wrapped grain. Of course, at the time I speak of, they would have stood a long time waiting for church bells to be rung three times, as in the war no bells pealed, except to warn of invasion. Shocking-up could be very painful on the arms, especially if the crop contained a copious supply of thistles - as was often the case.

Barley, on the other hand, often skipped this intermediate stage, with much being cut during a spell of good weather and carted straight away. In that case, the men would bring their pitchforks and set off in a like manner

Haytime and Harvest

to shocking, but this time one row would be thrown into the next, making a track wide enough to take a wagon. A pair of pitchers, one right-handed, one left, could then pick up the sheaves on either side without any grain being spoiled under the hooves or wheels. Dad and Charlie would work away for three hours, and often join in the big chase when the last few cuts finally laid the corn low and rabbits fled for dear life.

The great thing about those harvests was the fact that everybody, and I do mean everybody, was involved in it somewhere. In a very roundabout way even the tradesmen were worthy of a mention - one in particular. I laugh at the memory of my dad pursuing a rabbit almost the length of Middle Thirty Acres, and gaining on it at last as they approached the road hedge; Dad had prepared to strike, when suddenly a figure appeared and fell on the squealing animal. Dad slid to an amazed standstill, with his stick raised over the prostrate form of Jack, the baker. He had seen the chase from the road, and leaving his van had run out to head the rabbit off, but managed to make the kill himself. Imagine my father's frustration after running almost half-a-mile only to see his next day's dinner snatched from under his perspiring nose! Between gasping for breath he expressed the wish that his stick had got Jack's head for his cheek, but the jubilant baker cared little for Dad's bad grace and bore off the dinner to Pentney.

On another occasion, it was I who got his comeuppance. The old horse pasture bore some wonderful crops of wheat, and the rabbits lived there in abundance - often they would hide in very short holes dug in the corn, and one such hole appeared after the binder passed by. Down on my knees I went, pushing my arm down the hole, and feeling for the back end of the rabbit, as they always went in head first. A sharp bite on my finger shot my arm out again at the speed of light and sent me hopping around, dripping blood and cursing. I was so shocked that I retreated from the hole without further investigation, but I'm sure a rat, a much more formidable animal than the poor, little, terrified rabbit, had taken shelter there. I never remember putting a hand down a hole from then on, but always broke them open with the aid of my trusty stick.

All harvest long we would haunt the fields, and only return home for food, bed and a wash if it was forced upon us. Whether alone or with mates, I enjoyed myself so much it really defies description, but this chapter only paints a picture of the harvests seen by me before my ninth birthday; after that milestone I had to view the scene from another angle - that of a working man!

Chapter 12
Hey Ho! It's Off to Work I Go!

Having read the previous chapter, you would be excused in thinking that wartime harvests revolved around catching rabbit meat to supplement the meagre rations, rather than around cereal production for a nation desperate for bread - but, please remember that you are reading a boy's eye view of village life, and naturally our priorities change as we mature.

So it was, at the age of nine, that I became more involved in the real harvest, and partly left my carefree days of freedom behind. In those days, there existed a certain work ladder and pecking order for boys employed for harvest. The lowest rung, reserved for the youngest and least experienced, was as elevator boy; this entailed sitting at the base of the huge elevator all day with the specific purpose of ensuring that the horse driving the mechanism kept going round as required. This was a very dusty job with a great deal of dry dust and chaff dropping down as the elevator forks went up and down carrying shoofs on to the stack. I can see the dark curls of Cyril Jones covered with dust when he had the job for a short while. Some horses carried on their monotonous task unattended, obeying words of command from the unloader on the wagon, but if the animal was awkward then the elevator boy came into play, as Cyril did on occasions.

The second position on the ladder was that of 'holgy' boy. This much more important job entailed sitting on the horse's back out in the field and calling "hold tight" every time the horse and wagon needed to move on, so that the two men loading the shoofs wouldn't suddenly be jerked off the high load. The third, and most prestigious job, was to go solo and be the driver of a horse-rake out on the cleared fields, cleaning up the loose stalks of grain that had escaped from the shoofs in earlier operations.

It was to the middle order of things that my call came. Mr Wilson parked his bike by the front gate and came rolling (Charlie always had a distinct roll whether walking or riding a bike) round to our back door, seeking my mother. He explained the severe lack of holgy boys for the coming harvest, and wondered if she would allow me to go to work the next week when harvest was to begin in earnest. Hiding further up the garden I could hardly believe my ears - the honour of jumping straight up to number two post was unbelievable, since even the ultra-experienced Dilbury had served an apprenticeship as elevator boy (even if he had been only about seven at the time!). When Mum hesitated and almost said no, I could have wept. In the end, after much persuasion on the foreman's part, she agreed to my going, but not starting at the statutory 7 a.m. - only on

Hey Ho! It's Off to Work I Go

condition that my day should start an hour later would she agree, and the payment of £2-10s would reward me for the harvest of about one month's duration.

For the remainder of the week my stomach knotted up with the excitement of going to work, and with the anxiety about whether I could manage it. Not only had I jumped on to the second rung of the ladder, I was to join the head gang led by George Hall. George was lord over the whole harvest undertaking, and three gangs were involved altogether. Mrs Hall, on hearing of my impending job and proposed one hour late start, told Mum that her George wouldn't like that, only to be informed by my no-nonsense-mum that if he didn't like it, he'd jolly well have to lump it or go without a holgy boy altogether! Needless to say, no more was said on the matter. Anyway, George Hall may have been lord of the harvest, but Charlie Wilson was foreman over him, and he had struck the bargain. My very caring and thoughtful parent considered a twelve hour day to be too long for a nine year old boy. Of course, she was right, as sufficient sleep is very essential for growing children, and her family's health and welfare came before all else.

I was directed to report to the gang as they began work on the top section of the Hulver, which ran along the very extensive Soigné Wood. Covering the mile or so journey on my bike, part by road and part on cart track, I arrived at 8 a.m. to find the work already started, and the wagon out in the field. As my Uncle John was just taking an empty wagon out to the pitchers, I was helped up the shafts and seated on top of a huge shire horse between the large, leather collar and even larger wooden-topped saddle. A leather strap held the two pieces of harness together, thus preventing the collar from sliding down the horse's neck should it lower its head. This strap and buckle made a very uncomfortable seat, but, thanks to my thoughtful uncle, a thick corn sack was produced, preventing me from being too saddle-sore. Off we went with Uncle John guiding his trace horse in front by means of a long pair of reins. My docile mate plodded along behind without any help from me. I must say I felt both nervous and proud to be riding on the back of such a huge animal.

As we approached the loaded vehicle, my mentor gently took hold of the bridle and eased us over to draw close alongside, thus allowing the two loaders to slide down on to the bed of my empty wagon. Then, undoing the hooks on the chain ends, he transferred his trace, or front horse, to the loaded wagon, and away they went heading back to the elevator parked over a stack bottom in the field corner.

Suddenly I felt very lost and lonely as my uncle strode away, but I was so lucky to have four very friendly and helpful men on that first day. Knowing I hadn't handled horses before, Arthur Wright came forward to

103

help settle me down, before explaining that I must shout "Hold tight" in a very loud voice, before moving the horse on to the next shock. After loading the first one, he let me call out before leading the horse forward alongside the next - this he continued to do each time, having a short chat with me as we moved. He explained that to get the horse to go right, I had to pull the rein on that side, and vice versa to go left. When it was necessary to stop, I had to shout, "Whoa", quite loudly, whilst pulling straight back on both the thick, leather reins attached to my horse's mouth. It was a cool, fresh morning, but I lost a fair amount of sweat in the form of nervous energy.

Arthur's pitching mate was a more elderly man, Percy Barnes; both men cycled in from Castleacre to work daily. Our loaders were Ted Dack at the front, and Long "Stacks" Battersby on the back. The latter, younger men, came from Westacre village. By degrees, my erratic steering improved under the quiet tutoring of Arthur, although quite often the wagon was either too far away, or ended up with a wheel on the tail-end of the shoofs. Two of our three horses were quiet, and knew where they were going anyway, and took me around, rather than me guiding them. The third shaft horse was a young gelding named Prince, a grey who was quite new to the job and rather enjoyed being awkward with his inexperienced jockey. He got one or two quick jerks from Arthur to indicate there was a firm hand not too far away if he didn't behave.

After a couple or so loads we went to breakfast, a short break taken about twenty minutes to nine. With relief, I scrambled down to the ground. John showed me how to tie the horse to a hedge-bush using the kind of knot that could easily be undone when needed. Then, clutching my precious sack, I nervously joined the men seated under the hedge opening their white, cloth food bags. Each had a bottle of black tea encased in a sock to help it retain its heat for as long as possible. My neat little sandwiches looked puny beside their doorsteps of bread, but of course their appetites were very healthy, especially those who had left home at Castleacre just after 6 a.m. to bike up to Soigné.

At nine o'clock sharp, George Hall would rise and place his bag back into the hedge. Without a word, all the others would rise up and do the same. Uncle John untied the horse with the empty wagon and set me off to follow my men out to where their pitchforks had been left standing up in the field. For the next three hours work continued at a pace, for remember, the men were on piece-work which meant they were paid according to the amount of work done. Before harvest actually started, George Hall, the lord, Blackie Wright, his deputy, and Charlie Wilson, the foreman, would meet to agree on the price per acre to be paid for the harvest. This meant, in effect, that the agreed sum was paid into a central kitty for every acre of corn crop cleared and stacked. At the end of the week, George would calculate how much money had been earned, and how much could safely be paid to his men, for remember, wet days meant no earnings, so we had to take this all into account. If good harvest weather predominated, then after drawing average wages for the time put in, there would be a nice little lump sum to draw at the end. On the other hand, a very wet time often meant working at a loss and nothing extra to look forward to. Success or failure seemed to lie in the lap of the gods, rather than in sweat from the working man's brow.

After that short explanatory note, we return to the work in hand, namely to clear the rye crop on the upper Hulver. As we proceeded up and down the rows of tall shocks, the cleared stubble area grew apace. Looking back at the stack, we saw it growing almost visibly. As rye ears grow on a very long straw, it soon fills a stack and it grows much faster than one made of short, barley shoofs. By dinner-time at twelve o'clock the square structure seemed almost to have reached its eaves, with the elevator already threaded on to its second length of thread. The stack men slowly descended their long ladder propped up beside the elevator. As tradition would have it, George was always the last to come down as he would be on the stack's completion later in the day.

At this longer break the elevator horse was uncoupled and tied on to the hedge. Each horse pulled leaves from as far down the hedge as he could reach, champing green spittle around the iron bit across his tongue. Clouds of flies, attracted by the animals, annoyed both the horses and the men. After eating, some of the men lit up their pipes and puffed smoke around their heads to clear the pests from themselves. The horses flicked their tails, shook their heads and stamped their feet, all of which set the harness chains rattling. How nice it was to stretch out on my sack and rest my head on a shoof. Being able to stretch out legs that had been tucked up alongside the sweaty side of a horse all morning was indescribable bliss! One or two men took forty winks, for a wonderful peace settled over the gathering after the last piece of food had been eaten and bags packed away. Several half-closed eyes watched for George's first move, as his built-in alarm clock told them it was time to get on - no rest for the wicked, and little for the righteous either it seemed, as off we all went to our appointed places as if by clockwork!

Shock after shock was cleared as the noonday sun beat down. The men worked in shirt sleeves, their braces making a dark, damp patch across their backs. Arthur wore a cap, whilst Percy favoured a trilby to shade his eyes. Both pitchers kept a brightly-coloured neckerchief tied round their shirt collar to prevent grain and chaff from going inside as they lifted the shoofs above their heads. Each time Uncle John brought an empty wagon, I would climb from one set of shafts to the other, dragging my sack cushion with me. Dust and chaff would slowly settle on my head and back, coming in tiny puffs every time Ted Dack placed a shoof into the front of his load. I considered the need for a neckerchief around my shirt collar!

Half way through the afternoon we turned into the row of shocks leading back to the stack. Stopping at the end, we all took the opportunity of going for a drink. My, how wonderful that cool, milky tea tasted - mustn't drink too much as the day was far from over. Carefully measuring my bottle, I prayed that Mum would remember to send an additional drink with Mrs Hall when she brought her husband's fourses. Away I went, round the stack, with my empty wagon. I noticed with interest that Charlie Wilson had arrived to pace out another stack bottom on the end of the one almost completed. Already the middle had been filled and the roof was starting to take shape. Charlie strode his twelve paces and stuck a leafy stick at the end, ensuring his line was straight, then six paces wide marked with a second stick. Then, checking the square on his corners, he gave orders for a load of straw to be spread over the area. At the rate at which long rye shoofs filled the stack, the second one would be needed by tea time. After completing this task, Charlie strode up behind our wagon to enquire from Percy, his brother-in-law, how I was shaping. Apparently he received a reasonable report, for without more ado he set off to his bike and bumped off down the rutted track running alongside the wood back to the road. My steering still tended to be erratic - it was a good job there was a whole field to turn around in. Once or twice when my wagon ended up away from the shock, the younger men on top would laughingly ask Percy whether he needed his bike to cover the distance. Both pitchers would smile at me and reply to the effect that practice would make perfect. This gentle leg-pulling made me feel one of them, and made me determined to concentrate on improving, which I soon did.

At four o'clock, I could relax for a few moments, and enjoy my tea. How thankful I was that Mrs Hall remembered to bring my drink. The heat, coupled with the stress of a new job, had almost dehydrated me, so that extra-long drink was heavenly. As the harvesters always stopped at four o'clock, the break wasn't to eat our tea, but to have our "fourses" - a word kept exclusively for that particular break at harvest time. All too soon our half hour was over, and the wheels set in motion again. Shoofs were slowly sent up the elevator to George Hall, who, as chief stacker, remained alone on the ridge, slowly working back from each gable to finally seal the centre of the stack. As he descended the ladder, he would brush a bit here and whack a place there with his pitchfork. Only perfection would do since no stacker, worth his salt, would leave his handiwork in any way blemished; meanwhile, a few loads would be

Hey Ho! It's Off to Work I Go

thrown straight off the loaded wagon on to the new stack bottom. Whilst this was being done, the team-man would unhitch one of the wagon horses and back it into the set of shafts newly-fixed to the elevator. Slowly, the top-heavy machine would be eased from the stack and gently lowered on the handle. When finally clear of the newly-built stack, it could be dropped to its lowest level and pulled and pushed into place beside the new site in readiness to repeat its task once more.

These manoeuvres would take a little time, so that as our wagon was full before Uncle John could return with our replacement, Arthur suggested I go back and meet him halfway. This gave me the opportunity to at least have a break from the monotony of shouting "Hold tight" for a few minutes and off I rattled, pleased to be able to rest my dry, cracked voice-box. At half past six John announced the fact that he had brought the last wagon of the day. At a quarter to seven, we turned our conveyance towards the stack. I was surprised at the speed suddenly produced by my tired, slow-plodding mount. Horses always knew when it was home time, and increased speed accordingly as a long drink and a good feed in the stable became their one aim in life. They could hardly stand still as they waited to be unhitched, and the five of them to be tied together; off home to Soigné they went, with their team-man up on Prince's back. Away down the cart track they went, with chains jingling, heads nodding, and almost tripping over their feet in their haste to get home.

Before collecting bags and bicycles, the workmen would stand their pitchforks under the elevator, and lower the machine to rest on the stack, or take it down as low as possible. The stack itself would be left with a well-filled middle, just in case rain should come before work resumed. Placing my, by this time, very sore behind on the cycle seat, I set off for home, wobbling a bit from fatigue, for it had been a very long day in unaccustomed surroundings. Was I pleased to get indoors and also to have a good wash - without being badgered into it! - That was a surprise for my mother, I can tell you. A nice supper was soon put out of sight, and was ever a bed so comfortable as mine was that night?

There were so many things to tell my mother, but there was no strength left to talk about them. Long before Dad returned home, just after nine, I was fast asleep, much too tired to even think about all the rabbits that had escaped from the corn due to a mighty hunter like me being busy elsewhere. As my dad had departed for work before my sleepy head was woken by Mum the next day, I had to wait for the weekend to tell him all about it. I've no doubt that he'd had a word with George Hall or Mr Wilson to check on my progress. I hope he was proud of me, as I sought to give of my best and keep up the good Bumfrey working name from day one of my employment.

107

Hey Ho! It's Off to Work I Go

Oh how quickly that second morning came round, and I could hardly believe it was seven o'clock as my mother shook me gently to wakefulness. Dragging myself out of bed, I wearily washed and had breakfast before mounting my bike and going off up the Soigné road and along to the Hulver. As on the previous day, the men were already at work with Arthur leading the horse on each time. Parking my bike, I quickly gathered up my sack from beside Uncle John's bag and was away across the short distance to my post. Arthur Wright held the horse whilst I climbed the shaft to my perch on his back. "Hold tight", and we were off on another day's work, which I hoped would not be such a strain for me.

My steering steadily improved as the day wore on, but I did discover another hidden hazard which hadn't cropped up on the first day - this involved special care when turning the wagon. Two of the vehicles were designed with a free-turning front carriage, allowing a very tight turn if needed. The third one had a central, wooden bar which meant that the wheel caught up if a greater than ninety degrees turn was attempted. I only discovered this when the wheel jammed tight, thus lifting one rear wheel off the ground, causing my loaders to fall down - and me to panic! By straightening out slightly, the wagon regained its equilibrium, and from then on I took a larger circle when manoeuvring that particular vehicle. I felt very silly and lost some of my new-found confidence, but it was all part of the learning process which lasted all through my first harvest.

By mid afternoon, the last row of shocks was picked up and the second stack almost complete. The final shocks gathered were those along the wood side. Here, the rye tended to be slightly green, owing to the partial shade. These shoofs were used to top-up the stack, and could dry out a bit more before thatching took place a fortnight or so later. The big question now was, where were we going next? Well, as the weather looked to be set fair, Charlie Wilson had decided to cart the barley, freshly cut on the Little Strawberries. For the move, I was to take one wagon, Stanley Battersby another, and Arthur Wright the third. The team-man would bring the elevator, using the elevator horse - now reharnessed for shaft use - and his trace horse. Up went my bike on the wagon, as did the other two, and off they went down the track, with me bringing up the rear on our quietest horse. We turned off the cart track and along the road for a short distance before preparing the turn into the field gateway. Suddenly I was confronted with the second big problem of the day as I turned in too sharply and came to an abrupt halt, with the rear wheels stuck on the inside gatepost. More sweat was lost, until one of the men gently backed me off and instructed me to take a wider turn, thus swinging the wagon through the centre of the gateway.

After fourses, the men took their forks and went off round the field, throwing one row of shoofs into another, and making a passage up the middle for our wagon. This meant I could have a rest - much needed I can tell you, after having almost turned the wagon over and then stuck on a gatepost. My nerves were in tatters, and I already had a new system of work to be worry about. This time, of course, I had to look on both sides of the wagon to make sure both pitchers were up to the front and ready for me to pull on. In the event, this didn't prove too difficult, although occasionally I would pull on before Percy had caught up, and then he would politely ask me if I had developed a stiff neck, preventing a turn in his direction. Arthur would wink and tell him to speed up a bit, which would cause a laugh all round.

There were three, separate carting gangs, or companies, engaged in the harvest effort. Blackie Wright headed one, with Uncle Will Bumfrey as team-man and Dilbury as holgy boy. The third gang was led by Percy's brother, Bertie Barnes, with Old Laddie as team-man and Derek Winner, I believe, as holgy boy (but of that I'm not quite sure; I know Derek came up from the village to work at around that time). The latter two stackers came from Castleacre, so they tended to work the fields on the High House side of the farm, whilst George Hall stayed nearer Soigné as he lived next to us at Pretoria. This meant I didn't have too far to ride to work, and could often go home to dinner. Mum would push the pram into the nearer fields at fourses times, so that we could enjoy a picnic quite often. Michael and Brian would have their floppy sunhats on to protect their fair skin. It was very rare that more than one gang worked in the same field, although it might occur near the end of harvest. Great interest was shown by those cycling past in the progress of their fellow workers. I remember one occasion when Bertie Barnes' men were clearing Little Ash Breck. This "little" field was of forty acres and held a very thick crop of corn. Naturally, quite a time had to be spent there, as about seven stacks came off. When I heard my fellow workers remarking the job there had begun to stink, I was very puzzled as to how a nice, clean wheat crop could stink. Their meaning was that very little money was being earned for the kitty, and they were insinuating that the men in question were taking life too easily. By watching George Hall's actions closely, one could gauge how much money was in the kitty. If George rose five minutes before the meal break was due to finish, things were tight. If he gave the men a few minutes' grace after the allotted time, then money was flowing in at a reasonable rate.

We went from field to field, carting barley in hot, sunny weather, and oats off the shock when they were ready, if the weather was damp; or on mornings when a heavy dew existed, we went on to shocked wheat. This cereal never heated in the stack, due to its very stiff straw and would dry itself out, providing threshing was left until late winter. Sometime during harvest, the threshing tackle would pull into an oat field to thresh out oats for a day. This meant unloading the wagon straight on to the drum board instead of stacking the crop. Oats were used for feed and the previous year's supply would be used up by this time. The horses weren't too fond of standing beside the whirring drum and puffing steam engine. There was a job here for the elevator boy to hold their tossing heads and keep them still during the unloading process. One or two extra hands were drafted in to help the four stackers deal with the job. The engine driver usually helped out with the corn sacks, and his mate cut the bonds or fed the drum. The deep-golden oat straw was stacked as it provided valuable stock feed. The only unusable part of the oat was its chaff or flights, the light, feathery covers surrounding the grain. If used to augment stock feed, as other chaff was, it tended to float upwards as the animals breathed, to stick on their eyes and could cause permanent blindness. Therefore, oat flights were always collected up and burned.

When we were working close to Pretoria, I was able to bike home to dinner. If there was time, I climbed the dilberry tree and filled a bag with the sweet, little plums to share with the men. They were very partial to the fruit, and we had so many every year that it was a shame to leave them to the wasps. Mum had an old, lined shopping bag, home- made and very serviceable, which stood the wear and tear of fruit picking. A few over-ripe fruits stained the lining, but no-one worried about a small thing like that. The small, round fruit stone was also very useful as a missile when propelled by exerting pressure on them between finger and thumb. One or two nodding trilby hats were used as target practice by younger members of the gang, whilst consuming the fruit at break time.

One morning, towards the end of harvest, we were carting wheat on Twenty Five Acres, and I had Prince out in the field. Suddenly, without any warning, he started to gallop away across the field. Both my loaders, taken completely by surprise, fell backwards off the load. Desperately I hung on pulling vainly at his reins. A twelve-foot hedge loomed up in front as we headed in the cow pasture direction, and this must have caused him to slant towards the left. I could hear Arthur Wright shouting, "Pull him round, pull him round", and I hung on the left-hand rein. Still shouting, Arthur ran across to cut him off, just managing to catch his head and hang on (at no small amount of risk to himself from hooves and wheels). We slid to a halt in a cloud of dust and I sat with knees trembling and hands shaking.

Arthur stood almost breathless, trying to calm the frightened horse. Percy arrived declaring Prince ought to be shot before he killed somebody. The two loaders had picked themselves up and limped into view rubbing bruised behinds, whilst adding their highly-coloured opinions of the errant Prince. I think the least frightened was myself, as I hadn't realised the extent of the danger. Had I not held on or tried to jump off, the iron-shod wagon wheels would have crushed me and this story would have ended here without the author living to tell the tale. Uncle John came out from the stack to join our group who were trying to ascertain why the horse had run off, but we never found out and Prince couldn't tell us. Maybe a horse-fly stung him, or he imagined there was danger. The big question was, would I want to continue?. I quickly decided I would, and Arthur led the horse back to our row, and work continued with everyone casting wary eyes at the grey gelding. Needless to say, he was as good as gold for the rest of the harvest. Perhaps he had got all his badness out of his system. As everyone had to be run-away-with at least once before becoming a real horseman, I reckoned I had earned my spurs quite early on. It certainly didn't frighten me unduly, as I loved horses, and was never afraid of them.

So harvest drew to a close as fields became bare stubble with a group of neat stacks in one corner. Horrie Everard and his mate were well on the way to thatching them all - the long, orange thatcher's ladder could be seen up the roof, with the golden thatch newly pegged down on the right hand side, and the butt end of sheaves on the un-thatched, left hand side. Horrie, a veteran of World War I, did all the thatching, starting with the haystacks, and then continuing with all corn-stacks. I believe Jack Havers was his labourer then, although the much younger Jack Curl took over later on.

It was a bittersweet day when the last shoof of corn was picked up. We had been over many fields since that first day with the rye on the Hulver - fields with marvellous names, such as Long Elbreck, Honeypot, Ashtree Shift, Heron Hill, Waterpit, Squires Field, or Swaffham Breck. All the fields had their own individual features, such as surrounding woods, pit holes, inclines, trees - no two working days were ever the same, and the company was very good, with everyone cheerful and helpful. At the very last moment Mr Wilson arrived to pay me with two green one pound notes and a brown ten shilling one. How rich I felt - and not a bit aggrieved over the fact that I had worked on average for only two shillings per day (an equivalent of ten new pence for a ten hour day), and I had enjoyed every minute of it!

My work must have been satisfactory, because I stayed with the same gang throughout my whole holgy boy career. Faces changed as my two first-year loaders went on to greater things. Horses changed gradually as age caught up with them. I'm glad to say I never experienced a runaway again, and my driving became second nature. I worked a full day the next year and took home the princely sum of three pounds, rising gradually with experience and wartime inflation. Arthur and Percy remained my pitchers throughout the war years, and I remember celebrating V J Day on the Little Strawberries, with Percy vowing to have an extra cup of cocoa for his supper, whilst the others preferred the pub!

Yes, harvest holds many happy memories for me and remains my favourite time of year. I long to stride into a field being cut by a self-binder and to pitch sheaves on to a horse-drawn wagon. I know those days can never return, but I feel very favoured to have been there before progress wiped out all the happiness and comradeship from the agricultural scene. Those were the days when men whistled and sang at their work. I recall my Grandfather Bumfrey singing away on the stack whilst working on the Brooms (a field on the far side of High House) - he sounded a bit off-key, but I'm sure that he was so happy in his work, that his soul sang from sheer joy. That off-key singing was a much sweeter sound than the tinny transistor blaring out over the building site of today. On second thoughts, perhaps Alfred was a lead singer born before his time, as his near tone-deaf rendition was on a par with many, so-called, modern-day singers.

The author with Rip his faithful dog, High House cottages are in the background.

The author and his father in the vegetable garden at High House.

Checking young stock on the Codlings pasture, or were they checking us?

Mum in her London Days, a far cry from High House.

A High House workers group. Back row, left to right: Grandad Thaxton, Barney Hooks, Harold Plummer, Wesley Moreton, Jeff Thaxton, Dad. Front Row: Cyril Goose, Walter Williamson ('Wibby') and Ted Dack.

More High House workmen, left to right: An Icelandic student, Dick Everard, Herbert Moreton, Walter Williamson, Arthur Wright and Bob Mobbs.

Granny Bumfrey

Aunt Lucy, Grandad, Ivy and Jane

This picture was taken taken at the front of Westacre School in 1949 just before it closed. Mr Angell, the then headmaster, is pictured with, back row, left to right: Brian Wright, Jack Wilson, Peter Welham, Derek Curl, John Thaxton. Centre row: Mary Mills, Madeliene Overton, Margaret Thane, Jean Andrews, June Eagle. Front row: Michael Thane, Roger Taylor, –?– and Terry Eagle.

The children are standing on the lawn with a low hedge behind dividing it from the school path. The smallest window on the right was the infants room with the senior room window on the left.

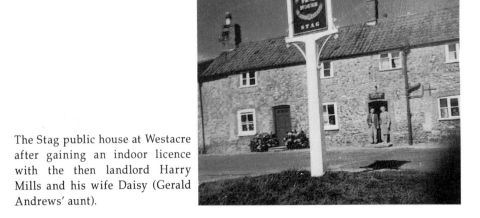

The Stag public house at Westacre after gaining an indoor licence with the then landlord Harry Mills and his wife Daisy (Gerald Andrews' aunt).

A close up of the 'watch and pray' church clock at Westacre.

All Saints Church with the priory gateway leading to Abbey House.

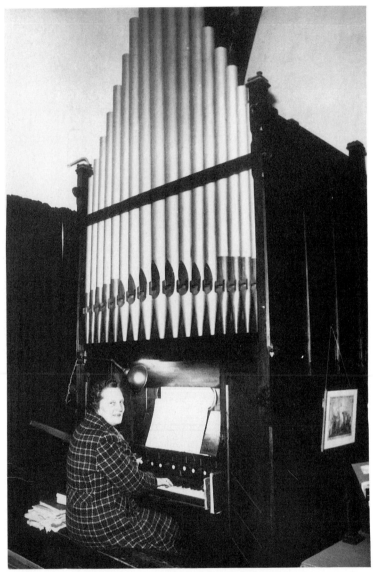

Miss Jean Plummer seated at the Westacre church organ. Note the pumping handle on Jean's left where Gerald dozed on occasions when the day was warm.

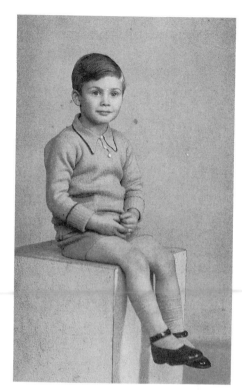

My school friend and farming mentor Gerald Andrews taken in the 1930s. Could you imagine such an angelic lad offering the head gardener 'A shilling for your old hook George?'

Jeff and Billy Thaxton, Joe Bly with Leslie Richardson on a day out.

The hoeing gang on Little Strawberries. Standing, left to right: Cecil Meek, George Hall, 'Larkie' Bennoit, Percy and Bertie Barnes. Seated: ?, Barney Hooks, 'Blackie' Wright, Walter Back, Fred Bumfrey, Aubrey Simmonds, 'Lightning' Smith, Bob Mobbs and 'Lijah' Bloy.

Working for Alfred Lewis, Uncle Will and Dad third and fifth from the left respectively standing at the back.

Harvest at Soigne, out in the field. Seated left to right: Geoffrey Rye and Cyril Goose. Standing: S Hilton, one of the Chase boys and Uncle Will Bumfrey.

At the stack, left to right: Grandad Alfred Bumfrey, Barney Hooks, 'Blackie' Wright and 'Lijah' Bloy.

On holiday at Tithe Barn, Michael, Dad and Granny Eke.

At work, Dad leading out a young bull.

Taken at Melton Constable Loco, left to right: E. Mallet, Uncle Fred Eke, B. Earls and H. Reeve.

Uncle Fred in the cab at Weybourne station, 1950.

Pre war hay makers, sitting, left to right: Ted Dack, Walter Back and −?−. Standing: Fred Bumfrey, Spencer Bly, Percy Barnes and Barney Hooks.

Dad and Granny Eke with the cats outside Tithe Barn cottages.

Granny and Waggs, our second dog.

Another world, 1966, Michael washing his car outside number 6 Pretoria, numbers 1 and 2 on the left.

The author with his father and mother taking the bracing Sheringham air, 1966.

A day at the show, Left to right: Albert Richardson ('Old Laddie'), Uncle Will Bumfrey, Jimmy Lane, Uncle John Bumfrey and Gerald Andrews ('Dilberry').

Chapter 13
Dark Days Before Christmas

As the gate closed on the last cleared harvest field, thoughts turned to harvesting and storing the precious vegetable crops grown on the garden. The late potato crop needed to be dug, dried lightly and picked up into hessian sacks. A good sack was a very precious commodity, especially one without the corners gnawed out by ever-present rats and mice. Most of our sacks were tied across at least one of the bottom corners to keep the potatoes from spilling. First the larger tubers were collected for eating, and then a number of well-shaped, clean potatoes were selected to be the seed basis for the next year's crop, for new seed potatoes were unobtainable at the height of the war. All small tubers were gleaned for use as boiled mash for fowls, and were called, very obviously, chicken potatoes.

The whole crop was stacked in the shed and had to last the family until the following summer when new potatoes were dug. Unfortunately our sheds, although dry and clean, were not frost-proof, so obviously steps had to be taken to prevent the stored potatoes from freezing and this meant putting them back into the garden in a hale or hod. This operation entailed digging a hole about three feet across and one foot or so deep. The hole was then lined with straw and filled with potatoes stacked up to finish with a dome-shaped pile well above ground level; a bucket of water was then thrown over them to prevent shrivelling. A thick covering of straw was kept in place by a good layer of soil, the whole structure ending as a round dome, with a trench all the way round the base where the soil had been taken out. A wisp of straw peeped out of the top allowing the precious potatoes to breath. Here they would lie for most of the winter, or at least until the sack-covered supply in the shed had been exhausted. We usually had two hales on our garden, and sometimes three if an extra heavy crop had been grown. A frost-free period was chosen for the opening of the hale, hod or clamp. I always joined my dad as we knelt on a thick pad putting potatoes into fresh sacks, discarding any rotten ones and complaining bitterly at any signs of mouse or rat damage. Sometimes these pests would burrow into the hod to spoil much more than they ate of the precious food stored therein.

Mum also tried to store as much of the vegetable and fruit crops as was possible. No deep-freeze facilities existed, and only a very limited sugar supply was allocated. Runner beans were sliced and packed into jars with copious amounts of salt to help preserve them. Salt was scraped from a large block, the knife making painful blisters on the youthful hands

113

allocated for the job. Even after much washing, the salty beans were only edible under protest and sheer hunger caused by tight rationing. Plums were bottled in Kilner jars, whose rings were becoming perished with no replacements available. Often the contents would turn black on the shelf and one knew air had entered, owing to a broken seal, rendering the contents useless and all the fiddling work wasted.

Jam was always made with what little sugar came our way. Victoria plum and damson were favourites as the fruit came from our own trees. These jams were always stored in my bedroom, standing in a large, cardboard box on top of the chest of drawers, the reason being that mould came on the top if kept in more conventional places, such as the pantry. So it was jam in the bedroom and apples in the front room. Yes, all the Bramley seedling apples were carefully picked and laid out on newspaper sheets on the front room floor. They would keep like that until winter's end, becoming yellow as they seasoned and quite nice to eat raw. I expect our unsweetened, wartime palates could suffer higher acid levels than our cosseted taste-buds would today.

Pickling was another form of harvest storage we used. Shallots were peeled and pickled, as was red cabbage. Surplus shallots and all the onions were dried and then hung in bunches under the wide eaves of the shed; red cabbages also were trimmed, leaving the head on the long stalk and hung there until required. Another adornment for the shed wall outside was our rabbit skins which were left inside out, just as they had been pulled off the carcass, to dry until a gipsy should call to buy them. These stiff, old skins were then sold on to Horace Friend & Company Limited of Wisbech for use in the fur trade. Dad also caught moles on High House pastures by means of traps. The black, furry bodies were skinned and the pelt nailed out on a board to dry. These were also parcelled up and dispatched to Wisbech for about fourpence each.

There were several wild crops to be harvested as well as those on cultivated land. The dewy mornings of autumn brought a flush of mushrooms to certain pastures. The Codlings pasture near our cottages at High House was one, and it was a great loss when the War Ag decreed it should be ploughed up. But our main supply came from the pasture, used in wartime by the horses, which ran alongside Charlie Andrews' garden. We would take a basket very early on Sunday morning and set out across Lightning Breck to the top of the pasture. There we would gather plenty of pink-and-white, newly-formed mushrooms. Mum would peel them ready to cook for breakfast. "Mmmm" they went down well I can tell you!

Grandad Bumfrey told us that the white, puffball fungi found in woods were very tasty when sliced and fried. These were never tried by our household. My mother said we never should pick and eat any fungi-type

Dark Days Before Christmas

food from under trees. Also, the so-called mushrooms must peel cleanly to be safely edible. Cyril Jones was always wanting to take home doubtful fungi, but we country boys managed to prevent him poisoning himself and his entire family to boot.

Nuts were also much sought after by marauding gangs of boys. Hazelnuts abounded on the bushes bordering the Westacre road and so were easy to collect on the return journey from school. Sweet chestnuts also fell on to the road, the impact breaking open very spiny cases to reveal shiny, brown nuts, so famous for their roasting qualities. Many a long, winter's evening was brightened up by roasting chestnuts on top of the cooking range; if someone had purposely omitted to cut a hole in the thick skin of a nut, it exploded loudly when well-heated, shaking everyone out of their heat-induced semi-stupor, and the poor old dog would leap up off the mat and shoot under the table! Walnuts could be kicked out of their half-rotten cases under the trees on the park and farm pastures. Care had to be taken not to get their stain on the fingers for fear Mrs Clark took umbrage and caned the offending digits. With care we had a good nut supply up until Christmas.

Blackberries were also very useful for cooking as they could be mixed with apples to make jam, or even eaten as a dessert. Stewed apples spread on bread and margarine was used at tea time when our jam supply had run out. A walking-stick came in handy to pull down the large fruit, just out of reach. Some lovely, fat berries could be gathered on the far side of the Mowing Ground. This rather rough pasture was known, for some obscure reason, as the Hundred Acres, although its area fell a long way short of this. Perhaps at some earlier date it had taken in another tract of land which had subsequently been hedged off. Huge bramble thickets grew there, and were so dense that no one could get to their centre. Rabbits burrowed underneath, throwing up great piles of sandy soil. The bramble thickets prevented rabbit diggers from getting at them during the winter months, so they lived undisturbed, probably eating more grass from the pasture than the grazing cattle. Large lawns of closely-nibbled grass surrounded each thicket.

One last crop which became very important in wartime was the rosehip. This fruit of the dog-rose was gathered from hedgerows and sent away for the manufacture of rosehip syrup, a children's medicine rich in vitamins. I don't recollect trying it myself; my tipple was a spoonful of radio malt, and later a foul-tasting concoction known as Famel syrup - these things being designed to strengthen and help clear my weak chest.

Home-brewed beer was made in the summer and I remember watching the live yeast, bought from Jack the baker, floating up and down the dark liquid. If a thunderstorm occurred during the making period the beer was rendered useless, though for what reason I never knew. The finished product was corked down in dark brown beer bottles with black screw tops, then stored on the cool, brick pantry floor. Very occasionally one would explode, sending glass and beer all over the floor. Home-made lemonade was made up using some kind of lemonade powder, but it wasn't until well after the war that 'pop', as we know it, became available from a King's Lynn firm known as Bestyett. This came in varying flavours, with the fizz being kept in the liquid by means of an elaborate, airtight cork held down by a metal, spring-like contraption fastened to the neck of the bottle.

Mum cycled to Castleacre or Swaffham to attempt to buy some off-ration foodstuffs. I remained at home taking care of my two small brothers. Of course, when Aunt Gladys came from London she stayed to keep an eye on us all. Mum had a "sit up and beg" bicycle with shopping bags hanging precariously from the handlebars. It was a good seven miles each way, but she would set off in all weathers without thought of her own discomfort. Her only objective was to find food to help augment the meagre, but essential rations of her family. It was no good the tradesman hiding goods behind his counter for her rather prominent nose would smell them out. The staff of Hannants, and Mallets the grocers, knew her well, as did those who worked for John Aldiss the outfitters at Swaffham. Mrs Joplin at Castleacre was also a good friend whose van had supplied us at High House before the war.

Returning to school after five weeks' harvest holiday meant checking the state of our wartime gardens which had been dug on part of the large playground. The soil was very poor and the length of time they had been left untended didn't help our crop prospects. Very little food was ever produced, but at least we had played our part in the Dig for Victory campaign.

For a start, the autumn term seemed very mundane after all the excitement of harvest. It seemed a long time to Guy Fawkes, and anyway there would be no fireworks. There were enough real fireworks lighting up our skies without adding to them.

We played very little organised sport at school and balls were frowned upon if they exceeded soft, tennis ball-size owing to the many windows overlooking the playground. A heavy, leather football, more often soft than not, occasionally came out for a game on the pasture, but the sloping and uneven surface made playing very difficult. A few games of cricket in the summer were made possible by sheep brought in to crop the grass. If you were chosen to be on Billy Battersby's side you always won, because Billy was chief batsman, bowler and umpire. Anyone silly enough to get Billy out early in his innings usually received a good crack across the backside with the bat for their pains. I remember Georgie Wright clean bowling him and then, after a good bat-whacking, deciding the delivery was a no-ball! Rounders were played more often, because mixed sides helped to hide the problems caused by limited numbers. In the playground we boys played all sorts of war games. On one occasion, just after Dilbury and I had moved into the big playground, we were forced to dig a deep hole to use as an air raid shelter. Branches and twigs were interlaced over the top, and then my mate and I had to take turns to crouch underneath while the big boys bombed us using huge, flint stones brought from the field behind the school. This physical and mental torture continued until one heavy bomber came over with an extra-large stone, which hit my head via one of the roof beams and almost knocked me out. It was then decided to discontinue the bombing raids for a bit.

Minor skirmishes still continued to break out, using smaller flint stones as missiles, until the fateful day we took cover in the toilets and a stone struck my chin sending me off to the District Nurse for treatment. A decree, issued by an irate headmistress, caused peace to break out for a time and some of the bullying to cease, making life a bit more pleasant for the younger element. In those days there was no supervision in the playground and bullying could go undetected as no one wanted to be called a tell-tale tit.

As the days became shorter and colder my friend, Cyril Jones, became starved more often and tended to whine and whinge around the house. One Saturday morning about 9.30 I went through the passage between numbers 4 and 5 to call for him. Just as I raised my hand to knock on the back door a loud scuffle erupted inside, and without further warning the door flew open and a gaggle of arms and legs (which turned out to be Cyril) flew down the steps, being soundly belaboured by an irate mother using a long nut stick. I leapt back out of the way as the stick knew no specific target as it struck out in anger and I had no intention of getting involved in the argument between the stick and Cyril. Laying full length on the muddy path, the unfortunate victim writhed and moaned to the effect that his back was broken in several places. The only reply he received from his mother wasn't in the least sympathetic, although the stick ceased to descend on its prostrate victim. Turning back to the house, the stick owner shouted, "You've got something to moan about now, so get on with it", and disappeared indoors, accompanied by a loudly-slammed door. Thinking discretion was the better part of valour I shot back down the passage, leaving my fallen comrade to lick his wounds and recover his composure as best he could. I am sure neither of the combatants saw me, or cared about me being there. When Cyril eventually appeared, limping and slightly soiled from his brush with authority, I tried to be sympathetic, but found it very hard to keep my face in a sympathetic mask. I must say

Dark Days Before Christmas

his moaning got on my nerves, so there was a certain understanding of how Mrs Jones felt that morning. Unfortunately, the short, sharp, shock treatment failed to cure him of the habit of a lifetime as he still felt starved on cold days.

As we lived on a large game-rearing Estate, shooting became of great interest to us during the autumn days. Partridge shooting came in mid-September and October, before too many fields of root crops were cleared. Even during the war there seemed to be a plentiful supply of cartridges for 12-bore guns, and quite a few gentlemen to use them. Eight sticks were placed at regular intervals just outside the fields to be driven by the beaters. Usually the guns, eight in number, stood behind a high fence, each stationed alongside his numbered stick. A line of beaters walked slowly towards them through the root crop putting to flight coveys of partridge living in the cover. Shots rang out and pathetic bundles of feathers would fall earthwards to be collected as soon as the drive was completed. Trained gun dogs soon picked them up, holding the small birds gently in their jaws. In all, eight separate drives would be staked out by the keepers beforehand as everything needed to be well planned. A great deal of prestige rested on the lord of the manor providing a good shoot for his friends. The grey partridge thrived on Norfolk land before the use of pesticides, but declined so rapidly in the 1950s that it was in danger of being lost altogether. In the days I speak of, one couldn't walk across any stubble field without setting up half a dozen coveys at least. The rather larger, red-legged French partridge was more of a rarity, but seemed to survive the poisonous sprays rather better than its smaller relative.

The main shoot came later in the year when the pheasant season started. Without doubt the pheasant was next to God and had to be treated with the same kind of reverence. To poach it meant risking home, job and almost everything else, for if you were caught and sent for trial, you could bet the magistrate was a sporting landlord, dead set on making an example of any felon daring to take the life of a lordly pheasant - but to shoot it out of the sky between October 1st and January 31st was sport, and as such was acclaimed by all born to take part in the sport as the highlight of the year.

Anyway, we boys enjoyed it for quite a different reason as you will see in a moment. The Estate was divided into five main shoots, which lasted a full day each - Westacre, East Walton, Gayton Thorpe, Pretoria and Soigné Wood, the last two being the best. For the Pretoria shoot the gentlemen and beaters met outside our cottages at 9 a.m. The cars would be parked alongside the road, and the beaters' bikes just inside the field. Gun dogs sniffed suspiciously at one another, and occasionally a disagreement would break out, but this was quickly quelled by a sharp word from an owner. If we were at home from school, we would be looking forward to the first

Dark Days Before Christmas

drive after lunch when the guns stood directly in front of our houses as the pheasants were driven out of the adjoining wood. Some came out quite high and it took a good shot to bring them down. Watching from the window we would see a strong-flying bird suddenly crumple in a puff of loose feathers and come plummeting straight down to hit the ground with a terrific bang. Lead shot would rattle down outside, with sometimes a pheasant crashing into our garden. Unfortunately it was never left for our consumption as, at the end of the drive, a keeper and dog would arrive to search it out. The expertise of the guns varied tremendously. One gun would seem to shoot every bird passing over his section, whilst another would hit thin air almost every time. Each gentleman had a pair of guns, one of which his loader held ready loaded, passing it over and receiving the discharged weapon for reloading.

Plus fours, stalking hats and whisky flasks were the order of the day, making a very typical country scene and one I always enjoyed, both as a boy and later as an active beater. The keepers would be dressed in their best keeping suits, which were provided as part-payment for their work. These of course were not renewable yearly at that time, as clothes rationing prevented this, so the existing ones had to be kept for shooting days and older garments worn at other times. The beaters, both male and female, were clad in all sorts of protective wear, but not of too good quality as the thorns and brambles to be negotiated in the woods gave scant thought to one's clothing and did their best to tear both flesh and cloth. Waterproof leggings were essential as there was always a field of kale adjoining at least one wood and this had to be walked through by part of the force. Only those who have had experience of a kale crop will realise how much water the huge leaves retain, even on a dry day. The beaters were mainly made up of pensioners, ladies and teenagers. The keepers were all above service age - in fact they were approaching normal retirement age.

The shot birds were collected and hung in pairs inside a very ancient, horse-drawn game-cart driven by Jimmy Reynolds who lived at Pretoria. The horse used was deaf, so the discharging guns had no frightening effect on it. The game-cart itself was shaped like a stagecoach with doors at the back, and was lined with rows of hooks on which the birds were hung in braces. Candle-lit sidelights dimly shone to guide Jimmy back to the game larder in the Abbey Farm, and he presented quite a ghostly silhouette as he drove home on a misty November evening.

But the best part came on the Saturday after the shoot when we boys were free to follow the path of the guns. The cartridge cases used by 12-bore guns came in all colours of compressed cardboard, with a shiny, brass base. These made very colourful and useful playthings, and we just loved collecting them. If the weather was dry we found them in pristine condition lying all around the sticks where they had ejected from the guns. They were red, orange, blue, green and often grey, depending upon the manufacturers. Standing about four inches high, they could be built into forts or garages, farm stacks or buildings. Endless hours of fun were had with these 'freebies', both in collecting them and playing with them. Off we would go with our bags, running from stick to stick, trying to outpace our mates and get the best colours first. Sometimes we would find special cases with double-depth, metal bases and these were valued very highly. Sometimes the ground was muddy as we slopped around, and often it was hard and frosty, with the cartridges covered in rime frost causing our fingers to ache with cold as we trudged from field to field. Foggy days made life difficult as it was hard to follow the line of stands, but we loved the fresh air and freedom, carrying our collection home like gold-dust to set them up for counting in the warmth of our living-room. If the cases had become damp they were set along a wide hob under the oven door on our kitchen range; there they could gently dry without losing shape.

One Saturday afternoon we were cartridge-hunting around the top of Tumbler Hill wood when we came upon a pile of shot pheasants lying beside one of the shooting sticks. A council of consultation was called and we hung around our find to discuss the best thing to do with them. As it was very misty we were sure there was no one observing us, so we toyed with the idea of taking them home and discreetly saying nothing, but weighing the risk carefully, and taking into account the godlike esteem pheasants were held in by the guardians of the Estate, we decided to leave them there and tell Clem Softley of our find. This we did, hoping for a reward, but I don't think we received anything beyond being complimented upon our honesty. But maybe Clem thought he had done us a few favours in the past by closing one eye to some of our escapades, so this made things even. If someone in authority had spotted the birds, it would have shown the keepers up in a poor light, as they all spent the day following the shoot "picking up". This involved going over the ground with their dogs, picking up any missed or wounded birds. To have failed to notice this number would have suggested that perhaps they had curtailed their duties considerably and gone home to tea rather early.

As we went through all these pleasures of the autumn of 1944, we little realised the heavy blow that fate would deal our family before the year ended. Aunt Gladys had fled London as the V1 and V2 blitz began in earnest. Our household now consisted of herself, her daughters Kathleen, Sylvia and Gill, as well as Mum, Dad, myself, Michael and Brian. It was towards the end of November when little Brian fell ill with a 'flu-like infection. Dr Thorpe came and treated him for influenza, but he became steadily worse and had to be admitted to hospital at King's Lynn. More

Dark Days Before Christmas

days of terrible anxiety followed, but our little brother never responded to any treatment. The death certificate gave the cause of death as tubercular meningitis. He was three and a half. We were all devastated. We just couldn't believe such a healthy, fair-haired little boy could be taken from us.

On the day of the funeral I took Michael for a walk and we collected some cartridges down near where we found the pheasants only a few weeks before. As we walked alongside the wood the funeral cars passed the end of the ride. Brian William Bumfrey could never enjoy the simple, boyhood pleasures we enjoyed, but he had lived in a loving family home for his short life, and had been loved by all who knew him. He lies at rest in the corner of the new churchyard at Westacre under the holly trees. Margaret Eagle and Brian Chase rest nearby for they also had very short lives on this earth, although slightly longer than our Brian. His death almost broke my mother's heart and cast a deep gloom over our lives for a long time. In fact the run up to Christmas has never held any joy for me, even to this day.

Aunt Gladys went away, and we somehow dragged ourselves into the New Year. Dad cut a small fir tree from the wood, holly was picked and put above the pictures, but Christmas was a sad, sad time. To this day, I'm always glad when Christmas is over, for I cannot rid myself of a deep sadness until November and December have gone, even after 49 years and as I write this chapter.

My mother never totally recovered from the loss. Perhaps if we had lived in an age of counsellors they could have helped, but I feel that genuine grief is all part of life, and must take its place beside all the happy feelings that we retain. My dad very rarely showed his true feelings, but I know he also felt the loss deeply, as he did also when his mother passed away. The only time I ever saw him drink a cup of cold water was just before her funeral. It was so unusual that it stuck in my mind so vividly; I can see him now with a deep-mauve scarf around his neck bending to dip a cup in the bucket under the pantry shelf. The tears were running down his face as he prepared to cycle to the little church at Gayton Thorpe.

Prior to that sad year, our Christmases had been small, family affairs. We always had a Christmas tree with clip-on candle holders which hopefully would stay upright to keep the flame from the pine branches -a certain fire hazard if ever there was one! Treasured decorations were retrieved from the cupboard under the stairs and hung up. Sugar mice and chocolate pipes or Father Christmases were used to decorate the tree when available, and some thin tinsel finished it off. Dad always bred and fattened his own cockerel which was kept in its own little run and killed a few days before Christmas. A particularly barbaric way was traditionally used to kill the bird. It was hung up on a convenient apple

121

branch by its legs, then systematically bled from the beak using a sharp knife. This medieval method drained the blood from the whole body, giving very white meat. I used to hate to see the poor bird that I had helped feed fluttering his life away thus.

Poultry was always hung in the shed for a few days, with a piece of brown paper tied around the head to catch the last drops of blood. Mum did the plucking, keeping the feathers for cushion or pillow stuffing. Some of the stiff, wing feathers made us Red Indian head-dresses, or bird scarers to twist in the wind in springtime. I conveniently forgot my previous qualms on the big day and enjoyed roast cockerel with roast potatoes, brussels sprouts and parsnips, together with home-made stuffing and Christmas pudding. This feast filled our war-shrunken bellies in next to no time. Dad always managed to remark afterwards that he would have preferred a lump of cheese instead. It's a wonder he didn't get crowned with a dirty saucepan after all the effort my mother had put in!

Christmas Eve was always exciting, with Santa Claus eagerly awaited by two little boys and a bigger one, who wasn't quite sure what to expect. I prayed every Christmas for a threshing engine and drum, but it never came, mainly because no one made a toy like that. I did have a mobile, anti-aircraft gun which showed a flint spark at every firing. I shot down many an enemy aircraft with that as they tried to bomb our forts made of spent cartridge cases! We also had a proper toy fort and some lead soldiers, and also a Meccano set with which we made many things. A shortage of nuts and bolts became a problem, as no replacements for mislaid components were obtainable. A big, wooden box with a lid held the toys, and this was the most useful item in the house. Coupled with our toys, we had a wind-up gramophone which played '78' records, of which we had a large selection and many of which had passed on from Rats Hall. Hours were spent playing with this, and Mum would change our needle every so often as the sound began to slur, indicating a worn needle. My favourite record had a lovely, bright-green label and was a rather sad song, whose name I cannot remember. Some of the words were:

> "A million miles I've travelled,
> and a million sights I've seen,
> and I'm waiting for the glory soon to be.
> Oh, I wonder, yes I wonder,
> in the glory way up yonder,
> will the angels play their harps for me?"

I presume they were words sung by a tramp or hobo reaching his final resting place. A much more lively record was about the day that

Dark Days Before Christmas

O'Rafferty's pig ran away. There were marches, love songs, comic songs and monologues. Some records had cracks, some had scratches and some had coloured stamps stuck on their labels which we watched spinning around. There was the little dog peering down the gramophone horn on His Master's Voice label, and the horse and jockey who had a record for a head on the Winner label. Centre rings came in all colours, varying through maroon, red, blue and green, depending upon the record companies. The colours sometimes meant more to my small brothers than the songs on the records. Often they would pick a colour to play, and we would have to endure an unloved recording just to keep the peace.

This form of entertainment passed away many a long winter afternoon until the fateful day when the winding handle turned with no resistance. The double spring had broken and war time shortages meant that no replacement could be obtained. Michael couldn't understand why it didn't work after he had turned the handle, but it was clear to everyone else that O'Rafferty's pig had run away for the very last time.

Chapter 14
Winter Sports, Norfolk-style

Living in Norfolk meant that we experienced quite a bit of real winter weather in most years. To us boys, some hard frost and snow meant a lot of fun and maybe a period when we couldn't even get to school. To the adults, especially stockmen like my father, it meant much harder work and hours of trying to thaw out pipes in the stock yards.

The year of 1947 was particularly severe, with much snow and high winds which caused drifting making many roads impassable. Pretoria was cut off by road for days on end as the wind whipped fresh snow from the large fields to deposit it in huge drifts, many feet deep, on the roads. Everywhere looked like fairyland as the drifts were cut into wonderful, curved shapes. A horse-drawn snow-plough could clear normal, lying snow, but gangs of men were needed to cut a way through the drifts. One day, towards the evening, Tumbler Hill was cleared only for the wind to have completely filled it by the next morning. The same applied to all roads leading to Pretoria - the only way to travel was to walk across the frozen fields where the snow had been blown clear.

Tractors brought our food and other essentials as the big freeze continued from about 12 January to 20 March. School was out for most of this period, because by that time I attended the grammar school at Swaffham, seven miles away. My lessons suffered badly, but I had the time of my life enjoying a cold-free winter, far from the germ-laden air of the classroom. We all hoped the snow would never melt, although my dad had other opinions and would get quite growly when we mentioned it. His bike was permanently left in the shed as he never risked life and limb on a bike if there was ice about - not since the day he fell turning the corner off the High House Road into Pretoria. As I was present, I can tell you how spectacular it was. Freddie was riding with one hand and carrying a can of milk in the other. As the machine began to slide he was more concerned with saving the can than himself. As the bike went one way, he went the other and continued to slide along the road on one knee, with his precious milk can held straight and high in a most ballet-like posture. I thought it hilarious and just couldn't contain my laughter as I slithered across the icy road to rescue the fallen. Dad suffered a badly bruised knee and severe loss of face, but was slightly cheered by the saving of the milk supply. Into the shed went the bike and there it stayed until a thaw set in.

As the High House road was on the north-west side of a wood, it was one of the last roads to lose its covering of packed down ice. The other

Winter Sports, Norfolk-style

factor against it was that it was on the extremity of Bert Pitcher's length, and consequently came last on the sanding priorities in bad weather. A thaw was always imminent by the time Bert and Norfolk County Council barrow had reached our neck of the woods.

A large snowman always sat on our garden opposite the living-room side window. With a body well packed together, he would outlast most of the drifts, defying the thaw to the very last minute dot of frozen snow. When that dot disappeared we felt spring must be just around the corner once more. Wonderfully long slides were cut out on the road, but we were never allowed to slide on any of the frozen ponds. Mum was very strict about this, and we never went against that particular rule.

After the war ended and John Thaxton came to live at Pretoria, we used to play ice cricket on the bottom road. Michael, John and myself were the only boys left in the row after the evacuees returned to their respective cities. But that fact didn't curtail our fun. The form of movable wicket we used, I believe, was a five-gallon, empty oil drum, the bat was a thick stick and we had a small, hard, rubber ball. Falling around was all part of the fun, although I think Michael broke his arm once and John suffered a bleeding nose when I returned the ball straight from my bat into his face. A full-blooded drive took on a new meaning as he bled like the proverbial stuck pig. A quick dash to our house for first aid soon sorted him out before sent him further up the hill to explain his blood-stained shirt to his mother. On another occasion we three were having horse races by jumping roadside drainage ditches. There had been heavy rain, but some of the ditches were drying out and were filled at the bottom by thick, semi-liquid mud. Unfortunately one horse fell at the third ditch and went into the mud - I don't know why it was always the unlucky John who came to grief, but his clean, blue shirt was a muddy mess when we hauled him up again. This time we could do nothing to help, and he had to return home alone to face the wrath of an exasperated mother!

John was a carbon copy of Just William when it came to being accident prone, but was a great mate to Michael and myself. Game for anything, he enjoyed all our country pursuits, especially our rabbiting expeditions on cold winter days. Never starved like poor Cyril Jones, he would enter into all our winter sports. It had been very hard to get Cyril motivated on any but warm, sunny days, but I suppose being born and brought up in Devon meant that Norfolk felt two coats colder to him. John came from High House to live at No 8 Pretoria shortly after the war ended and helped fill the gap left by the return home of the evacuees.

Field Barn was one of our favourite haunts at all times of the year, but especially in winter time. It lay on the border between High House and Warren Farm land, being under the jurisdiction of the latter when in use,

Winter Sports, Norfolk-style

and consisting of various open and closed bullock yards and a lone cottage. At the time I speak of, the cottage was empty and had ceased to be suitable for human habitation. The last person to live there was a Mr Jex and his blind wife. Being about two miles from the road and three miles away from the village, life must have been very hard for them. Mr Jex spent his winter months grinding swedes and mangolds by hand, then feeding them to fattening bullocks in the yards. The roots were sliced in a machine turned by a handle attached to a large wheel. Mixed with chaff, they were then carried by bushel-skep to the yard feed-bins, or mangers, where the bullocks could slowly feed all day. As spring approached, the best of the animals would gradually be weaned off and sent to Lynn fatstock market. How long Mrs Jex had been blind I don't know, but we all felt very sorry for the couple. Eventually, I believe, she had to go away, and I hope it wasn't to the workhouse, but that would be very possible in those pre-National Health Service days. When the property fell vacant, Dad spotted the decent, galvanised-iron shed in the garden, and, as the house was condemned, he asked if he could remove it and put it in our garden. This he did, and we gained a bicycle shed on the end wall of our existing buildings. Having just an earth floor it was very dusty, but dry overhead, and made a useful addition to our shed space.

As soon as breakfast was over and chores completed, we three musketeers would collect our trusty, many-notched sticks and set off through the Squires Field gate and up beside the wood in the direction of Field Barn. Sometimes we followed the wood round to the very top of the field, and along a short cart track. On other occasions a track through the wood brought us to the Mowing Ground gate, and across we went via the duck pond where hides had been specially built for shooting wild duck lured on to the water. Occasionally, cartridge cases could be collected from the floor of the hides, but overall, very little duck shooting took place. Climbing the end gate, quietly we would creep around the side of the silent bullock yards. Fairly large areas of rough grass and nettles ran alongside the buildings making a wonderful hiding place for rabbits. Creeping stealthily into position, we would walk into the tall grass from different directions, hoping to confuse our quarry and making a killing more likely. On one occasion a rabbit ran out near to us, and John yelled, "There he goes, run like the b******". Well, for the life of me, I couldn't run - it sounded so funny! The rabbit left me doubled up with laughter, and a very red-faced John demanded the reason for my unusual behaviour. Swearing wasn't one of our normal vices, but I suppose it just slipped out in all the pent up excitement. It appears that John often told his grandfather, Mr Thaxton, of our hunting expeditions, as he, in turn, told Dad that every other rabbit around Field Barn had broken bones and nine lives as they all narrowly

Winter Sports, Norfolk-style

escaped from we intrepid hunters.

After exhausting all the likely areas hiding the next week's dinner, we would go across to the house. Having been empty for quite a time, it was very damp, smelling of soot and mildew. Great lumps of soot had fallen into the hearth, whilst the broken, kitchen range was rusty. Obviously we searched diligently for any treasure poor old Mr Jex had left behind, but found very little, apart from a few empty jam jars in the pantry and some old newspaper on a cupboard shelf. Upstairs, the water had come through the roof in places, but parts of the wooden floors were dry. A lookout could be kept towards the Warren where a very long cart track wound over the hill to the farm just out of sight. Should any enemies approach from that direction we could take evasive action well before they came. The yellowing newspapers from 1936 gave us some football results and league tables showing Norwich City up in the dizzy heights of Division 2 of the Football League - almost unbelievable to us who only knew them in their parlous state of applying for re-election to Division 3 South. A team called King's Park were in the Scottish League and, to top it all, there was not yet a league place for our arch enemies of all time, Ipswich Town. That very thought almost made up for the earlier disappointment when all our rabbits got away.

On drowsy summer days we would lie looking out across sunlit fields, with heat-haze shimmering across the distant woods. We made up imaginary cricket teams, of which John was captain and opening batsman. Michael, already a fast bowler in mind, if not in body, would claim a hat trick in the first over. Both Michael and John became leading cricketers in the village with ball and bat respectively - almost as we had dreamt it many years before. My imagined prowess remained a dream, and I spent my village cricket career making up the number when a shortfall occurred.

Let us refrain from dreaming and return once more to the white fields of Norfolk and the winter pastimes of youth. All the stacks we had helped build at harvest had to be threshed out during the winter months. This operation came after the sugar-beet and other root crops had been cleared from the land in the months leading up to Christmas. All through the muddy days of October and November, gangs of men had been knocking and topping sugar-beet in readiness for it to be transported from the roadside to the factory at King's Lynn. I recollect one beet crop on Swaffham Breck, the field in front of our house. A very foggy, November afternoon hid everything from view. Standing on the bank under the oak tree, directly outside the gate, my eyes strained to see the workers. A steady slice, slice, could be heard as the hooks cut beet from tops. The rattle of beet thrown on to the board bottoms of the tumbrils, the jingle of horses' harness, and muffled orders shouted to the animals, came to me, but

Winter Sports, Norfolk-style

no movement could I see and it was very uncanny. Blinking my mist-covered eyelashes, at last blurred figures appeared and a ghostly horse came towards me. Suddenly there were four men, led by my Grandfather Bumfrey complete with cap, and Protos sacks around his waist and shoulders, and the damp mist gave the whole a white halo. His moustache bristled with tiny drops of moisture and I expect his nose held a drop as well. He could well have been a Norseman or Viking coming out of the mist, but his approach was nothing like that of our fierce ancestors as he recognised his little grandson. With the gentleness associated with all Bumfreys towards children, he came over and talked with me, wiping his muddy hands on his sack-apron and filling his pipe with Darkie shag, or whatever foul concoction he smoked at the time. His huge figure, slightly bowed with age and hard work, towered above me, but it was as equals we stood and discussed the awful weather and what we would have for tea. Perhaps he was looking forward to his favourite pea soup which Aunt Ivy once told him he had on the brain! As I turned back across the road, the men bent their backs once more and disappeared into the mist, accompanied by the juicy swish of hooks through the beet. Who the other three ghostly figures were I don't recall. They could have been any of the men mentioned in the harvest chapter, or Elijah Bloy, Larkie Bennoit, Bob Mobbs or Barney Hooks. There was a large number of employees to choose from in those days.

The sound we most looked forward to in the days coming up to Christmas was a low rumbling far away in the distance. It came from the Tumbler Hill wood direction at about 4 o'clock in the afternoon. As the rumble grew louder, we would stand on the bank, with eyes glued to the spot near Short Row Pit where the Westacre road came into view through the trees. A small spiral of smoke appeared first, rising up through the leafless branches, and then it rolled into full vision - the threshing drum and elevator, pulled by a huge, black steam-engine, with flywheel spinning and mammoth wheels grinding along the highway. Up on the footplate stood Fred Petch senior, and the smaller figure of Harry Forster, his assistant and drum feeder. Smoke curled out of the tall smoke stack or chimney slowly melting away in the air as the magnificent machine rolled along the level stretch towards Pretoria. Where were they going? Which way would they turn? These anxious questions were asked one to another.

As the tackle reached our corner, Fred would give the steering wheel several quick turns to the left and the chain steering would pull the slightly smaller, front wheels round into the Soigné road. Extra power was now required to haul the load up our hill, so huge chuffs of black smoke and sparks would fly into the air. The whole ground shook with the power and weight as the huge conveyance lumbered past. Any weak road surfaces

Winter Sports, Norfolk-style

were broken by the massive, rear engine wheels. Little boys' thin legs shook inside their short trousers, but one could never miss the magnificent sight of the passing threshing tackle, however young we were.

No sooner had the machines passed, than off we went behind to ascertain their destination, up the hill and away towards White Gate Corner where the engine cut speed to slowly turn into the gate between Middle and Lower Thirty Ares where up to four or five stacks had been built. This was great and we knew where we would spend the next few days of our holiday. Our attention would turn from pursuing rabbits to the nation's biggest pest and public enemy number one, the brown rat. Corn-stacks provided a perfect home for rats and mice, giving not only dry shelter, but an in-house food supply as well. Stacks became infested as soon as cold, autumn weather restricted the food supply in open fields and hedgerows. Runs were cut along the sides of stacks, and holes dug under the stack bottoms as well; also, one penny was paid by the farmer for every rat killed. The law stated that a wire netting fence had to be erected around any threshing operation to enable rats to be caught. We just couldn't wait to get our sticks into operation.

The drum was reversed and pulled alongside the first stack, and the straw pitcher hauled up on to the rear end. The engine itself was damped down, and left facing the machines in readiness for an early start the next morning. After pulling a tarpaulin over the back end of the machine, Fred and Harry would untie their bicycles that had hung under the elevator during the journey from Westacre, and ride off along the green road towards East Walton where they both lived.

The men would return well before 7 a.m. in order to pull up the fire in the engine and get up steam for the coming day's threshing. Steam coal was supplied by the farmer hiring the tackle, as well as the clean water required to keep the machine working. Before threshing began, the drum was uncovered and a medium-sized, leather or canvas belt was fitted between it and the elevator. This had to be at the correct tension, and some adjustment was necessary to the machines. When correctly positioned, wedges were placed in front and behind the wheels to keep the machine steady. The drum needed to be level, this being checked by a bubble set on the drum top. A jack could be used to rectify any serious deficiency. Finally, the wide, leather drive-belt was connected from the large engine flywheel to the small-diameter, drum drive wheel.

Whilst all this technical work was being done, the three men working on the corn-stack would have been on the roof pulling the brorches and clearing the well-weathered thatch. Brorches were the nut sticks used to hold the thatching string in place over the straw. These sticks were gathered up and tied ready for use the next year. A few were left out and used to peg the rat-catching, wire netting in position around most of the site, although a large gap was left on one side for access as wagons came and went with sacks of grain and chaff.

At last, all would be ready, and in the half-light of a December morning, the flywheel would turn slowly, breathing life into the drum and straw pitcher. As the wheel gathered pace, the various belts, pulleys and riddles whirred and shook, miraculously changing shoofs of corn into sacks of grain and chaff, and spewing out golden, barley straw at the back. A great dust was raised in all departments and neckerchiefs were the order of the day, especially for the three men on the corn-stack when later they would be lifting rat-ravaged shoofs above their heads. It was the practice to place the drum on whichever side helped to take the dust away from the stack, but sometimes a change of wind direction would make life very uncomfortable for Arthur, Percy and Elijah Bloy. It required ten men to run a threshing gang - three on the corn-stack as mentioned, two on the straw-stack if barley was being threshed, and one extra hand for wheat, rye and oats. Bertie Barnes and Horrie Everard were the usual straw stackers, with perhaps a younger man coming in on occasions. Blackie Wright was always in charge of the grain sacks, with an assistant, weighing up into 12, 16 or 18 stone bags, depending upon the type of grain being threshed. Oats, barley and wheat filled railway sacks in those weights as indicated. The thick, stiff sacks were hired from the individual railway companies, although in wartime they were well assorted and even more patched as the years progressed. London North Eastern, London Midland Scottish, Great Western Railway and even a few Great Eastern sacks came off the pile. Quite a number sprang leaks and Blackie would have to leap to plug the gap with rolled wisps of straw before too much precious grain poured on to the ground.

The worst job of the lot was attending to the chaff. This was collected in large bags from a chute often placed between the stack and the drum. Here the dust was thickest and conditions far from enjoyable. Poor old Pat Easter, who was as deaf as a post, attended to it sometimes, or at others perhaps some unfortunate youth, who had fallen foul of Charlie Wilson and faced a punishment worse than death itself for his indiscretion, was given the job. The last two men in the gang were positioned on the drum itself. One man received the shoofs from the stack-man on to a board, cut the string holding the corn together, and pushed it towards Harry Forster who fed it, ears first, into the rapidly- turning beaters. These beaters immediately knocked the grain from its ear to fall on to a series of various-sized riddles which separated grain from straw, chaff from grain, and eventually head corn from tail corn, and despatched each item into its own, individual chute where it was bagged or sent up the elevator, as was

Winter Sports, Norfolk-style

required. All weed seeds and tiny stones were shaken through the whole machine to drop down under the drum. These seeds made a wonderful feast for hoards of different finches after the operation was complete.

As the drum began to turn at full speed, a wonderful humming sound went out through the frosty air. Getting up as early as possible, I would quickly breakfast and get outside to feed the chickens and complete any other allocated jobs. The hum of the drum two fields away would add wings to my heels. At the time when Cyril was billeted in the row I would then have a long, tedious wait for him to surface; later on, in the John Thaxton days, John would be calling for me, raring to team up with Michael and myself and be away to the scene of action.

Not many rats appeared early in the day because there were hundreds of runs down in the body of the stack for them to retreat into. Occasionally one would leap off the edge when a forkful of shoofs was lifted up. We would then set off in pursuit, until our victim hit the wire- netting guard, and then we would almost demolish the net with sticks flailing the air and only occasionally making contact with the rat. As in rabbit catching, a great noise was made to terrify our intended victim and, in this case, to give us Dutch courage, as a cornered rat could be a very nasty customer indeed.

In fact, on this very day I had a nasty experience and one I didn't forget in a hurry. Pacing up and down the stack side, we kept vigil until we spotted a very large, scabby, ginger-backed rat creeping away towards the end of the netting. Quickly taking up the chase, I followed him over the frozen ruts as he made tracks for the nearby pit hole. Taking an extra long swipe at him, I tripped and fell on the rough ground. As I lay face down in a deep rut, I suddenly saw the foul creature coming down the rut towards me. Frantically I tried to roll away, but couldn't get a grip on the frozen earth. The rat, hell-bent on getting to safety, ran right over my face and I can feel his feet now and the scrape of his scabby tail. John carried on with the chase, but was defeated by the ruts and a very wily rodent who knew how to use them to his advantage. Small brother Michael stopped to help me up and watched me spitting imagined rat fur from my mouth. This I continued to do for the rest of the morning, as my imagination relived the nightmare again and again. My ribs were sore where they had crashed on the hard rut edges, but otherwise my much deflated personage was okay. Needless to say, I declined to chase any quarry that made it clear of the netting on that particular day.

At about 10.30 the drum would slowly run down as Fred Petch took the engine out of drive, for the men to have a drink, and then he helped load the first wagon with sacks of corn. The sixteen stones of barley were lifted by two men on to a stool set under the open back of a wagon. The driver, probably Uncle John, would pull the sack up on to the vehicle,

Winter Sports, Norfolk-style

with the two men below giving a push up on each corner. When loaded, the wagon would set off to the farm, pulled by a shaft and trace horse. The sacks would be stored on the first floor of the barn until a lorry called to transport the barley to a mill for grinding. Some of the barley crop would be allocated to the farm for grinding into meal for pig feed, and this operation was carried out on the premises with Dick Welham in charge.

After the short break, the drum would be started again and threshing would continue until 12 o'clock, which was the universal time for dinner to be taken. If the day was quite chilly, a fire would be built in the nearby pit hole and at about 11.30 one of the gang would have been spared to gather small twigs from the scrub bushes growing in the pit to get a blaze started. Larger pieces of dead wood were added, and by the time the gang stopped, a lovely, blazing fire would be going. Donning their overcoats, the workmen would carry dinner bags, and sacks for seating, into the hollow to enjoy a rest and maybe some toasted bread as the fire warmed their fronts and coats protected their fast- cooling backs. We boys would set off for home where dinner was swallowed at high speed to enable us to be back ready for action when the men rose again at twenty minutes to one, resuming their work on the stack.

One stack was threshed per day, and when the task had been completed and all grain sacks loaded, the men had finished for that day. Mind you, after sweating all day in such a dusty atmosphere they needed any time gained to use in washing the grime away, having no proper bathroom facilities to help them.

The early afternoon was the most important and exciting time for we rodent killers. As the corn-stack became lower, the rats were forced to run for new cover, and the action became intense. As each forkful of shoofs was lifted from the stack edge, we stood with sticks raised in readiness to strike. Often two or three rats would be uncovered and shoot off in various directions. Once, in my excitement, I struck Elijah's pitchfork and earned a growled reprimand for my pains. His precious pitchfork was a valuable tool of trade and had a very bowed handle, I remember, caused by continuous heavy lifting.

Every rat caught was kicked over into a pile for eventual counting. The farm paid the gang one old penny for every rat killed, so it was important to keep a tally. All pink, young ones were scooped up from uncovered nests and died from cold on the boot hill of the rat world. By about 3 o'clock the last of the very flat shoofs would have been lifted from the stack bottom, leaving a flat bed of straw, twelve feet by six feet, on which the barley-stack had rested since that lovely, warm harvest day when we started the whole cycle off.

Now came the finale of the sport, as the men slowly turned up the stack

Winter Sports, Norfolk-style

bottom to reveal rat runs cut into the soil resembling a complicated, under-stack road system. Rats fled, sticks flew and shins cracked if too eager legs got in the way. Charlie Wilson's little, white terrier joined in the mêlée, until a wild stick sent him howling away with a very sore back. Neither the dog nor Charlie were too happy, but, with the shock soon forgotten, the little dog was back in the fray. Some of the old rats were fearsome to look at, with red eyes peering out of holes, daring the enemy to come near. A well-aimed pitchfork tine through the straw soon had them skewered on the end and a heavy boot squashed fight and life out of them. Of course, every long trouser leg was tied at the ankle with string to prevent a rat streaking for cover up the inside. The mind boggles at the very thought of what would have happened when a great, sandy rat reached the point of no return!

Sadly, at last, the stack bottom would be turned and every last moving rat and mouse slaughtered. One of the gang would count the bodies with white bellies turned up to the sky. Soon, when peace returned to the field corner, crows and surviving rats would return to eat their fill on the pile of carcasses. Pink rat and mouse babies made a good supper for winter-hungry rooks in their colonies, or lone carrion crows and magpies seeking to feed away from the keeper's gun.

Slowly the huge engine would manoeuvre the heavy tackle along to the next stack in readiness for an early start on the morrow. It was miraculous how that machine, with fire in its belly, turned and ran over dry straw without starting a fire accidentally. I know a spark-guard covered the chimney, but even then a stray cinder seemed ever likely to drop from below the fire box. After watching the last of the corn sacks being loaded, the threshing tackle relocated, and the men thrusting their pitchforks into the end of the next corn-stack, we made our way slowly on to the road. Dusty, tired and triumphant, the three musketeers, Michael, John and myself, set off for Pretoria and the warmth of a good fire. The crimson sunset away over East Walton would tell us of a sharp frost that night, and a fine day to follow, when we would be back on duty killing the grain-eating vermin and doing our bit in wartime for King and Country.

As we moved away from the White Gate Corner, I felt what might be described as a fluttering sensation on my shoulder. Pulling off my coat and jersey, to our amazement we found a tiny mouse inside my shirt. How on earth it had got up there was a mystery to me, but the little creature caused me much less concern than my brush with the old, sandy rat earlier in the day. Whether my mother would have been quite so calm about it had I undressed indoors, is questionable.

And so our holidays were mapped out, for we knew that as long as the threshing tackle remained at Soigné we would be ever present with it.

133

Winter Sports, Norfolk-style

Only a return to school could keep us away, and even then heavy snow might help to reunite us for a few days. Modern families can keep the thrills of breaking limbs on the Swiss ski slopes - my idea of an ideal winter sport will always be a few days with rat-infested corn-stacks and a steam threshing tackle to help with my enjoyment.

Chapter 15
Hamonds Grammar School

To most pupils at the village school, education meant staying in the same classroom from the age of seven, until the school leaving age of fourteen. The brighter pupils reached quite a high standard, but obviously the scope was rather limited, with only one teacher covering pupils from such a wide age range. For most of the boys the only objective to aim for was reaching one's fourteenth birthday. The most senior pupils sat at the top of our room, both girls and boys. One or two very large pupils stuck out like sore thumbs amongst the younger ones, being the slow learners unable to keep up with their contemporaries. We younger ones watched the senior pupils say goodbye to their classmates and go off into the working world. Gladys Curl, Olwen Leighton and Olga Winner went off at the end of one term. Dan Softley, Ted Thaxton and Bob Clarke also left en bloc one Friday lunchtime; they were each guaranteed farm jobs, and, when asked by Mrs Clark when they were starting work, I well remember their replies. Dan, the Abbey Farm foreman's son, intended to start that afternoon, Ted Thaxton plunged in on the Saturday morning, but Bob, with fifty-one working years in front of him, decided to have a week's holiday first before adding his name to the Soigné staff.

Prior to the war, grammar schools were all fee-paying, catering in Norfolk for farmers' and small businessmen's sons or daughters as fee-paying, girls' schools existed as well. However bright the agricultural labourer's children might be, they were forced to stay at a local school until hard, labouring work quickly dulled their brains after reaching the age of fourteen. But, during the war, a very few scholarships became available through an eleven-plus examination. My parents knew very little about it, but Mrs Clark entered both myself and Eileen Softley for the test and gave us special tuition for it. The exam was to take place at Castleacre school and we were directed to present ourselves there at a given time. I didn't intend to go, as my inbred shyness didn't allow for those sorts of nervous extravaganzas.

On the morning of the exam I got up, told my mother I was going, and off on the bike I went. With great trepidation I found the school, did the exam and returned home, giving no thought to the eventual outcome. Anyway, I knew there was no chance of me passing, and failed to understand why Mrs Clark felt it so important anyway. To me, as to all my contemporaries, school was just something to get through because the law said so. Imagine my surprise, and Mrs Clark's joy when both her

135

Hamonds Grammar School

entrants passed the written part of the exam. The second stage of gaining a grant-assisted place was an interview with the headmaster of the school itself, in this case Mr Tom Welburn, who welcomed my mother and myself into the inner sanctum of Hamonds Grammar School at Swaffham, the market town about seven miles from Pretoria.

I was very nervous as usual, and wished fervently I had never agreed to sit the exam in the first place. The headmaster's study was rather dark, with a high ceiling and long sash windows covered with lace curtains. We were invited to sit on two chairs in front of his large desk and he proceeded to ask all sorts of pertinent questions and I tried hard to remember the things Mrs Clark had suggested would help me. Knowing how shy I was, she was certain I wouldn't attempt to sell my best points. What were my hobbies? Stamp collecting and ornithology (she had turned my original egg collecting into a much more scientific- sounding hobby). What type of books did I read? Well, I liked books by George Henty, such as The Last of the Incas. While he talked over the financial commitments covering school uniforms and sports gear, I took an interest in the large cupboard behind the headmaster and wondered if it was full of canes. As it happened, there was at least one hidden somewhere, although I never came anywhere near it - or it near me! As we came to realise, Tom Welburn wasn't averse to using it when civilised law and order was flouted by individuals. It had the necessary effect on most occasions, and no boy would ever be tempted to let the school down in public more than once. At the end of our interview, Mr Welburn shook hands with us, saying that he would look forward to having me at his school. In due time, confirmation of this arrived with a letter setting out all the requirements needed to start school in Swaffham in September, 1944.

I didn't realise then what a big difference the move would make to my life. It was to be the first real insight into the world outside the confines of Westacre Estate, which was in effect a little world of its own, which even the war had affected very little. I owe a great debt to my parents for the sacrifice they made to send me there and also to Tom Welburn who was the fairest and firmest man any boys could wish to have over them. His wonderful influence has stayed with me throughout my working life, even though the academic things I tried to learn there have long since left me.

But before we set off to Swaffham, let us have a last, long look at Westacre school. Looking back, I shall always remember one bright, March day when the Abbey men were threshing a wheat-stack at the back of the school. At dinner time we boys climbed over the wires and joined the workforce to enjoy some rat catching. Wheat-stacks always had a lot more rats than any other type of corn, so we were kept very busy pursuing the vermin. The drum noise drowned the tinny ring of the bell on the

Hamonds Grammar School

school front and so we stayed past the 1.30 deadline. Obviously Mrs Clark enquired why her classroom was half empty and completely devoid of male pupils. The girls, being only too eager to help, soon told her where we were, and one of the senior girls was despatched to bring us back. One or two younger or more nervous boys returned, but the main pack (which included myself) remained at the stack. The fun was fast and furious with rats running everywhere. If a second messenger came we didn't hear her through the dust and noise of battle. When the final rat lay dead and the drum ceased to turn, we slowly returned to the school, with dust in our hair and straw sticking to our woollen jerseys. The school clock stared at us accusingly, with its silly hands pointing at twenty minutes to three. Mrs Clark stood behind her desk with a face like thunder as we filed in with heads sunk into our shoulders. We certainly didn't look the same valiant hunters who, an hour before, had told the innocent messenger to take a two-fingered sign back to our schoolmistress.

We were halted in our tracks as we made our way back to the empty desks. "Where do you think you're going?" barked the diminutive sergeant-major. "All stand along the front". Reluctantly we shuffled into a ragged line, looking more like street urchins than scholarly pupils. I found myself on the farthest end from Mrs Clark, and was at first glad of it because I would receive less of an ear-bashing down there. But when the instruction came for hands to be held out in front with palms uppermost, I changed my mind. I couldn't stand and wait for my turn to be caned, listening to the howls of others further along the line. Quickly I raced up to the top position as the irate teacher took up her nut stick cane. As the switch came down across my palms I realised what a fool I was to volunteer to take the full force of the fresh arm muscles. The cane whistled down with some force and stung like a red hot poker. "Keep your hands out", came the order, as smarting palms were rubbed on buttocks after the first strike. I was sure then that I had made the wrong decision by changing positions, for no lady of such slight build could keep up that kind of power along a row of more than a dozen boys. All through the mass corporal punishment, the girls sat and smirked at our discomfort. Perhaps the rats we had so recently whacked also had a smile if they looked down from the great rat run in the sky. With smarting palms and severely dented egos, we slumped back to our respective desks. Mrs Clark put her cane away and faced the class, knowing that no one would flaunt her authority for a few days at least.

Most of the village children went home to dinner, but those from Pretoria, Soigné and High House ate sandwiches in the schoolroom. In winter we sat around a large fire and warmed our toes. Bob Clarke, Georgie Wright, Ted Thaxton, Dilbury and myself made up most of the dinner party. One day Tich, as we called Ted, decided he would like some toast - but how to hold it near the fire was the big question. Something quite long was needed to reach through the bars of the fireguard. Why not old Ma Clark's cane? So Ted made his toast without blackening the stick too much in the process. His crunching of burned and smoky, buttered toast made the other older boys envious. Why don't we all cut nut sticks tomorrow and bring them in at dinner time; we could all make toast at once then. So the plan was carried out and we all sat like men in the field making toast by the fire. Suddenly the middle door opened and Minnie Wiskerd came through to collect something. "What do you think you're doing?" she cried, with arms rising up with mock horror. "You look like a gang of navvies, put those sticks outside at once". Our lovely dinner was ruined before it had hardly begun. Back to our dry, national loaf sandwiches we went, muttering obscenities between the chewing. For the life of us we couldn't imagine what rules of etiquette we were breaching as we were in private, but I suppose standards had to be kept up on school premises - even if we slipped back into the gutter when we left school to join our elders on the land. We were only thankful she didn't find Ted with the cane stick the previous day - she would have gone up, never to come down again, and Ted would have felt the cane for good measure. So our efforts to spice up our very mundane lunch fare were thwarted by authority.

As luck would have it, I was soon considered old enough to cycle home for dinner, this move being accelerated by my newspaper delivery service taken on just after this event. W. H. Smith, who supplied the papers, were forced, through lack of labour, to restrict deliveries in country districts and would only come to one central point in each village, namely the post office. From here we collected the papers at dinner time and rode home to deliver them, myself to Pretoria and Dilbury to Soigné. The delivery charge was at the rate of two old pennies per house per week. The Sunday editions were brought up from the village by Dilbury, who pumped the church organ and had to travel down and back anyway. And so it was that we called in at the post office for our papers on the day that Reggie Wright was reported killed in action. I remember vividly how stunned we were as we cycled home and each Armistice Day brings back our journey along that road, not knowing quite how we felt, or should feel at that kind of news.

One highlight of the school year was the ripening of the small pears on the tree situated just outside the bike shed. This huge tree stood on the edge of Mrs Clark's garden, beside the large, covered tank which contained the school water supply. It was clearly understood that we were allowed to eat any of the small, sweet, juicy pears that fell to the ground (which they did in large numbers). One operation, carried out at the tank, was the washing out of the paint pots and the need for this increased enormously towards the end of the summer term, which coincided with the ripening of the pears. One afternoon saw quite a gang of us at the tank enjoying a skive in the warm sunshine. As the supply of fallen pears had dried up, I decided to throw a fairly large, flint stone up into the branches hoping to shake more down. Swinging my arm in an arc with the missile on the end, I prepared to launch it into the centre of the tree. Just as my arm reached the launching point, the sound of an opening door in the schoolhouse caused the whole operation to abort and my arm almost left its socket as I attempted to bring the stone back to earth. Gillian Clark came out to the garden, oblivious to the intended destruction of her mother's fruit tree, and must have been very surprised by the sight of a contorting boy throwing himself to earth in a cloud of dust. Confusion reigned as we all hastily put ourselves back to the glass jar-cleaning task, with faces slightly redder than the heat of the afternoon warranted.

The warm, summer days allowed the class to sit out on the lawn to do some lessons. The lawn, belonging to the school house, ran along the front of the buildings and made a lovely setting for the children to work in. I fear we didn't produce much in gratitude, but the warm air and country sounds lifted our spirits on those very grim, wartime afternoons. Another summer term adventure was in the form of a nature walk. Sometimes the route taken was along the track on the western side of the school and up to the triangular-shaped wood, known as The Heater, the name possibly being derived from its shape which resembled the pre-heated piece of metal placed in an ironing box. Following the dusty farm track lined with wild flowers, such as blue bugloss, wild poppies, knapweed, and cornflowers, we would go up one side of the wood, around the north side and back down towards the school. As we made our way along, as slowly as possible in order to extend our break from the school desks to the limit, Mrs Clark would point out various things of interest. Truth be known, we probably knew more about it than she did, being born and bred in the countryside, but she always made things as interesting as possible. Another route walked was down past the front of the school, and along the road for a short distance, before turning right into the leafy lane which would take us towards the watercress beds, where the River Nar gently flowed through large, clear beds of watercress. This delicacy was cut for sale at certain times of the year, making a nice addition to salads, especially in wartime. This walk was especially nice, as the shade helped to take the edge off the hot, July sun. Wild flowers would be collected and placed in jam jars on burning- hot windowsills where they quickly died and the water turned brown and smelt horribly. These jars were the bane of Millie Everard's life. She was our school cleaner and was usually left to clear them away. In passing I will mention that Millie, sister to Horrie Everard the Soigné thatcher, kept house for him and her daughter Kathy in a cottage directly opposite the church. It was second in the row of rather "Heath Robinson"-type houses, which appeared to have been added to each other in a seemingly haphazard way. The first dwelling was almost end on to the road and really faced into its garden. This was occupied during the war by Mrs Smith and her family from London. She went to Lynn on the bus and brought her shopping home in a sack, which seemed very strange to us locals; her two boys, Buddie and Sydney, went to school with us. Then came Horrie's abode, being perched up on a bank, with three or four concrete steps down to the road. Little Miss Harriet Curl, Derek Curl's Aunt Harriet, squeezed in next. She was a tiny lady with a very humpty back, caused no doubt by some childhood deformity which would have been cured in our present day environment; nevertheless, she was a lovely, little person. I seem to remember the rest of the row was 'front door-less' and one had to gain admittance round the back. Edgar Coe lived there, as well as Billy Spooner, and a man who cut hair whose name I cannot call to mind at the moment. These houses were later condemned and knocked down, causing Horrie to move fifty yards further from the church, taking up residence in the very ancient dwelling known universally as the wooden hut. When choosing to live there Horrie, who had a very dry sense of humour, expressed the view that as he was advancing in age, he didn't want to move too far from the churchyard and incur extra travelling expenses on his last journey!

Mrs Clark lived in the schoolhouse with her family. Her husband was in the services, and the two elder girls, Hilary and Gillian, were away at school. Ian, the only boy, spent a short time at the village school before moving on to complete his education away from home. The youngest daughter, Jean, studied with us, as did an evacuee relative, Jan Stratton. One afternoon Jan, who sat directly across the gangway to me, broke wind on the wooden seat with a resounding, rasping sound. His face went ruby red and it sent Dilbury and myself into a fit of uncontrolled laughter. Tears rolled down our faces as we tried desperately to stifle our mirth. A furious school-marm turned on us, demanding to know the cause of our sudden outburst. Eyeing the unfortunate Jan sitting red- faced and guilt-ridden at his desk, she then forcibly dragged him out in front. Obviously he dare not admit to his indiscretion and we couldn't speak, even if we had been willing to. Getting no joy from us or her victim she began slapping his bare legs in a most unseemly manner, giving enough whacks to punish whatever crime she may have thought he had committed. The prolonged leg slapping of an innocent man tended to take the hilarity out of the situation and eventually order was restored. Jan was a bit of a lad, so perhaps the punishment did some good, although I doubt it as he failed to learn much by the experience.

On another occasion a wasps' nest was discovered in the bank near the school and everyone was warned not to go near it. At the weekend Jan took a stick to poke at it and received several stings to face and head. On Monday morning he came into class, looking for all the world as if he had acquired Chinese ancestry overnight as he peered through swollen slits where his bright-blue eyes had been on Friday. His aunt held him up before his classmates as a prime example of the fool who could not take good advice and do as he was told. I don't think Jan worried too much, as his ways didn't make any noticeable changes, which helped him to be one of us despite the unfortunate fact of living in the same house as his "school-marm" aunt.

On the whole, we weren't a cheeky gang of schoolboys, although we had occasional lapses of conduct. Walter Dack, the publican, farmed some small fields alongside the road out of the village towards Pretoria. His elderly father worked in them sometimes and, for some reason, we began to shout rudely at this bearded gentleman. This name-calling went on for a day or two, until one afternoon our shouts were cut short by an irate Walter Dack who had lain in wait for us behind the hedge. Our bikes sped off up the road at high speed and we lived in fear and trembling for days after, just in case we were reported to Mrs Clark. No more shouts or jeers were directed at Mr Dack senior after that!

Some time later, on the same road, we ourselves were subjected to an uncalled for attack. It appeared that someone at school had been bullying Sydney Smith, the youngest of the evacuee family living next to Horrie Everard. As we pushed our bikes up Tumbler Hill, an elder Smith brother, David, came off the adjoining field carrying a thick ash stick. Taking us by surprise, he attacked us with the weapon in no uncertain manner, issuing threats to all and sundry who dared bully his brother. We tried to leap on our machines to escape the onslaught, but the steep hill towards home prevented us from speeding away and many a good bang was received on legs and bikes before we made good our escape. We sped past that field just as fast as the hill would allow us, until the likelihood of David working there had passed. Our already bent rear mudguards were even more dented after the ash cudgel had done its work. We certainly didn't yell the well worn, local, cheeky expression against the wartime incomers to the effect that all cockneys kept coal in their baths. It put the wind up us and no mistake!

If one lad stood out for cheek it had to be Dilbury. You may remember his brush with Freddie Sculpher. The head gardener, Mr George Wright, was cutting his roadside hedge with a reef hook. As we all cycled by Dilbury yelled out, "Give you a shilling for your old hook, George". I couldn't believe my ears and instantly wished the road would open up and swallow me, bike and all! The bellowed, "that's enough of your cheek, young man", followed us down the road. I prayed nothing would be said to my parents, for I knew there would be big trouble if there was. It was alright for my mate Dilbury, but I had to deliver the Wright's newspaper when we returned. How my heart thumped every time I went to their door, expecting the tall figure of the head gardener to question my part in the affair, but my fears were never realised.

Suddenly, all these school friendships were to change as a new school beckoned and a very different environment had to be dealt with. Prior to my starting at the grammar school, my mother and myself cycled to Narborough, where I had to stable my cycle before catching the Swaffham bus. We called at a roadside house, which had originally been a forge. The good people there agreed to look after my bike and, as it was to be locked in a large shed attached to the house, we asked whether I could collect the key, secure my bike and then return the key to their door. This key, I remember, was on a string, with a huge, wooden block acting as a key ring. One certainly couldn't lose it as one would soon trip over the block, it seemed so large. Narborough was roughly four miles from Pretoria and set on an angle to Swaffham itself, but it was the nearest point on the Lynn/Swaffham bus route. The education committee paid my fare, so the roundabout journey saved me three miles each way on my cycle, but extended my time from home quite considerably.

The first day saw me sick with apprehension, which gave me the usual bilious headache well before night. I followed the half-dozen or so boys from the bus and entered the wide, double gates of my new educational home. A huge beech tree overhung the cycle shed and lawn. A wide, Tarmac pathway-cum-playground stretched alongside the classrooms and away towards a relatively new, two-storey building at the top of the school grounds. There were boys of all sizes everywhere, milling and shouting to each other, as greetings were exchanged between friends kept apart by the long summer holiday. Where should I go? Why had I come, was more to the point? Oh, for the gravel playground of Westacre and a quiet life in familiar surroundings. I was almost petrified with fear as I joined the throng being shepherded towards the newest part of the school which housed the large gymnasium, where morning assembly was always held. The new boys gathered in the front rows and waited for events to unfold. All the masters sat at the front, wearing black gowns on their shoulders, with one woman teacher, the headmaster's wife, amongst them. As the hands of the wall-clock reached 9 a.m., Tom Welburn swept in through the door, resplendent in gown and black mortar-board. As he took his place behind the central lectern, silence fell upon his audience. Prayers were said and a hymn sung and the members of each class were read out in a very loud voice, beginning with the sixth form and working down through forms 5, 4 and 3. A new system had been devised for the new intake, as numbers had swelled with grant-assisted boys coming in . Form 2 was subdivided into classes A and B, with 30 boys in each section. My name was called with the other 29 for the B section. As we left, the remainder of the small boys under eleven formed Form 1, which consisted wholly of fee-paying youngsters. The remainder of the day was spent in a blur of receiving books, pens and pencils, instructions and a timetable for the term. My head ached terribly and my stomach churned as my long since taken breakfast threatened to return from whence it had come.

Dinner was eaten in a large dining-room, where we were allocated table places which we had to keep permanently and queue accordingly outside. A master or prefect sat at the end of each table to keep order. Dinners were served at a large hatch and collected by two boys at the end of the seated diners. This chore lasted for a week and then everyone moved up a place, allowing the previous week's dinner orderlies to sit at the bottom end. What we had on that first day, I don't know, but I had no appetite anyway, so it didn't really matter. Playtime was a nightmare as I knew no one at the school. We had a fifteen minute break mid-morning, a longer period after lunch and then the afternoon of full lessons, I believe. My break-time was spent with my back to a wall, trying to be invisible and praying for lesson time to start again. A bigger boy, dressed like a wasp in a black and yellow striped blazer, the school colours, repeatedly found me out and tormented me, saying my ears were like jug handles, my teeth stuck out and I was a farm worker's son. What a specimen and, in his opinion, a worthy recipient for all his wit and bullying in front of his hangers-on. This was my first lesson in the hard facts of life, and that our community was a divided one, very definitely 'them' and 'us'. At Westacre school we had all been equal, whether foreman's children or cowman's. Here it was very different and we grant-assisted children were to be the butt of monied bullies, until the new system worked through a few years later.

It seemed that we were the first batch of boys to have the advantage of free, grammar school education, and the staff treated us with a very fair hand in the classroom. In fact, it may even have been a pleasure to teach youngsters who had arrived by their own hard work and mental ability, rather than boys sent there by the power of parents' purses.

At the sound of the last bell, I picked up my satchel and made for the gate, where boys were spilling out into the quiet Swaffham streets. It was, however, very orderly with no one attempting to run or create horseplay.

143

Hamonds Grammar School

I wondered how to fill my time whilst waiting for the bus back to Narborough in almost an hour's time. A long crocodile of boys passed on their way to catch the Dereham train, masters and older boys walked alongside as the large contingent marched towards the station some half mile away. After wandering around aimlessly for some time, a voice broke into my worried thoughts, "Good afternoon, Bumfrey. I fear you have lost your way" - it was Mr Welburn, the headmaster, who stood before me, having spotted my forlorn figure from his study window. He led me back into the school and took me to a large classroom where the other Narborough boys, along with a larger group awaiting the later departure of the Watton train, were working. As we walked, the headmaster explained that the waiting time was productively filled by doing homework, under the watchful eye of a master. When the appropriate time approached, we were released to walk across the road to our bus stop, under the eagle eye of Geoff Shirley, the senior boy in the group. Any fooling around outside would be seen from the headmaster's study and dealt with very severely. A boy in school uniform represented the school and no one, large or small, was allowed to besmirch the school's good name in any way.

At last the double-decker bus ground into view up the incline from the Dereham direction. Sitting on the bus, I managed to team up with Donald Bootman, a farmer's son from Pentney, who was in the same class as myself. A fee-paying boy who had spent a year previously in Form 1, he was a great help to me and I owe him a great deal for his friendship which helped to make that first year a little less traumatic for me. My nervousness meant that I never dared ask a question in class, so many things went unexplained in a group of thirty boys. My monthly marks were poor and left me very near the bottom of a very substandard class. Once more I felt a blockhead who couldn't learn anything, and consequently didn't learn much. I couldn't draw, couldn't do carpentry, or play football because of my weak chest. Playtimes were purgatory, as I tried to make myself invisible for fear the yellow and black wasp would arrive to tease me in front of his mates. My one hope was that an apple a day would keep my tormentor away and I brought a supply to school and stood by a wall gnawing one to give me something to do. I was desperately unhappy, both at school and at home, for my Westacre school mates soon drifted away from me as our worlds separated and interests changed. I spent more and more time with my small brothers, which pleased them no doubt, but it meant that I became isolated from everyone. Then in December of that first term at Swaffham, Brian became seriously ill and died, knocking the bottom out of our little world, and leaving us devastated and needing all our resources to go on living, let alone anything else.

My life dropped to an all-time low that Christmas, and has tended to take an annual dip in mid-November and December of each year since that time, causing me to make a very unpopular statement that, "I hate Christmas", on many occasions.

Chapter 16
Neither Fish, nor Fowl

Before we become too involved in life at the grammar school, I would like to step back to the time when life had no real problems, and was there to be enjoyed in the company of good friends. Our little gang at Pretoria consisted of myself, Cyril, Terry and Dulcie Jones, David Bunker, Hazel Hall and Ann Mann. Sometimes we played as sex-segregated groups, but often it was one for all and all for one, as we ran wild on the near traffic-free roads or roamed in surrounding woods. We owned no watches to keep track of time, but tummy rumblings seemed to be just as effective in sending us home when the meal was nearly ready for serving.

One occupation we all enjoyed was hut-building in the woods, the favourite site being under a large holly tree by the Squires Field gateway. This particular tree had very low branches, which hung to ground level, making a very good, natural shield. Long-fallen branches were used to make a hut framework, this being tied to living branches on the host tree. Thinner sticks then made a second layer, with twigs finely intertwined to seal the walls. The same system made up the roof, but here the last layer was made of straw, carried from the stack, which was nearly always built in that corner. Being situated under the thick canopy of evergreen leaves meant that very little rainwater penetrated the roof, so straw bedding, placed inside on the floor, remained fairly dry. A sack fixed over the doorway gave Robin Hood and his Merry Men plenty of privacy from the prying eyes of the Sheriff of Nottingham's men who occasionally passed by on the road. A lookout, seated high in the topmost branches of the holly tree, sent down a message of warning to the outlaws below and everyone froze until the danger had passed. Pretend-campfires (real fires being banned by common consent of children and parents) were tended and sat around by the camp entrance. Bows and arrows were cut and made up from nut sticks, for every boy had a selection of shutknives in his pocket. Rabbits were hunted for food and expeditions undertaken to our other hut situated deeper in the wood. This construction was under part of a fallen tree, on the edge of a shallow pit hole. Thick ivy, growing from the ground and over the tree, made quite a good shield.

I remember the first time the girls were allowed to visit this rather male-exclusive dwelling. Very gallantly, I offered Dulcie Jones my chief's seat, as I took rather a shine to her at the time. Possibly it was her long, wavy hair that moved my male hormones for the first recorded time. Clem Softley, to his credit, never interfered with our games, whatever the time of year, and left his pheasants to fend for themselves in that section of the wood. This action alone set Clem apart as one of the most human of gamekeepers, and earned him much respect from us all.

Dilbury had worked on the farm during all holidays, whilst we other boys played our free days away, with the exception of harvest. Cyril, David Bunker and myself suddenly felt that we needed gainful employment (and the money that went with it!) so we decided to ask Mr Wilson if he had a job for the Easter holidays. Hanging around the Soigné premises, we tried to pluck up enough courage to do the asking. Eventually, the asking took place, and after a bit of wheedling on our part, he decided to set us on as crow scarers, working on three adjoining, newly-sown corn fields, namely Big and Little Strawberries which were on the opposite side of the private road to Fifty Acres, the third field to be patrolled. Off we went out of the farmyard as pleased as puppy-dogs, with our newly-acquired status of workmen. Taking one field each, we walked around, yelling loudly enough to scare every rook in the county, let alone those in our field. The heavy, clay soil soon adhered to our boots and leg muscles ached with the extra load carried. Sticking it out until dinner time, we all walked home to Pretoria, proudly announcing that we were crow scarers. My parents weren't too happy as I then had to cycle to the village, collect papers and deliver them, before returning to work. Bolting my dinner, I tore to Westacre, and semi-tore back as the steep Tumbler Hill hampered my headlong dash. Having distributed the news at a record speed, I flew through the farmyard to rejoin my comrades who had walked on ahead. All the afternoon our cracked voices and rapidly tiring limbs attempted to rid those muddy fields of crowds of black scavengers. No sooner had we disturbed them from one end of the long fields, than they flew to the other end! By dusk, the shine had begun to come off the magic of being employed, and by the following afternoon the glitter had completely gone and we found ourselves together in the belt of trees running between Little Strawberries and the tiny farm pastures. Heaps of fallen branches inspired the idea of a hut for shelter should it rain, and so we set out enthusiastically to construct one. Charlie Wilson, riding back to the farm in his trap, was unpleasantly surprised to see the three fields around him black with rooks and conspicuously clear of boys! Tying his horse at the end of the belt, he walked the short distance to the side of the half-built shelter. "What's this, my fellows? I can't see any crows in here to scare!". How we jumped, and with very red faces explained why we weren't at work. "You can spend all day building huts from now on", was the terse reply. "You're all sacked!", and with that damning statement he turned on his heel and left us gaping open-mouthed at one another. We dare not follow him to ask for wages, nor did we dare tell our parents of our disgrace. Instead, we concocted a tale to the effect that, as there were very few crows around, our labour was surplus to requirements. This lie turned out to be useless, as by the next dinner time my dad had met the foreman and the truth was out. For the second time in twenty-four hours I was made to look very silly. Was it any wonder that Dilbury's total reliability gained even more praise than usual when it was measured up against such clowns as we? Admittedly, we weren't sorry to give up the cloying mud picked up in the fields, but the loss of face didn't help our public image and we went down in our own estimation, if not in anyone else's.

Great games were played out on the many, mature trees in the woods and on the pastures. Branches swept down very near the ground, making lovely swings and climbing frames in a natural environment. The only risk we ran was on the pastures, where cattle rubbed itching backs on low branches. This danger came from picking up ringworm from the bark where infected places had touched. Ringworm in cattle was rife and could also infect humans with a red, itchy, skin condition in a circular pattern, which was both annoying and hard to get rid of, even with special ointment. The other curse of pasture fences was barbed wire, and many an ugly scratch showed on bare arms and legs, or three- cornered tears made in jackets or trousers. I remember well my first pair of long, grey flannel trousers being ripped at the knee when negotiating a barbed wire fence on the Mowing Ground. It was a Sunday evening and we met Mum and Dad out for a walk with my small brothers. I could feel my mother's eyes homing in on my flapping trouser leg, long before we limped into speaking distance. My woeful countenance must have melted her heart, because the expected torrent of recriminations didn't materialise and we turned for home, discussing the best method to repair those almost-new, Sunday trousers, for clothes rationing meant that, even if money was available, new clothes were not.

Discarded pram and Tansad wheels were a most valuable item in our boys' world. Every family owned an old pram which was used for wood cart. Even when the body of the pram had broken, the wheels went on to new life under a wooden box body, propelled by youthful legs and used for racing or to carry a younger family member on a ramble too long for little legs. Our cart raced from the shed and round a sharp corner alongside the house. Sometimes Rip was the passenger who risked life and limb on the bendy course, as the speeding cart slid on the dusty path, turning over on occasions and flinging the old dog out in the process. Faithfully he would return to the top of the run and jump into the lethal contraption. When Michael grew a little he took over the hot seat, and miraculously escaped splitting his head open on the brick wall of the house as the speeding reached higher and more dangerous levels.

Neither Fish, nor Fowl

At other times the cart was converted into a threshing engine, by having an old, square biscuit tin inserted, complete with metal smoke pipe. Dried grass and any other smoke-emitting material was lighted in the tin, causing smoke to rise from the chimney. This tackle moved from fruit tree to fruit tree as these pretend corn-stacks were threshed by our gang, with Rip, and later Waggs, there to catch pretend rats.

When Uncle Ernie Eke came on a day visit from his home in King's Lynn, we always went up the High House road before cutting through under the lovely beech trees behind the chalk pit. Here we re-enacted scenes from Robin Hood and he joined us for practice with bows and arrows on targets marked out on beech tree trunks. No time for him to sit indoors and gossip with womenfolk - just for a few hours he could be a boy again and join in our games with all the enthusiasm of youth. What a change it made from his life in wartime railway workshops at South Lynn where he was an engine fitter and shop steward for the NUR. A wonderful character, being self-taught to a high degree of education, Ernie was the eldest son and almost an extension of Grandad Eke, who was also a very deep thinking, well educated and well read man for his time. Aunt Cissy, who hailed from London, wasn't country-minded, so she left Ern to play at outlaws in the beech wood and declined any effort to get her to play Maid Marion.

Around the time I started at grammar school, the Jones family returned home to Plymouth, and although David Bunker stayed slightly longer, the little gang disintegrated. Not meeting at school meant that I lost contact with Dilbury and Bob Easter from Soigné. It certainly wasn't because I felt any better than my late schoolmates, it was just differing circumstances that caused the break. The shock of Brian's death of course didn't help matters, and it wasn't until John Thaxton arrived on the scene that normal, youngsters' adventures got under way again.

Losing some schooldays in December, 1944, and a few weeks during the winter of 1945, through chesty colds, meant that my lessons fell sadly behind. Basic words and grammar in French were lost, and with them the interest to learn. Physics seemed to suffer in the same way, especially as I failed to gel with either of the masters. The same reasons for failure could have applied to chemistry, but I enjoyed working with the master, Mr Boyle, so it was in that subject I excelled. History and geography I liked. English language and literature were passable. Art and woodwork were abysmal! The only item produced from the carpentry workshop in five years was a tiny, wooden scissor rack, which my mother used on the fire many years later saying that she knew I didn't want it. Five years of work gone up in smoke - what sacrilege!

During the summer term I tried valiantly to salvage something from my

Neither Fish, nor Fowl

first year. Our form master, Mr "Billygoat" Newman, the rector from South Pickenham, encouraged me all he could and I managed by excelling at the subjects I liked, although failing miserably at the ones I didn't, to finish in second place, but with only 49% - the top mark was 50%, so you could see the form, as a whole, was pretty substandard. Poor old Billygoat didn't have much to be proud of that year, but neither did we, with only one prize awarded in the whole form, and that to a Master Fitt B., I believe, for his 50% form-topping effort.

Sports day came and went. My sporting prowess failed to get me a place in any of the races, having been eliminated at earlier trials. The school was divided into five houses, namely Wilsons, Bells, Drurys, Hamonds and Lee Warners. The house colours were green, yellow, dark-blue, light-blue and red, corresponding to the houses in their order. I was in Wilsons House which, if rumour was to be believed, had carried all before them in the years prior to my arrival, but in that first year had sunk to an all time low in every sporting event. This trend continued for the five years of my secondary education, although in the last year fortunes began to pick up. On that first sports day a super athlete, called Dodds, won everything within sight, collecting the victor ludorum cup and helping Drurys House to take the House Cup.

But it wasn't just the fact of Wilsons House finishing at the bottom of the pile that made the day miserable for me. My parents weren't there, Dad certainly wouldn't have attended if he could, and Mum wasn't able either. All the posh parents paraded around, talking with the staff and hanging on every word their stuck-up sons told them about the school. It just wasn't my scene and I made every excuse from that year on to miss the most important day in the school calendar. Just one thing else sticks in my mind, and that is when Dodds did a victory handstand and all his pencils fell out of his blazer pocket to rattle on a wooden floor. If only he had been captain of Wilsons House, the day would have looked so much brighter!

After that first year, I decided to cycle the seven miles to Swaffham by myself. The long ride was never lonely, as I could see so much going on in the fields along the way. Setting off around 8 a.m., the first mile and a half took me down into the village, with steep Tumbler Hill giving me a good, downhill start. Then, crossing the river, a long climb faced me as I rode up the narrow road towards Swaffham. One hill, then a second took me off the Birkbeck Estate and through light-soiled farmland belonging to a Southacre-based consortium. For almost four miles I cycled without passing a cottage, just field upon field along the rough, semi-tarmaced road, dotted with pot holes and often covered in mud and sand, either washed or blown from those same fields, then joined the Narford/Swaffham road, where the surface improved, until the town became visible on the horizon, over the railway bridge and into town, past the garage, Howards Saddlers shop and the post office. I had arrived at school, very wide awake and with lungs filled with clean, fresh air. The part of the day I enjoyed most was over, even if the wind did always blow in my face, no matter which way I was travelling. Cape and leggings were needed for wet days and handkerchiefs were semi-dried on the handlebars when streaming colds soaked them before the day had hardly begun. On the return journey, I had the advantage of mainly downhill travel into Westacre, but had to contend with the dreaded Tumbler Hill on the very last lap. That hill always lay between myself and a lovely tea, prepared for me, and very much needed after the long cycle ride.

A couple of hours' homework set the seal on my day, and was it any wonder I had no time to make contact with any of my late mates from Westacre school? My homework session was carried out in the relative quiet of the front room, albeit surrounded by stored apples in the winter months, but warmed by an open fire lit especially for me on cold days. The lovely smell of apples, coupled with the crackling fire and warm lamplight, made a cosy study to work in which was rather more conducive to a sleepy head after the long, cold cycle ride home, followed by a well-cooked, tasty meal. The summer evenings brought their special distractions, when the sound of children playing outside tended to draw my mind away from academic problems and on to more frivolous thoughts. Later in my school life Dick Barton, Special Agent came on to the scene as a thriller serial broadcast five nights a week on the BBC. At 6.45 p.m. the introductory music would allow me to down my pen and nip into the living-room to join the rest of the family for fifteen minutes' respite from the real world. It seemed as if everything stopped for Dick Barton - the whole nation switched off from work, and we were no exception. Dad came from the garden, Mum from the kitchen and Michael left playmates to go to their own sets at this appointed hour. Only in summer, when Dad worked overtime, did the ritual waiver, and then strict instructions were left for us to note the action and pass on this vital information to him the next day. Can you wonder at the uproar caused when the early 50s brought about the demise of Dick, Snowy and Jock on the lame excuse of excess violence! The Archers, which replaced our favourite, had a lot to answer for!

The General Election of 1945, which resulted in a landslide victory for Labour, was an education in itself. Having come from a staunch socialist background, I naturally hoped 'we', the Labour Party headed by Clement Attlee, would win, but was wise enough to keep my mouth shut in the midst of such a true-blue establishment as a 1940s grammar school. The

Neither Fish, nor Fowl

Daily Herald, which was the foremost Labour newspaper, put forward all the socialist plans for a new Britain, based on a fair deal for all, but with quite a bit less for those deemed to have been born with a silver spoon in their mouths, which included quite a large proportion of my class fellows. Of course, this wasn't really the case, as those conceited little prigs, who lorded it over such as myself, were only one step up the so-called social ladder, but it did seem at the time as if they lived in a different world.

The Labour candidate for the Swaffham area was Mr Sidney Dye, a Methodist lay preacher and a well-known, local man. His opponent, with the blue rosette, was of no consequence to me, and being unable to remember his name leaves me with no regrets. Everywhere in the school roughbooks contained caricatures of "Kidney Pie", as the budding young Conservatives derided the silly oaf, hoping to break the stranglehold of Tory monopoly in this rural constituency. Of course, all the farmworkers and their wives would troop into the polling booths and place their cross where their masters had indicated. Their homes and jobs depended upon this allegiance, so there was no question about the outcome. Anyway, how could a bible-thumping, Methodist yokel enter the corridors of power to represent them, the cream of the blue bloods? This jaundiced Tory view in no way described Mr Dye, who was held in high regard locally.

I read the headlines trumpeting the hopes of such stalwart Labour men as Ernest Bevin, Herbert Morrison and Aneurin Bevan, and felt they must win. Then, back at school, the constant, derisory comments of all and sundry sent my hopes crashing into dust. How on earth could the undistinguished figure of Clement Attlee defeat the flamboyant and ultra-successful Winston Churchill in the fight for Britain's post-war future?

That election, so different from the present day, computer-calculated ones, took a longer time to sort out. Votes had to be brought from around the world from soldiers still fighting in the Far East, or sorting out the aftermath of war in Europe. Eventually, with all the counting done, Labour came through as the victorious party, with a landslide majority in parliament. Sydney Dye emerged as the new MP for South West Norfolk, much to the disbelief of the majority at Hamonds Grammar School, but to the delight of a few incomers who were forced to keep their jubilant feelings well under wraps.

One thing I did learn from the election was that the so-called upholders of the stiff upper lip and "that isn't cricket" syndrome made very poor losers if the results from the ballot box failed to go their way. It was worth all the jeering comments poked at "Kidney Pie" to know that at last the worm had turned, and real democracy had almost reached the far flung, rural areas of Norfolk. Of course, the farmers' sons decreed that their paters were planning to sack all employees. Of course, the cloth caps of

Neither Fish, nor Fowl

Labour couldn't run the country, as the majority couldn't read or write. This last, often repeated jibe, leant new impetus to my determination that, whether I could speak French or not at the end of my schooling, I would make sure that reading and writing were mastered to as high a degree as possible, and this I eventually did.

Mixing and listening to the type of boys who would eventually be my employers did much for my future understanding of how their minds worked, and would stand me in good stead in many a trade union and work situation later in life. Their strengths and weaknesses became apparent and I managed to work out a few employers' Achilles heels through being able to tap this lucrative source of experience.

After Easter in my first year, the worst nightmares seemed to be over, and I began to enjoy the new experiences. That isn't to say the thought of a double algebra lesson with Mr Newton didn't fill me with tummy-gripping dread as I crossed the railway bridge in the morning. Geometry and algebra were so much useless double Dutch to my brain, whereas straightforward arithmetic had its practical uses and was therefore worked at. I recall one afternoon when Mr Newton had set us a test in algebra. As usual I was completely at sea with it, and sat idly staring into space, my pen hand dangling down, with sharp nib directed forward. Mr Newton, backing slowly up the aisle, failed to notice the impending danger and brought his leg back into the resting nib. With a yell like a stuck pig Sandy, as we called him, leapt forward, clutching the wounded limb, believing a death-inducing blow had been administered. I led the class in jumping up in shock, especially when he and I realised my pen had been responsible. I couldn't convince him it had been an accident, and had to suffer his wrath, whilst several toadies smirked their condolences to the wounded man. After the lesson my mates congratulated me for such a daring escapade, so I didn't over-emphasise the accidental nature of the incident to them. I quite enjoyed my hero status, and secretly wished I'd thought to do it in the first place. I fear my poor marks were even poorer after that, but it was worth it just to hear him yell and see the few hairs around his bald pate stand on end. The couple of hundred lines stating that I must pay more attention in class weren't so funny and achieved the desired effect in blunting my pen nib somewhat by the time they were finished.

My friendship with Donald Bootman faded a bit after I ceased to travel on the Narborough bus. A wider group developed to include Leslie Tufts from Bradenham, Derek Rant, Cooky, a boy Ives, Wilf Gathercole and a Welsh lad named Griffiths. I remember standing in the dinner queue when Griffiths remarked to Wilf on the strange fact that he had been to gather sticks, but never to "gather coal". Wilf laughed as, I expect like me, he was

Neither Fish, nor Fowl

used to people taking the mickey out of his name. Only one of the masters was definitely a working man's champion and that was Harry Carter, the art and woodwork teacher. His lessons weren't my cup of tea at all as my carpentry was bad and my drawing worse, but an afternoon with Harry was always interesting, especially when one of the more intellectual members of our class drew him into some deep discussion on current affairs, which incidentally never had any connection with the lesson in hand. No other member of staff ever gave any indication of his political leanings, but Mr Carter never failed to be led into championing some cause on behalf of the underprivileged. I am sure that Harry Carter will always be remembered in Swaffham for making the wonderful, wooden, town sign, depicting the Pedlar of Swaffham with his dog, that stands on the small, tree-lined area opposite our school buildings in the town centre. I believe he made signs for other villages in later years, and was a very clever and hard-working man whose suit always carried a dusting of chalk or sawdust, which also adhered to his brushed-back, curly hair.

The main object to aim at in the carpentry workshop was to obtain some small, offcut, blocks of wood to use as football pucks on the tarmac surface playground. We spent hours of playtime kicking our shoes to pieces with this game. I became very adept at scoring goals into the big, grey gate at the very top of the school premises. No time to stand around like a wallflower now as we transformed ourselves into the Tommy Lawton or Stanley Matthews of the playground. Yet, despite being a leading light at this form of soccer, I played very little real football, although I did score one goal on a very rare appearance for the form team. Most of my winter sports afternoons were spent sitting in a classroom reading, owing to my very weak chest.

Cricket was more my forte, and I loved the warm summer afternoons with the smell of new-mown grass and the crack of ball on willow. House cricket matches were usually enlivened by the batting feats of Morrie Grief who played for Bells House, and took such a dislike to the cricket ball that he tried to hit it out of sight every time it was bowled at him. Once more I sighed with a wish for him to have been in Wilsons House and flying the green flag. Leslie Tufts did play for us, and we gave him great support when batting, which he did with a stubborn resilience so typical of his character. "Come on Bradenham", we shouted, at which everyone thought we were likening him to Don Bradman, the prolific-scoring Australian captain. In actual fact, we were using our nickname for him which was the village of his home.

Talking of Don Bradman reminds me of the fateful day in 1948 when the all-conquering Australian cricket team needed in excess of 400 runs to win on the last day at Leeds, and they did it with time to spare. The

154

Neither Fish, nor Fowl

England attack was decimated and, as we ate lunch, Norman Yardley, the captain, turned in desperation to Len Hutton, our wonderful opening batsman. Our hopes sank visibly as poor Len's bowling was a succession of fours and sixes as Don Bradman and Arthur Morris raced on towards their target. No one had any appetite for dinner that day! I then questioned fate - was I always destined to support the losing team! Looking back almost fifty years, the answer is unquestionably yes, I was, and still am.

It was widely known that Keith Miller, another famous name in that Australian team, wore his cricket shirt with the collar raised, so we all wore ours that way as well. It was part of the Keith Miller cult that swept through our ranks, making us feel good but having little, if any, effect on our cricketing prowess.

Most of the masters I have already mentioned. Of the others, Mr Jones, the French master, gave copious lines for any and every misdemeanour, whether in the field of discipline or academics. If I had continued with the subject after scoring 10% at the end of term exams mid-way through my five year course, I would still have been writing lines for him now. Luckily for me it was decided that I and the French language should part company, and as I have never had cause to use that tongue to date, I think it was a wise decision on my tutor's part. Mrs Welburn took geography and was teaching at a boys' school, owing to a chronic shortage of male teachers caused by the war. Mr Edwards took English with the more senior boys and was deputy headmaster.

Discipline was hard, but fair, starting with line writing and ending with the headmaster's cane as a last resort. A look from the head could quell the more riotous horseplay. At one maths lesson Sandy Newton had been delayed and a real noisy exchange developed in his absence. That is until one boy looked up at the window and spotted the mortar-board and eagle eye of Mr Welburn looking in. Just as oil calms troubled waters, an uncanny silence fell over the whole class and no one dared utter a sound until the missing master arrived. On another occasion the whole school was gathered in the parish church for the school service. Tom Welburn was acting as organist sitting behind the curtains at the organ. A noisy buzz grew amongst the boys, until the curtain parted fractionally and a nose showed out. Again the uncanny silence fell upon the multitude until the service commenced. That is what I call discipline - it was built on respect much more than fear. Everybody knew where they stood with Tom Welburn as his standards never varied, rules were made and understood by all, so there was no excuse accepted from anyone who blatantly flaunted them. No one person was allowed to spoil things for the majority as the occasional transgressor found out to his painful cost. I and all my contemporaries were taught to respect others' lives and properties,

155

Neither Fish, nor Fowl

hopefully becoming better citizens in the process.

A grammar school education did me a power of good in many ways, but it left me wondering sometimes which life I was really part of. In fact I often wondered whether I was fish or fowl, but by the time I left school my life had come down heavily on the side of my roots - a man destined to do, rather than to order others to do for me.

Chapter 17
High Days and Holidays

Grandad Bumfrey, Aunt Ivy, Uncles Will and John all lived at Rats Hall during the war, so we could walk down to visit them on a Sunday afternoon and then stay for tea. Dad would follow us after his milking stint was over, riding his bike and then pushing it back when we returned in the evening. My uncles would save me cigarette cards when they were still included in the packets and later, any new type of packets when we had the craze to collect one each of them. Players Navy Cut, Woodbines, Gold Flake, Black Cat - such intriguing names they had! Smokers had to make do with whatever brand became available as war shortages began to bite. We always enjoyed those walks and the nice tea Aunt Ivy prepared. On some weekends Ivy would come to us for a change, as life was very lonely for such a young person shut away in the back of beyond; then, if the weather was fine, we would take the pram and dog along the road, in various directions as the fancy took us. It was in preparation for one of these walks that I attempted to take the pram, full of brothers, down the steep incline at the front gate and tipped the whole lot into the dust.

On another occasion we went on a picnic to Westacre Mill. For some unknown reason I was in a foul mood, and allowed the bile in my system to ruin the whole afternoon. Having taken a jam jar for fishing, I did catch a couple of minnows, but still retained my ill-temper. When it was time to pack up the picnic, one of Brian's socks was missing and we eventually found it flung through a wire fence; how it got that far away I don't know, but my foul mood may have had something to do with it. By whinging most of the way back, I made everyone as miserable as possible. When Mum accidentally upset my jar containing the tiny fish, I howled and kicked about. At last my mother's temper flared and a few hearty slaps gave me something to howl about. Straight to bed I went and poor Aunt Ivy must have sighed with relief as she cycled back to the relative calm of Rats Hall to prepare the washing for Monday morning. It wasn't very often I was out temper, so perhaps that is why I remember the incident so clearly.

Aunt Jane and Aunt Marjorie, or Mick as she was always known, lived at Mileham about 15 miles away. On odd occasions Mick might cycle over to see her sister Ivy, but normally both aunts were dropped off the Litcham to King's Lynn bus at the Patch Corner from where they walked the mile or so to Rats Hall. It wasn't until Grandad moved to Pretoria in 1947 that we saw much of them. The move into semi-civilisation for Ivy meant a

157

much longer walk for her sisters on their visits, but it seems you can't have everything in life your own way. We boys were so shy that we used to hide when they came, as we did when Uncle Jack and Aunt Lucy came from Bunwell on their motorcycle combination. They must have thought we were oddities and no mistake. Aunt Jane had four children, namely Basil, Maurice, Raymond and Jean, but we didn't see them much either, although Raymond came to stay for a holiday after the Bumfreys moved to Pretoria. Aunt Mick and her husband Sid Cason had one daughter, Maureen.

Day outings were a rare event; as previously mentioned, pre-war finances were so poor that an annual trip to King's Lynn after harvest was probably the limit for most families. But one trip to Hunstanton with the Sunday School comes to mind. As I never went to Sunday School, we must have helped to fill the third coach, as I am fairly sure there were three. A picture of the Rev. Ainsworth, complete with black, knee-high boots and stick, shepherding his flock into their respective vehicles, stays with me. Those jackboots, as we thought of them, caused much giggling and German spy speculation as we small boys peeped through holes in the front church pew on one wartime Sunday afternoon. Suddenly a hand gripped the collar of Barry Beck and we saw him being yanked back to another pew where he sat, crimson faced, beside Mrs Ainsworth. Our foolish giggling ceased forthwith and we sat very straight, with red ears flashing like beacons in the dimly lit church.

Only once did I attend the small Sunday School run by Mrs Sybil Birkbeck at the Hall. Much pressure had been put on my mother to send me, as it was painfully obvious to our betters that my religious education was suffering badly. At last I decided to go, and accompanied Georgie Wright up the Hall Drive, through the park and into the huge house. Obviously I didn't like what I saw, and never went again. Perhaps I couldn't memorise the text given for that purpose. Mrs Wright spent ages each week trying to cement the text into son George's mind, but she admitted that by the time he reached the holly bush across the road it had gone again. Being the head gardener's son meant that poor Georgie had to go weekly, as house servants' families were expected to set a good example to the more heathen labourers. To its credit, the Estate gave the tenants' children a Christmas party, but I was never well enough at that time of year to attend one of them. A little present and a few cakes came back for me, so I never felt deprived, especially as I never was a dedicated party-goer.

The onset of World War II prevented organised outings to the seaside, as all beaches were mined and barricaded with barbed wire. Concrete pillboxes guarded vital routes, both on the coast and inland. Trenches were dug across large fields to prevent enemy aircraft or gliders landing. Ribbons of white chalk were turned up by the mechanical diggers whose long necks dipped and rose as the metal scoop loaded and discharged. Very soon, red poppies and yellow charlock adorned those freshly-dug heaps, and seeds that must have been buried for years burst into life as sunshine and moisture combined to revive them. (Our Norfolk name for the fore-mentioned, yellow weed was carlick.)

But all this wartime activity failed to stop the most important event in the Bumfrey family's year. That was the annual holiday at the home of my mother's parents, Grandad and Granny Eke. In our little community this holiday was almost unique, as not even the hierarchy on the Estate had holidays away from home. Usually taken between hay cart and harvest, this annual trip to Briston was a great adventure for we boys, and a veritable lifeline for my mother as she loved her home village of Briston and the people living there. I am sure it was mentioned previously that Mum never really became a native of Westacre, but remained a Bristonian living in exile 25 miles away. As June advanced, the progress of haymaking was noted very closely and estimates were made as to when our holiday could be taken. Sometimes the gap between hay and corn harvests was narrow, being governed by weather variations both in spring and summer. I must confess, a great fuss always seemed to be necessary to produce one man to milk the cows during Dad's absence. At first it was only for one week, but later on a fortnight came to be the norm for seven-days-a-week men, as stockmen were called. Of course, all this buildup made the event all the more exciting as letters sped from Mum to Granny and from Granny to Mum. On one occasion it seemed Aunt Edith, Mum's sister, somehow convinced Granny she was too old to deal with us all and so our holiday looked like being cancelled. Mum was devastated and then roaring mad with her sister, who had an unfortunate habit of poking her nose in where it wasn't needed. Needless to say, the letter despatched to Edith made this point very clear and also pointed out that Mum continued to work through the holiday and didn't sit on her bottom end and allow Granny to wait on the family all the time. As was the norm when Mum wrote a rather hot letter, the sharp nibbed pen went through the paper a few times! Let me explain that the Eke family, unlike the Bumfreys, were very hot tempered, but the storms soon blew out and were forgotten. By the time we arrived in Briston that year the two sisters were back on normal speaking terms and Aunt Edith accompanied us on at least one outing to the seaside. Being a single lady, in service with Miss Cook, spinster of the parish, she had no idea of the stresses and strains of bringing up a family, and didn't realise just how much the annual break meant to the health and sanity of her married, younger sister. I'll bet Edith's ears burned whilst Mum composed her fiery letter. I must also add here that

High Days and Holidays

Edie suffered from a nervous complaint which caused permanent hair loss and a very snappy attitude at times, through no fault of her own. At heart she was very kind and tried to make the best of her rather sad life through reading and attending chapel where "Miss Eke" was well respected.

My first recollection of Briston was when Granny lived at Plums Cottages where, incidentally, I was born. The cottage was on the end of a row, with a large vegetable garden across the loke which ran down into the road. In the Briston area, a loke was the cart track which connected a property with a tar-surfaced road. On arrival at my grandparents' house, I was so shy that Dad had to walk round the garden with me for quite a time before I would venture indoors. The cockle shells, used to bind the paths, crackled under our feet as we walked.

Granny often spoke of the wonderful time I had putting coal in and out of her metal saucepans. I must have been a sight to behold at the end of my game. "He'll wash", was Granny's verdict, for she never worried about a little dirt, as long as we were happy. My Uncle Billy Eke was a tiny man, and I remember sitting with him on stools, him on the taller one and me on the smallest. I thought it was wonderful to have a grown-up sitting down as low as me. Mum had grown up at Plums Cottages and my having seen the house helped me to relive her stories of childhood adventures when she told them in later days. Some of the characters of those days were Jack Pipp, the fishmonger, who called on Saturdays at lunchtime and rubbed his fishy hands into Mum's face, Steven Crask, whose cart shed had mysteriously caught fire whilst none of Granny's boys knew anything about it, and Robert Neale who built a donkey cart in his attic, then obviously failed to get it down the stairs. "Walter, Walter, what shall I do?" he cried to Grandad. "Take it to pieces again, Robert", was the only answer to give him. How I loved to hear the tales of those Briston characters.

By the time our more memorable holidays began, Grandad Eke had retired from Melton works and moved to a better house just outside the main village, at Tithe Barn. This house was the first of four, all brick and flint, very square-set houses, with good sized rooms downstairs and three bedrooms up above.

At last the big day would arrive and our journey begin; although only 25 miles had to be covered, the actual journey had three stages. The first job was to get to Massingham Station to board the train. When Michael and Brian were small and needed a pram for transport, we walked the four and a half miles to the station situated on the far side of Massingham village. As we passed Morris Brothers Butchers shop on the right and Nelsons Grocery on the left, we could check the time by the church clock. Sometimes we had a stop at the butchers to order meat for collection on our return, and then were waved on our way by the cheery, red faced Charlie Fitt. Past the large pond and off to the steep hill down towards the station we went, the pram loaded with children and parcels and Dad pushing his bike festooned with more luggage. Mum always counted the number of parcels, cases and children and took stock at every section of the journey. How my stomach lurched when I caught sight of the shining metals and the neat station buildings nestling in the valley. Over the far side of the line was the Railway Inn where Dad left his bike to await his return only a short week later.

Off the road and along the gravel track to the booking office door we went, with third-class return tickets to Melton Constable bought at the ticket office window, then out on to the platform, down the slope at the end and across a wooden path to the far side platform to await the train from South Lynn. We would anxiously peer up the line for the first sign of smoke, and await the bell that told us the train had left Hillington, the next station up the line. Smoke would at last appear in the distance, and, with a rattle and a roar, the huge engine would steam past and squeal to a halt, throwing surplus steam into the air as it came to rest. Little eyes would try to catch a peep into the engine cab as it passed, just in case Uncle Fred Eke was at the controls, but not this time; it must have been a Peterborough or South Lynn crew on their way out. Perhaps Uncle Fred would be at Melton and give us a wave when we arrived. Quickly the pram would be emptied and given over to the guard, with its label tied firmly on to the handle. Children and parents would find a carriage and bundle in, with luggage carefully counted as it was stacked on the racks up above. With a sigh, Mum would sink down and gather the little ones safely on to the seat before the train jerked on its way. The whistle would blow, the green flag wave and very slowly Massingham station waiting room, store house, huge name board and finally, goods sidings would slide behind us as we glided out into the countryside on the way to a new life, even if it was only for a fortnight.

We were the lucky ones, for we had a holiday, thanks to careful parents who saved the money to go, and caring grandparents who gave us such a wonderful time in their welcoming home. So much love and caring on my dad's meagre agricultural wage and Grandad Eke's ten shillings per week old age pension, a sure reminder that it's not what you have in life that's important, but how you use it makes the key to happiness.

As the train gathered speed, the telegraph poles flashed past and the workers in the fields stopped to watch us, using our passing as an excuse to straighten their backs for a few minutes. Almost before top speed was reached, the brakes were applied and East Rudham station slowly came into view. At the next stop a very smart porter called, "Raynham Park", in

High Days and Holidays

a posh, clipped, un-Norfolk-like tone. Perhaps Raynham Park was the home of some peer of the realm and so warranted a higher class accent! Another short run onto a double lined stretch of track would bring us to the larger station of Fakenham. The double track also meant that another train could flash past in the opposite direction, frightening us with its sudden roar and passing carriages so near our windows. The last stop before our destination was Thursford, and then we would realise that the first highlight of our holiday was nearly over. On towards Melton Constable we would go, past the Gunthorpe gatehouse where Uncle Fred demolished a linesman's hut when delivering the man an unofficial ration of coal in the form of one big lump, thrown off an engine going at full speed through the dark night. What tales those railwaymen could tell! Slowly, under Melton Bridge and into the junction we steamed, coming to a gentle halt beside the buffet hall and bookstall. Dad would release the wide, leather strap securing the window and reach out to open the door. Mum, myself, children and luggage were handed out and, after a stock count, we all moved towards the barrier where our tickets got punched and then retained safely in Dad's purse for the return journey, which would be so far back in our minds that it was not even contemplated.

Several railwaymen would recognise my mother and greet her like a long lost friend and help carry some of our luggage and pram up the wide, steep steps to the road high above the station. Reloading our vehicle with its human and dead stock contents, we would all set off down Melton Hill and into Briston village which joined Melton Constable at the hill bottom. Leaving Uncle Fred's house at 149 on the right, still without catching a glimpse of him in his oily overall jacket and driver's cap, we would press on past the new school and proceed beyond the village and into the side road leading to Tithe Barn.

As the little caravan wearily rounded the bend near Duffields Farm, we would all look up and see Grandad Eke in his panama hat and Granny with woollen beret, apron around her ample body and sleeves rolled up showing ham-like arms ready to give us boys a cuddle of welcome once again. "My how they have grown. Alice, you look tired. Lovely to see you Fred", from both, as my dad was a much loved son-in-law. The extra hands helped us over the last lap, in the gate and round to the back door. Peter and Fluffy, the two cats, looked on as they saw their peace shattered for the next two weeks, but also knew there was plenty of cosy shed room for a quiet nap far from the madding crowd. Grandad, being very deaf could retire to his chair in the shed after lunch and rest up while Granny would take the rush of young life in her stride and enjoy every minute of it, being the epitome of a matriarchal grandmother who liked all her family to be under her wing at some time or another. Already her plans would have

162

been made to make our holiday as happy and comfortable as possible, and this she always did even when she had reached her eighties and we were grown up.

How homely the house always smelt, the cooking oil stoves giving out a quite different background aroma from our own kitchen at home. After the hot walk, it was nice to sit in the cool, north-facing living-room with some lemonade to quench our thirst. After a few minutes' rest, the great outdoors would call and off we would go round the garden to look at the chickens and then peep under the leaves on the raspberry canes to see if any red fruit was hidden there. Not having raspberry canes at home, the soft fruit came as a treat. Many times a day during our stay we would lie on our backs under the canes to gaze upwards to find the largest and most luscious fruit hiding under the leaves. Granny would loudly remark that there seemed to be no raspberries to pick as the birds had taken them all. We would lay very still, believing no-one could see our legs sticking out under the foliage, and sharing Granny's oft-used joke.

Walter and Florence Eke had eight children, five boys and three girls. Ernest, the eldest, was married and lived in Friars Street, King's Lynn, working as an engine fitter at the South Lynn depot; he had one son, young Ernie. William, or Billy as he was known, the second son, was a very small man, already mentioned, who was forced to move into lodgings in Doncaster when the Melton Constable Railway Works closed in 1936; he was a wheel tapper. Herbert, the third son, was married and had two daughters, Joyce and Florrie; they lived for a time along the row at Plums Cottages and then moved into a council house just across the back fields from Granny's original home. Herbert, or Douchie, ran the gas house down at the Melton rail junction. Fred, alias Sheddy or Bones, was an engine driver working out of Melton depot, and lived with his wife, Violet, and son, Douglas, at 149, Fakenham Road, almost on the Briston parish border with Melton Constable, very handy for his shift work. Uncle Billy was never accepted for service in the army, but the other three brothers served their country in the Great War. After Uncle Fred, came three sisters, Gladys, Edith and my mother Alice. Aunt Gladys married and lived in London, rearing seven children, six girls and one boy. Aunt Edith, of whom we spoke at length earlier in the chapter, lived out her life in Briston after earlier years of service in London. My mother came next in line, followed by a fifth boy, Alfie, known to the family as Shirts, pronounced "shuts", who worked as a local postman. Alfie fought in the Second World War, being one of the youngest men in the post office group at the outbreak of war in 1939; he was married, but had no children, and his wife, Paddy, worked on the station staff during the war years.

So you can see, all the male side of the family had some connection with

High Days and Holidays

the railway, making life at Briston completely railway-orientated. Railway was shouted from every part of their lives: the garden sheds were made of boards from broken-up trucks, tarred with gas house tar and sand; tarpaulins covered wood, etc, and had been cut from truck covers, torn and discarded; sheds stood on sleepers; clothes posts were sawn-down sleepers, and this gave everything a tarry smell, especially when the sun shone. Watches were checked by various whistling trains, as everyone seemed to know the timetable, which also seemed to mean something in those days, even if Mr Hitler did his damnedest to upset it at times. Everyone who came in talked of trains or engines, smelled of steam and smoke, and generally exuded railways from every pore. How I enjoyed every minute of it, taking in all the gossip and fervently hoping to become an engine driver when I grew up. What a terrible blow lay in store for this community when Dr Beeching's axe fell in the early 1960s, completely wiping away a whole way of life in one fell swoop.

The first day of the holiday, being Sunday, would be spent in the garden, or on a walk along the quiet byroads. We always planned our walks so we took a different way each time, making sure we covered them all before Dad returned to his Rats Hall lodgings after the first week. Usually, the first day took us up the lane and along a field footpath leading on to a small wood, called The Patch, beside the Norwich Road. Probably, we would meet up with Billy Duffield whose farm it was at Tithe Barn and he and Dad would discuss farm matters whilst we boys poked around hoping they would soon break off, allowing us to get on with our walk. We would only peep out at the top of the path, because the Norwich Road carried some traffic and it was considered busy compared with the roads we were used to, but the traffic was only spasmodic really. Sitting on the stile by The Patch we could see the village of Briston spread out below us. On week days, trails of smoke showed us where the Norwich and Yarmouth lines ran on to Melton Constable. The heavy puffing of an engine would come to us, as it toiled up the bank into Melton, hauling a long line of goods trucks across the county. Screwing up our eyes, we would try to count them as they passed the distant gap in the trees. Why was it we always seemed to get a different number? As soon as Mr Duffield had returned home and reported that Mrs Eke's relations had arrived, John and Clifford, his schoolboy sons, would call for me to come down to the farm. A dairy herd was milked twice a day, which meant that the two boys had work to do in the dairy and they fed the stock as well. It was fun helping them and as a reward, their dad invited me to join them for a ride out in their old car after tea. What a thrill for me. My little brother, Michael, had to stay at home, much to his annoyance. Granny Eke did some washing for Duffields and this came in a large suitcase. On one occasion, when

High Days and Holidays

Michael had been left behind, he vented his temper by kicking the innocent container and exclaiming, "Old Duffelfield's case".

When Grandad Eke called at the farm to collect the milk, he used to sit in the dairy and pump gallons of water up into a storage tank by means of a handle-operated mechanism. This water was needed to run through the cooler, over which the milk ran before going into a large, metal churn. These churns were, in turn, collected from the stand outside the farm every day by the milk lorry. This lorry rattled its way along the narrow roads, calling at all the small farms in the area. In and around Briston, almost all the farms were what we called "one man" farms, so different from the huge acreages of the Estate farms in the Westacre area.

Very soon after the end of the war, our seaside towns began to open for visitors once again. By 1946, the large pram had been discarded as surplus to requirements. Michael, being six years old, was very independent and was a good walker, although I believe we did borrow an old pushchair from Aunt Violet to help out over the near three mile walk from Tithe Barn to Melton Station. Also, by this time, Dad would be entitled to a fortnight's holiday and Waggs, our crossbred spaniel bitch, had been added to our company. If the first Monday was fine, we would set off to take the train to Sheringham, our favourite destination, and much loved by Dad as he had lived near there as a boy and delivered milk to hotels as his first job of work.

Down the steep Melton steps we would go, and on to the platform to await the arrival of our train. I was always drawn to the bookstall and the thrill of buying a comic was something to savour. Just across the line from our platform was the turntable where the huge engines were turned round by the driver and fireman pushing on a wooden handle, one being at the front and one at the back of the engine. To get the table started was very hard work and many men ruptured themselves at this task, but nevertheless this manual task remained long after the use of electric motors had become commonplace. We boys loved to watch as the huge, sizzling monster was slowly, oh so slowly, pushed round to face the other way.

Another item of interest was the small platform and waiting room on the opposite side of the track from the main station buildings. This was a private waiting room for Lord Hastings and his family who lived at Melton Hall. I believe this facility was offered as an inducement to allow the railway through his land in the early days of steam progress. Incidentally, I never saw anyone on that platform, so I must presume the incumbent Lord Hastings travelled by road, or stayed at home pretty often.

As soon as the train pulled in, the number one priority was to get a seat by the window, so as to miss nothing on the journey. The pictures just

High Days and Holidays

below the carriage luggage rack were always of interest as they depicted scenes from all over Britain. As the train began to roll, I was always sure it was the station moving, and we who were standing still, but as speed picked up, this optical illusion was always shattered. Under the bridge and away to the right we steamed, with the carriage wheels clanking over the points. As the sea could be seen from the top of Melton Bridge on a clear day, it wouldn't be long before we caught sight of it and the event would always raise a cheer on the first trip out. The first stop was the small town of Holt and, as the porter called the station name, the train would do just that - halt. This schoolboy joke was trotted out religiously, both going and returning, much to the amusement of the fellow passengers. The next station was Weybourne, pronounced Webben by the locals. This time the sea was in full view away to our left with fishing boats dancing on the waves to increase our excitement and anticipation. Running along the cliff top, with only the famous golf course between us and the sea, our train eased into Sheringham station, and off we trundled, armed with buckets, spades, coats and packed lunch. I just cannot describe the deep, swelling joy I felt as our little party left the station behind and walked down the road into town.

The first shop we came to was a greengrocer's where Mum always stopped to buy some fruit. The man who owned it had a tradesman's bike which he used regularly to carry goods to and from a second shop in the town centre. Wearing a wide-brimmed trilby hat and long apron, he would hop on his machine and wobble off down the street between the many pedestrians jay-walking, as holidaymakers think they are entitled to do in someone else's town.

Following the main street past the clock tower, our noses picked up the smells of the sea. The wonderfully fresh, salt-laden air brought with it a mixture of fish and tar from the many small fishing boats pulled up on the shingle. The beauty of Sheringham was the wonderful stretch of clean sand when the tide went out. This sand was washed with every tide which came right up to the bank of round pebbles below the sea wall. Off down the steps we went, and on to the stones where our coats were soon spread and preparations made for the first paddle of the season. Clear pools could be found near the breakwaters and here Michael could splash around to his heart's content and I could help him build the obligatory sand-castle or hunt for a collection of shells. The air was very bracing, for Sheringham was a resort much used by the rich and famous in need of a health cure, especially in pre-war days. Uncle Billy Eke had once worked at the golf course in his youth and told us stories of the famous names he met up with. Being enamoured with golf, he acquired an old club with which he drove a ball straight through Granny's window. Giving the order, "Hold my club,

High Days and Holidays

caddy", to small brother Alfie, the budding golfer set off down the loke and wasn't seen until much later in the day, by which time he hoped the furore had died down.

Having a packed meal not only kept down the expenses for us, but also meant we could spend longer on the beach, which was the sole purpose of the trip. Mum was convinced that if the ozone-laden air could help cure the rich, then it would also help strengthen the poor and we should have a good dose of it. When the tide came back in, the temperature tended to drop, so a trip around the amusement arcade was next on the agenda. I wonder if that wretched crane which took our pennies, but never ever picked up a prize to drop down the chute, is still there. On rare occasions we had pennies returned from some machines, but they eventually all ended up in the pockets of the proprietor and we drifted away as losers once again. If Aunt Edith came with us, tea was taken in a little shop away from the sea front, but we were warned in advance to take no more than one fancy cake as the prices were above our expenditure level. Limited funds had to be stretched to last the fortnight. These holiday funds had been saved from the money earned by Dad working those three hours' overtime each day during the summer.

Just before six o'clock, it was time to retrace our steps and make for the station. Crossing the line, we would sit in the evening sunshine to watch the desultory life of the station staff as they moved slowly about their allotted tasks. The box of fish lying full in the sun would slowly leak its ice water on to the dusty platform. The mail bags would be flung down by the postman on to one of the metal-wheeled trolleys that used to rattle along all station platforms. Eventually the busy little train would bustle in from Cromer and our party would find a seat and sink wearily on to the hard, rough, third class upholstery. The bucket containing our shell collection and a large piece of brown seaweed was wedged upright, and away we went, watching the train speeding along as the westering sun put its shadow out on to the flat fields. With smoke streaming back we would make good time on our return to Melton, just as if everyone was longing to get home and be off to bed. After the long walk back from the station to Tithe Barn, we were certainly ready for our beds, and the sweet-smelling, white sheets soon wrapped us into a well earned deep and peaceful sleep.

Chapter 18
Those Hazy, Lazy Days of Summer

Every day of our holiday, whether on an outing or staying at home, held its own excitement and interest. So much of Briston life was different from our Westacre normality, and it was a life I longed to be part of. I suppose that all holidays have the same effect, seemingly full of new things compared with the mundane chores of home. When the fishmonger called, bringing a wonderful variety of freshly-caught wet and shell fish, Grandad would cook some bloaters for tea, setting them on a griddle over the fire. Cockles would be left to spit in salt water overnight and then he would cook them for breakfast. The rattle of their shells on the enamel dish would bring the cats crying in from the garden and we boys clattering down the stairs. Salt, pepper, and vinegar were put on the steaming delicacies as they slid out of their open shells on to our plates. Grandad would always give his cats some first, as he was a great cat lover and would have gladly given his whole breakfast away if Granny hadn't called a halt to proceedings. I can smell the wonderful aroma now as the salty steam rose up, making our mouths water as we waited for the cockles to cool. After breakfast, the white shells went out on to the path where our feet helped to crush them into the surface with a lovely crunching sound.

Then we would go off for a walk, this time up the steep hill behind the houses, following a narrow road between high banks, down past the end of Cunifer wood as far as Albert "Tute" Rudd's farm on the Saxthorpe road. This farm was called Roper Farm. Tute was a fairly stout, jolly type of man, very good-hearted and a great friend of Uncle Fred who often shot rabbits on his land. All sorts of fowl and duck roamed the farmyard, amongst them some guinea-fowl whose tiny heads and squeaky voices made them amusing to me. Often, Tute and his brother-in-law, Fred Catton, would be busy in the fields and would stop to have a word when they recognised who we were. On the very first occasion we met up we were mistaken for visitors from London, but as soon as we spoke, that myth was dispelled, although our accents weren't so broad as their own. Sometimes we would cut through the loke opposite the farm and return to The Patch along the Norwich Road, which was quite a good walk, despite the traffic. Otherwise, we would return the way we had come, allowing us to view Tithe Barn from the top of the hill and watch Grandad busy in his garden, with panama hat pushed back to let out the heat generated by his efforts in the late July sun. Usually, one of the cats would sit watching him from the path or top of the shed whilst the fat, brown, Rhode Island Red hens took

Those Hazy, Lazy Days of Summer

dust baths in their spacious run. Granny might come bustling out of the back door to fetch the washing, or to empty a bucket of water on the muck heap. This made a very peaceful, domestic scene, typifying a wonderful retirement after a long life of unremitting toil in both engineering and domestic fields.

We would return both hot and thirsty, with Waggs' tongue hanging out after she had tugged at her lead all the way out and all the way back, almost choking herself for no good reason at all. Unlike Rip, she was deaf to any commands once off the lead, and so had to endure the restriction on most walks, and yet if she went with Dad alone, there was no trouble and she would follow him at heel. We never understood why our presence caused her mind to blow, and all training to be forgotten. Granny's walk-in type larder was like an Aladdin's cave in a ration- restricted environment: it held seven pound jars of pickled onions and red cabbage, two pound jars of home made jam of various sorts, and biscuit tins containing fruit cake, short cakes, and tarts with the home made jam; there were also a crock of brown eggs, cold bacon, fresh fish, shellfish, and rabbit under the shelf for later. Our holiday menu never lacked a thing as all the goodies listed above were augmented by fresh vegetables from the garden, fruit from the trees and bushes, and milk from the farm. I don't think food rationing ever came to Granny's family for she was such a wizard in the kitchen that it hardly ever showed, a truly remarkable lady whose attributes could fill a whole chapter and still not run out.

Wednesday would bring another outing and as the weather always seemed to be warm and dry, there was no need to vary our set pattern of alternate days' outings. Yarmouth would probably be our destination and this would give us our longest train ride of the holiday. I know we enjoyed the railway journey just as much, if not more, than the stay by the sea. Yarmouth was, of course, much more commercialised, even in those days, than either Sheringham or Cromer. This time, the train would ease out of Melton in the opposite direction, showing us the back of Briston as we cruised past the common near Joe Rudd's farm. This common provided heather flowers, which in turned allowed bees to make the nutritious heather honey which Mum bought for us from the bee-keeper nearby. We couldn't actually see Tithe Barn because of its sheltered position, but the tall pine trees in The Patch showed up and we knew Granny would hear the rattle of the carriage wheels as we passed by in the distance. As we trundled our way across the landscape, a new type of vista emerged as we approached the Norfolk Broads. These flat, fen-like areas, interspersed with reed-fringed dykes, slowly gave way to larger water courses and patches of open water where brightly-painted cruisers and high-sailed yachts lit up the scene. At Potter Heigham, the heart of the Broads,

Those Hazy, Lazy Days of Summer

holidaymakers would be very evident where every "one week sailor" wore shorts and a sailor's cap while trying to look every inch a seafaring man despite white legs and a semi-pallid face. Leaving this unfamiliar scene behind, we launched out once more across the flat, green landscape, with only the fat cattle grazing quietly on the lush summer grass well supplied with moisture by the high water table.

The Yarmouth excursion meant a little less beach play and more window shopping and amusement arcades. There was much more concrete along the sea front, with the usual glitter and noise associated with commercial venues where people need these garish amusements to enjoy themselves. Some famous Yarmouth bloaters, or kippers, were needfully purchased, but they usually turned out to be a lot less fresh than those purchased from the cart at Tithe Barn. They often ended up inside the cats as Grandad Eke was just as fussy with his fish as he was with his cockles. Some funny old ice-cream was just beginning to appear after the war, and although we kiddies ate it, the quality left much to be desired.

Thursday, being another rest day, meant a lie in for us all. How Dad loved this, after getting up before 6.30 a.m. every day during the rest of the year. If I woke up earlier then I could content myself by rummaging in the cardboard boxes under the bed. These held all the books awarded to the Eke family as Sunday School prizes. Although slightly old-fashioned, they provided me with sufficient reading matter to last the holiday. The gaily-decorated sticker inside the front cover told me who had been the lucky recipient and from which chapel they had been awarded. Although neither Granny nor Grandad were worshippers, their offspring had been sent to Sunday School very regularly as was borne out by all those awards for regular attendance. In fact, I believe my mother often went to three different venues, not for the religious guidance, but to qualify for three outings and three parties at Christmas, not that the teaching did much good, for often when little sister Alice was running wild, Aunt Gladys, who was rather pious at the time, would confront her in the street with a dire warning, "Be sure your sins will find you out!". All poor Gladys received for her soul-saving message was a stuck-out tongue and a gang of girls prancing up the street behind her giving vent to all the catcalls they could think of.

The headmaster at Briston School once remarked to Ernie Eke, his star pupil, "Your sister Alice is as bold as brass", when she slid across the icy playground, defying the no-sliding rule. Fred Eke had to be carried to school under Granny's powerful arm, howling all the way. I doubt whether his regular attendance at any schools swelled the number of books under the bed. Rumour has it that he was too busy up the lane, setting fire to dry, grassy banks, to attend a place of religious education. Granny had seen life, bringing up her brood, but had retained her sense of humour and was still very young at heart, which enabled her to see life surprisingly clearly through youngsters' eyes.

After a lazy breakfast, we male members of the Pretoria contingent would set off walking another favourite route. Again, we might set off up the steep hill as far as the pightle which was a small, triangular, gorse-covered area, where the narrow Pack Horse Lane joined the Saxthorpe road. This time we would turn right to proceed down the sunken lane which led to the outskirts of the main Briston village by Henry Williamson's farm. Pack Horse Lane was so narrow that we had to get on to the steep bank should a motor vehicle decide to come along, although this was the exception, rather than the rule. Stunted oak trees topped the banks at intervals, and steep gateways led into the fields. In springtime these banks would be yellow with primroses, whilst bluebells grew in profusion in the Cunifer wood we mentioned when describing one of our other walks. If Henry was working in his field, a short chat would ensue before he resumed his work.

Henry was a very conscientious small farmer whose methods were mainly based on hard, manual work as mechanisation didn't lend itself to the tiny fields of almost all the village farms. It wasn't until one reached the extremes of the parish boundaries that the fields grew slightly from pocket-sized to a reasonable acreage on which a tractor and implement could get a good bite at its work. Tute Rudd worked the twenty acre plus fields and in one or two instances had removed a dividing fence or bank. Meanwhile, farmers such as Henry, who we should class as smallholders, would be seen with two-hoed push machines, powered by themselves, killing the weeds in root crops, and on one occasion I witnessed a very light harrow being pulled by a man. Don't forget, these jobs were being done by the farmer himself, and not by some unfortunate, hired labourer. Many of these small concerns had been passed from father to son and were proudly held on to, even at the expense of the farmer himself working like a slave and his family likewise in their attempt to wrestle an independent living from the soil. Compared with we labouring men, who were practically owned body and soul by the Estate, these "bossmen" were the slaves, and yet they had the one thing I was soon to crave for when I began my working life, and for which the holidays at Briston lit the flame. That commodity was freedom - the freedom to get up every morning and decide for myself exactly how and at what task the day would be spent. For this doubtful honour I had to wait until I was almost 54 years old and then the employment situation, or lack thereof, forced my hand, but by then the whole working environment had changed, even beyond the wildest dreams or nightmares of Henry or Dad, the men caught in an age-old time warp of

Those Hazy, Lazy Days of Summer

British farming which had changed so little since man first began to till the land.

Our returning steps would take us past the house of Mousey Massingham, a dealer in all sorts of scrap and surplus materials. The garden was decorated with all manner of ornaments picked up on his rounds. Mousey was, without doubt, of gipsy origin and very well known in the district as he toured many villages, piling his small motor truck high with seemingly useless pieces of metal. I remember on one occasion, when the Duffield boys and myself were on a craze of collecting car numbers, we carefully noted down Mr Massingham's van number as it stood in the drive. How shocked we were when an irate figure burst out of the house, waving and shouting at us to clear off at the double. This we did without a second bidding and left any other of Mousey's vehicles out of our numbers list. Perhaps he mistook us for young sleuths intent on solving some unconnected misdemeanour that had been committed in the area. That day, as we passed, the ever present, chained-up dog gave us a warning bark, but this little party was more interested in getting home for dinner than in anything else.

There were many dealers in and around Briston, living on pieces of waste ground in a wooden, self-built bungalow or disused railway carriage. These small, independent dwellings were normally kept very neat with roses trailing over the doors, and these also helped fire me with the independence which typified the inhabitants of Briston village. Everyone seemed to be his own man with his own niche and essential place in the community. When Mrs Grey, the so-called Queen of the Romanies, called round riding in her pony trap, Granny always treated her with great respect, as indeed she did my Grandmother. A piece of lace or ribbon was bought to keep on the right side of good luck for another year, but overall the event held the atmosphere of a royal visit and something that hailed back many hundreds of years through which the local and the wandering gipsy people had lived in partnership, their lives only perhaps touching on these annual occasions. When Mum was a girl she hid from Mrs Grey, but to Granny she was a special friend, and, more importantly, a kindred spirit.

It appears that Granny once reputedly told Uncle Herbert that her great grandmother was known as a wise woman and that ladies came in carriages to have their fortunes told. But of course, by the time Herbert retold the tale, there had been numerous black cats involved and tudds (which were toads) sitting in the copper hole. There must have been some truth in the first part of the story, because Granny clammed up about it when the suggestion of ridicule crept in. I know she was quite superstitious and felt there were some things in heaven and earth best left undisturbed. Grandad Eke on the other hand pooh-poohed any idea of superstition, much to

Those Hazy, Lazy Days of Summer

Granny's displeasure, especially where the Romanies were concerned. We saw very few real Romanies in the Westacre area, but received frequent visits from the "didicoys", who were the equivalent of today's new age travellers. These people bought rabbit skins or scrap metal and very often there would be one person at your door and another scouting around the shed backs on the lookout for anything worth pinching. Even in those days our shed was always kept locked at night, although we weren't as security-conscious as today.

Even more common on our roads around Westacre were tramps, making their way from one workhouse to the next. Many made for Gayton Union, although the rule of a bath before bed kept many others sleeping under the hedge. One old chap carrying a white stick called to sell Old Moore's Almanac. Dad bought one from him for sixpence on one Saturday dinner time, but when he called a fortnight later with another, and, on being questioned, informed Dad that the previous copy was last year's, he met with some opposition - "You thieving old b-----", roared my father, "get out of my garden". The blind man found the gate with such speed that we were sure his eyesight had miraculously recovered under the tongue-lashing given out by his irate customer. Incidentally, that old tramp was nicknamed "Isah" by Aunt Ivy. On one of his numerous calls at Rats Hall, Ivy made him a cup of tea, and after guzzling it down, he called round the door, "Isah, have you got another one?", so from that day on he was always known as Old Isah by the Bumfrey fraternity.

A trip to Norwich on either Friday or Saturday would finish off our first week in Briston. Again, the train ride was the highlight of the day. On the first visit to Norwich after the war, we were amazed when we drew into the city station. Apart from the platform and a few temporary station buildings, everything else was flat and empty, just an odd wall or two to show where homes or shops had been before the German bombers had razed them to the ground. As we left the station area, we saw partly-damaged buildings left standing, and I remember gazing up at an exposed bedroom that showed the tiny fireplace and torn, rose-patterned wallpaper hanging and moving in the wind. It looked so pitiful and forlorn and was the only live picture I had of the war through which I had lived so happily while others' lives had been torn apart and their homes desecrated.

On one occasion we must have holidayed after harvest, because the football season had started and Dad took me to Carrow Road for the first time, which helped to fan the flame of football support which I have given to the Canaries over many seasons - through thick and thin you may say, but with a great deal more thin than thick! That day I saw Bristol City as the visitors, and I believe Norwich won by 4 goals to 1; I know Bernard Robinson, the Norwich captain, scored from the penalty spot. Sitting in

173

Those Hazy, Lazy Days of Summer

the stand, we had a grand view, and the only thing to mar my afternoon was the cigar smoke from a neighbouring fan which gave me one of my sick headaches. "On the ball City", I learned to shout, and have worn a green and yellow scarf proudly since that day, despite the good-natured banter and ridicule heaped upon my head by supporters of more illustrious football teams that seem to carry all before them season after season.

The evenings at Granny's were either spent playing games on the big, central table, or listening to our visitors' tall tales. The main game played was dominoes, and Granny was a dab hand at placing a 5 next to a 4 if she couldn't follow by fair means. If Grandad noticed her sleight-of-hand, a great shout would go up and Granny would plead bad light or failing eyesight. We boys would wait for the eruption and for Granny to tell him to keep his hair on (of which he had very little on top) - at any rate, it was all good, family fun. Meracne, as his children rudely called Grandad out of his hearing, fell for the trick every time. If Uncle Herbert or Uncle Fred and Douglas called, then the games were forgotten and we listened enthralled to their stories; all the characters of Melton station would be paraded before us, as well as of many at stations up and down the line.

Fred also had poaching tales to tell, for he was a great man with his gun which always stood in the corner of Granny's living-room. Many an early morning saw Fred creeping along hedges and through woods, trying to catch a long-tailed rabbit. It was no wonder he suffered from rheumatism in later life, for he would lie for hours waiting for a pot-shot at a prospective pheasant dinner. He had shooting rights for rabbits on Tute Rudd's farmland, but, from the tales he told, there was more fun in risking his gun licence in other places as well. The tale I often laugh over was the one where he and Douglas were out walking quite a way from Tithe Barn, and Fred reckoned he could see a rabbit sitting at the bottom of a hedge. Keeping his quarry in sight, he sent son Douglas running back to Granny's to get the gun. Arriving back at the scene of action with the gun and cartridges, the breathless Douglas watched as his father took aim and shot dead a piece of rotten wood. I doubt Douglas was very complimentary about his father's eyesight, but Fred often told this tale against himself and never failed to make us laugh. "Silly fool", said Granny, "making that boy run all the way back for nothing".

Fred had a little, white, terrier dog which rode in a wooden box on the back of his bike, bouncing around as the old bone-shaker set off down the loke with Fred waving over his shoulder to we boys. He loved children and he enjoyed our company, as we always loved him. Uncle Fred was painfully thin, whilst Herbert was just the reverse, being stocky and well built and very strong. When they were boys and lived at Plums Cottages they all slept in one bed. When the pre-sleep horseplay became too noisy,

Those Hazy, Lazy Days of Summer

Granny would shout up the stairs, and, if this had no effect, a nut stick would come out and a few stripes would be delivered across the bed. Roars of semi-mock pain would come out, with Herbert making the loudest. What Granny didn't know was that Master Herbert, being much the strongest, held Fred and Billy's legs up above his own, so that they received a stinging stick. When the bustling figure of their mother returned downstairs, the man in the middle would tell his smarting-legged brothers to, "Shut up, for goodness sake", because he didn't feel any pain. I can see him now, with his cap peak half turned over one eye and grinning in his engaging way, as he poked his head round the door. Both those uncles were grand characters in their own very different ways.

It wasn't until well after the war, when he had been eventually demobbed, that we saw Uncle Alfie delivering the letters once more. He used to cycle around all the outlying farms in the days before mail vans became the norm. This long delivery round may have been idyllic on balmy, summer mornings, but the dark, wet, winter days must have been purgatory itself, especially after a life-threatening, pre-war bout of pleurisy left him with weak lungs which weren't much improved by his wartime privations. Still, he battled on until eventually delivery vans came in to lessen the load considerably. In fact, Alfie, after he had passed his driving test, was the only member of the Eke family to have a motor car. Never a man to be over free in the money-spending field, he ran around in a little car with near bald tyres, until MOT regulations forced him to become the owner of a roadworthy vehicle. As a boy he used to hide behind his father's chair when he was having a snooze, and tickle the bald pate with a feather, causing Grandad to wake up cursing those wretched flies disturbing his well-earned rest. On another occasion, Fred, still living at home, had his shirt half-way over his head, when little Alf woke up with a start and shouted that a ghost was in the room, hence his nickname, "Shirts".

Brother Fred, who was always a bit of a tease, upset my mother before she was married. Unfortunately for Fred, she was cleaning mackerel at the time, so she whacked him over the head with one of the wet fish. He often laughed about my mother's "mackerel temper" after that. He wasn't so amused at the time though, and Granny had to step in by telling him to leave the girl alone and get off home to his own house. As Granny always had the last word in any dispute, I expect that's what he did. Yes, the Ekes often fell out amongst themselves, but it never lasted and no one outside was allowed to say a word against one family member in the hearing of another, and when Granny said "enough was enough", then it was she who ruled the roost and they all knew it. I was very lucky as I had four wonderful grandparents, though of course I regrettably only knew Granny Bumfrey for a few short years, but her wonderful, cheerful character was mirrored in Aunt Ivy instead.

Now the first week at Briston seemed to go quite slowly, mainly because, as each individual day passed, we knew there was another one still to be enjoyed the next week. But once the first Friday had passed, the holiday was on the slippery slope and began to disappear at an alarming rate. If we were lucky and the weather and funds held out, then a trip to Cromer and one more to Sheringham were still to come. More walks had to be fitted in, and another ride out with Mr Duffield was still possible on the Sunday evening. As it happened, this wasn't to be, as, after we had all piled into the big, old car, the steering wheel failed to function because a pin had sheared whilst backing out of the shed. How lucky we all were that it happened in the farmyard. I doubt if I would have been writing this tale if the pin had sheared half-way down Hunworth Hill or some other steep incline with a sharp bend at the bottom. I'm afraid the thoughts of being lucky to be alive did little to salve our disappointment, but there we are, thank goodness we are still here to tell the tale. I suppose I felt a bit miffed, as did my small brother Michael the week before, and would have liked to have kicked old Duffelfield's car.

Our trip to Cromer was really an extended ride beyond Sheringham, the railway running along the north Norfolk coast, past the Runctons and into Cromer Beach Station. On one occasion, the driver was Uncle Fred so we were lifted up on to the footplate where the fire roared and the steam hissed - just a little frightening really, but a great and memorable experience nonetheless. Cromer boasted two railway stations, the second being Cromer East where trains on the Great Eastern Railway came in, cutting across the county from the opposite direction to our track. After a long walk along the cliffs, Mum took command and led us back to the station via a short cut known only to herself. Dad raised a faint objection, but was quickly overruled by one who knew better, although he had the last laugh when the so-called foot-saving short cut led us out at the Great Eastern station, leaving us an even longer walk over to the other side of town. Many a joke was made over Mum's short cuts. One item of special interest at Cromer was a visit to the lifeboat station. We always enjoyed looking at the boat and equipment, and being allowed to sit in it, which sent our imaginations into overdrive.

As I said, the last outing would be to our favourite watering place, namely Sheringham, so famous for its crabs and beautiful sand. Cromer was of course famous in the first category, as Cromer crabs are well known the country over, but the beach isn't in the same class as its neighbour. As the train steamed back towards Melton on the last trip, a certain melancholy settled over us, for our lovely holiday was almost at an end for another year. Our strip of brown seaweed would go back to Pretoria with

Those Hazy, Lazy Days of Summer

us, to hang by the door to forecast the weather, turning damp if rain was in the offing. A few large shells and coloured stones on the garden edge would serve to remind us of our carefree days. All too soon we must return to Melton for the journey home.

One game we played quite often in Granny's garden was marbles. Some beautifully-coloured, glass alleys had come to light from one of the numerous tins stored in the "long place" cupboard under Tithe Barn stairs. Added to these were more marbles bought in the village from little Mrs Coble's shop. This lady was very old and almost blind, but still managed to run her tiny sweet and oddments shop from a room in her house.

The Duffield boys played as well when their farm chores were finished. Often we went to help them first, and on one occasion we pulled turnips for stock feed and threw them into a tumbril, when Clifford became over-enthusiastic and hurled an extra-large one over the other side, hitting poor Michael on the head in the process. With knees buckled the stricken worker staggered around, not knowing what had hit him. John was very cross with his younger brother for fooling about, but the incident marred the day for Michael, for he was much younger than us and was pretty shaken by his experience. The job always undertaken on one of the last days at Briston was to cut the long hedges around the perimeter of Grandad's garden. These hedges were set up on a bank, which made them quite high from the roadside. Dad used the shears on the high side and Grandad did the inside. We boys were in charge of the clearing up, taking great care to remove all thorns from the loke for fear of causing punctures to the faithful bone-shaker bikes ridden by uncles and residents further up the row. Grandad was always very grateful for our help, but it was the least we could do for a man who would give his all away to those less fortunate than himself.

Just before we leave Tithe Barn, I must give mention to the privy situated at the very bottom of the garden. Grandad was meticulous over its cleanliness, making sure lime was sprinkled in the bucket, the wooden seat scrubbed and the interior lime-washed at least once a year. When we sat there, never a trace of foul air assailed our nostrils. The neat squares of Eastern Daily Press newspaper hung on a string and the only complaint I could raise was the fact that the squares didn't run in sequence. I could start to read an article on one square then find the square that completed it had already been used by the previous customer! Waggs always accompanied us to the toilet and would sit by our feet until we were ready to go. She was a funny little dog, but, like Rip before her, so very faithful.

When the fateful return home day arrived, all bags and parcels were re-packed and stacked by the door. Dinner was eaten in a restrained atmosphere as parting from our grandparents was such a sad affair. They

Those Hazy, Lazy Days of Summer

both kissed us goodbye, with Grandad's moustache tickling our faces and Granny smelling of cooking and loving kindness. Turning at the bottom of the road, we all returned their waves, and a near-to-tears silence wrapped us until we were well up the road towards the station. All too soon the village was left behind and home beckoned as the sounds and sights of the busy junction came to us.

Down the steps and into our carriage we went, with Waggs peeping out from under the seat and Mum hoping no one would notice we hadn't purchased a dog's ticket. Under the bridge we rattled, and away through Thursford, Fakenham, Raynham Park, still with its posh porter, East Rudham and finally, oh so finally into Massingham and back on to home soil. What a marvellous holiday we'd had, with not a minute wasted and so much enjoyment packed in. I wonder if the very tired Granny and Grandad Eke sighed with relief as we disappeared up the road. They could now sink back into their peaceful and happy retirement, with those two cats vying with them for the best chairs. But if peace of mind comes from helping others to enjoy their lives, then their rest must have been of the highest order, for they had given their all to make us welcome.

Chapter 19
Back in the Groove

As soon as we had gathered ourselves and all our luggage together and passed through the booking hall, giving up our tickets on the way, the holiday was officially over. Suddenly, the one thing on our minds as the train rattled away towards Hillington was to get back to Pretoria as fast as possible. In the days before our motorised travel to and from stations, Dad would nip around to the pub, retrieve his trusty bike and load up in readiness for the four and a half mile trek back to base, far into the hinterland of rural west Norfolk - this was a nice way to describe what the rest of the world would call the back of beyond.

On one occasion a flat tyre greeted him , but some fresh air pumped hastily in seemed to do the trick, and off we went up the very steep Little Massingham Hill, but on reaching the top the offending tyre had already almost deflated, so, after upending the machine on a level bank, Dad set to mending the puncture. To find the tiny hole in the inner tube he always partly inflated it, then worked his way around stretching it across his forehead in order to feel the escaping air. This he proceeded to do, until an apparently weakened section protested against the stretching and burst with quite a loud bang. The expression on his face was a picture, and one I never forgot. His cap shot back on his bald head, and his eyes almost popped out! This calamity meant a semi-push, semi-carry of the wretched bike on into the village where a new tube could be purchased and fitted. I expect there was much under-breath swearing about the inconvenience and expense incurred, but eventually our journey was resumed. Meat would be collected from Morris the Butchers, and a long walk beside and around Massingham Heath completed before the old familiar High House Road was reached and Pretoria hove into view sheltering at the front of its narrow belt of fir trees.

The first few hours back home always felt strange, but by the next day, everything was back into the groove and the onset of harvest thoughts relegated the wonders of the Briston world to the back of our minds until the next year's holiday blew the dust off them once more.

The garden always appeared to have been untreated for months, rather than fourteen days, the paths seemed un-walked and the weeds grew everywhere having relished their new found freedom from Dad's constant pulling and hoeing. In a very short time order would be restored and one could see that Freddie was in control of nature once more. Once this state of affairs had been confirmed, life took on its normal, day to day, season to

179

season pattern which was the way Dad loved to live. Not for him the joys of the unknown, or the kick of surprises - he liked to hoe a straight row and see any problems way up ahead in order to deal with them in his own methodical way, and allow sleeping dogs to lie as often as possible.

One of the first things to be done by we boys was to check the dilberry tree for ripening fruit. The very first one appeared as a red dot amongst all the greenery and this one plum just had to be obtained, so the clothes prop came into play to dislodge it. Sometimes, after hitting several lower boughs, it would divert at the last moment and fall in the hens' run where half a dozen watching matrons would converge on it, much to our dismay. More often than not, the reddening skin would hide a still green and sour interior and our efforts would be wasted by sampling too soon. As I have indicated before, once the fruit really ripened, plums could be picked by the bagful, but we just couldn't wait for another week. Those plum-gobbling chickens weren't really hungry, because Uncle Will had fed them well during our absence, being a most caring and responsible man towards any animal under his care. After 1947 when he moved to Pretoria, it was easier for him just to walk down the hill, rather than cycle in from Rats Hall, though I'm sure he never minded as the two brothers were very close friends.

Having previously described my holgy boy harvests, I will now move on to the heady days of my horse-raking harvests. In the pre-combine harvester days, as many as three horse-rakes would have been used to rake up the loose straws of corn, dropped from the shoofs when carting. These rakings were normally collected after the conclusion of the main harvest and stacked separately for threshing out later to provide grain for pheasant feeding. As the two red Massey Harris combines reduced the acreage of bound corn, the need for multiple horse-rakes declined, and by the time I qualified for the job, only I followed the two companies of carters.

My first field to rake was the Twenty Four Acres, at which I arrived in due course, after Mr Wilson had harnessed the horse used by Charlie Andrews, the shepherd, and backed it into the rake. My instructions were to proceed across the longest side of the field, then, when the rake was full, to put my foot on a pedal designed to activate a ratchet causing the rake to lift, thus depositing its contents. This action continued until the far fence was reached, and then on the return trip the rake was emptied level with the first deposit, making sure to keep as straight a line as possible for future ease in carting. The horse, feeling skittish at first, set off at a good rate, which occasionally caused the rake to shake over a rough furrow and activate the ratchet by accident, leaving the gathered straw out of line. This meant circling round to pick it up again, much to my embarrassment, although I doubt if anyone was around to see.

Back in the Groove

My whole day, through dinner and fourses, was spent alone with my horse. Gradually the field narrowed, and the gathered rows grew longer with a few of them reasonably straight, but others resembled a dog's hind leg! Raking through a cultivated pit hole was a bit scary and I felt my precarious perch on the iron, sack-covered seat wasn't the safest of places. At 6.30 p.m. I realised the work must stop for a return be made to the farm in readiness for leaving off at 7 o'clock. Unhitching the horse held no problems, but then I made a fatal mistake. Bending to pick up my coat and bag from the hedge bank, I let go of the horse, and up went his head and away he galloped towards Soigné, with the young greenhorn, Derek, running behind almost weeping with frustration and shame at being caught short of basic common sense. Would Dilbury ever have been made to look so foolish?

Up the side of the Hulver we trailed, my errant steed always keeping just ahead of me, as I continued my fruitless pursuit, weighed down by encumbrances such as dinner bag, sack and coat. Turning at the top of the track, horse and sweating boy entered the farmyard, the former with a final burst of speed, and the latter with leaden footsteps. The animal's final flourish caused his breeching harness to slide off his back and trail unceremoniously alongside as he made his way up to the new horse pasture gate which was just alongside Mr Andrews' house. By the time I had made good the lengthening gap between us, a widely-grinning Charlie "Lop" Andrews had come out to secure his horse and enquire as to the cause of such unprofessional behaviour. Slowly I led the now docile wretch back to the stable where even more problems awaited me in my unbelievably untrained state. Do you think I could get that wretched collar over the horse's head? Every time it began to nip my charge's neck, he whipped his head up as high as possible. I petted, cajoled (and swore I expect), but no, it just wouldn't come off. Then, at last thought replaced sheer panic and I reversed the collar and off it came like a dream. Why hadn't I paid attention in the morning when the stupid thing was put on? At last I was able to lead my by now bewildered horse out and along to the pasture where he ran and rolled from sheer joy at being freed from the hands of the biggest greenhorn ever to set foot on Soigné farm. Charlie Andrews gave me one of his wheezy chuckles as I set off for home, vowing to make a better job of the next day.

I am pleased to say the poor horse and I soon struck up a better understanding as we spent the next three weeks or so working away in the large, open fields, with only the continuous rattle of the horse-rake tines to keep us company. It was a job I really enjoyed, and the solitude never bothered me as I wasn't alone when a horse was there for company. Each day I started work in the relative cool of the morning, and could see my

Back in the Groove

day's work stretching out before me across the sun-kissed stubble. My eyes could survey the wonderful vista of rolling woods and fields as I rode backwards and forwards across the field, not noticing the jolts and rattles of my ancient, rusty machine. I was as near to heaven as was possible, in my estimation at least. As the sun became fiercer, a break could be taken and dinner eaten under any welcoming shade given by a hedgerow tree. My trusty sack gave me a rug to lie on, and a comic helped break my solitude. To lie in the shade and look out at the shimmering heat was heavenly. My horse would be tied securely to a sapling, thus allowing him to chew leaves to his heart's content. Charlie Wilson might come across occasionally, which would mean I took extra care in depositing the raking in a straight line. Up and down we went, with the sun beating down and reflecting up from the packed earth, but usually a little breeze helped to make it bearable.

Four o'clock and fourses meant another break under another tree, and so away until 6.30 when the rake was set down beside the neat stacks in the corner. Taking the horse out of the shafts meant extra care should be taken not to let it go, and after hanging bag and coat on the sails of his collar I would climb from the rake wheel on to his back and jog off to the farm. Gradually the cleared stubble was raked until the last field was reached and another harvest ended. These halcyon days of raking continued for another year or so, until the fateful day came when a much wider rake was purchased, and as this was designed to be pulled by a tractor, another enjoyable harvest task was terminated by the march of mechanical progress.

The introduction of the larger rake meant a promotion for me to driver in one of the remaining company of harvesters. As horses were still used there, I was the person delivering empty wagons and returning loads to the stack. I had at last graduated to the job my Uncle John had performed when first I took up harvest work as holgy boy. By this time Uncle Will Bumfrey looked after the only team of horses left on the farm, and this meant I was working with him - an arrangement we both enjoyed. Handling the trace horse with some skill now, I loved my job, and felt the pull of the land and especially the company of horses. I never gave tractors a second look, but a horse drew me like a magnet. It was this love of horses that kept me so close to Will as I sought to learn horse-sense from him. Whereas Uncle John turned naturally to tractors when the day came, Will pined for the horse years and remained with them until the sad day when the very last one went. With it, I fear, went Will's spirit, and he declined rapidly in health, succumbing to a modern disease suspected to be farmer's lung. But who knows what gives us life or a will for living. I do know that Billy Bumfrey was, for me, the very epitome of the horse age and I can never picture him without the faithful Gypsy there beside him pulling that

Back in the Groove

dark-green, pneumatic-tyred tumbril he used so often in and around the Soigné yards. If spirits return, then without doubt those two faithful, friendly ones will appear from time to time.

All too soon harvest was completed, and the time to return to school came round. Life at the grammar school became much less fraught after the first year. Admittedly, all my subjects were seen in either black or white, in that I either liked them and did well, or hated them and fell woefully short of the required standard. Chemistry, history, geography and religious knowledge came into the first category. French, physics, maths, art and woodwork fell into the second group in the order listed. Only English language and English literature could be spoken of as grey areas, depending upon the master taking them.

As I worked my way up the school, I lived up to my own definition of myself - never quite fitting into any category. By working hard at the subjects I liked, I kept near the top of Standard 2B and a year later 3B. A promotion to 4A failed miserably, as I lost confidence and hovered around the base of that year's class. For my final year, I spent the time in form 5B and it was decided to let me concentrate on my good subjects, which gave me just a sufficient number to enter the Cambridge School Certificate, although two extra subjects, art and woodwork, were added to give some semblance of a varied syllabus. I knew they were a dead loss, which meant all the others had to be passed in order to obtain the Certificate.

Poor health had held me back in all my years at school, I still suffered from streaming colds in the winter months, and these almost always turned to chesty coughs or bronchitis. Michael suffered even more severely than I did, and my poor mother battled away to keep us in this world on many occasions when breathing became almost impossible at night. Coupled with this was a running battle with the attendance officer who declared we must improve our attendance or court action would be involved. On one occasion she showed Dr Townend the letter and he glared at it and bit on the stem of his square-bowled pipe. An ex-naval man just returned from war time service, he closely resembled Winston Churchill in his pugnacious manner, especially against bureaucracy. "Just refer him to me, Mrs Bumfrey, I'll deal with his sort, you won't hear any more from him". He was dead right, we didn't.

Dr Townend was the champion of the worker and underprivileged. His partner, Dr Hallsmith, almost always attended the monied patients. Dr Townend didn't have the same bedside manner, but he helped us through some narrow squeaks. "When they leave school and get out into the air they'll be fine", was his diagnosis, and my goodness he was absolutely right. After leaving school I went until my 57th year before suffering any chest complaint at all, and my brother still runs half marathons well after his

183

Back in the Groove

50th birthday! There was just one strange twist to the story of Dr Townend: he would not join the National Health Service when it was introduced in 1948. He retired rather than work under Aneurin Bevan, the first Minister of Health. I often wondered if they had crossed swords at some earlier time for our heroic doctor spoke so bitterly about the Minister and ground out his name in a most Churchillian manner.

Incidentally, at the insistence of Grandad Eke, we children all belonged to the Oddfellows Club which meant that, for a few pence per month, we were entitled to free doctor's treatment. We certainly had our money's worth from the organisation. Grandad Eke was a very keen Oddfellow, and gave his sons short shrift should they ever raise tongue to complain over their subscriptions, which they did on occasions when times were hard. Grandad would have paid it himself, rather than let them be foolish enough to drop out.

But despite my poor health I worked hard at school, especially in the last year, when my efforts were rewarded by gaining my Cambridge School Certificate, with three distinctions and three credits, which upheld all the high hope of Mrs Clark, my village school mentor. Owing to my suspect health, Mum battled long and hard to get free school transport for me, and I was taken by car to Swaffham for the last year or so. An ancient, grey taxi came out from Braybrookes Garage to pick me up, collecting Roddy and Rosemary Welham from Southacre and finally the Butters children from an isolated cottage well outside Swaffham. Roddy had also started at the grammar school, being younger than me, and on one occasion, whilst waiting for our lift in the street, Roddy peeled a banana, a rare treat in post-war Britain and began to eat. As if by magic an apparition in dark overcoat, trilby hat and glasses stood before us. "What do you think you are doing, boy", roared an irate Tom Welburn, our headmaster. Poor Roddy was so shocked that he could only mumble the obvious which was, "Eating a banana, Sir". "You do not eat in the street whilst you are wearing school uniform, Welham; you are a disgrace to the School", thundered the paragon of Victorian rules. Needless to say, the half-eaten, forbidden fruit was hidden from sight, not to see the light of day, until Roddy was safely on the farm track leading to his isolated, gamekeeper's cottage home in the backwoods of Southacre.

I wondered many years later what Mr Welburn would have made of the long-haired, slovenly crew of boys I saw leaving the church to return to school. Their appearance did little to generate pride in the old school in me, and any thoughts of returning to look around, as old boys did in my schooldays, went from my mind. I doubt if there would have been anything to compare with the neat, well run establishment I knew and was proud to be part of. Victorian-type rules might have seemed harsh, but even I believe that a tidy appearance helped to generate a tidy mind. I am sure our brush with the headmaster helped we boys to develop a "keep Britain tidy" mentality at an early age. I dread to think what fury would have descended upon us if Roddy had cast the banana skin upon the pavement.

Having had the privilege of living long enough to have seen life turn almost full circle, I would back the type of fair, if severe, discipline meted out by my headmaster. That discipline helped enormously to shape my life, as did a stint of two years' National Service later on. We had rogues, we had jokers and we had cleverdicks, but they were never allowed so much rein that things were spoiled for the majority. For that I am forever grateful.

Continuing school after the normal leaving age of fourteen made me into something of an oddity, as work was the one thing uppermost in everyone's mind, and the average thinker just couldn't understand why a body should be wasted at a school desk when it could have been used to work and earn money. It was common understanding that after fourteen years of parental support, the least a body could do was to earn a living and start repaying the unasked for debt. Obviously, with large families coming up behind, this was very necessary and not to be condemned. But things were slowly changing, and not least in the size of families. Unfortunately, country mentality did not seem to have changed and many times my dad was embarrassed by questions as to when I was going to earn a living. If it had been my mother, she would have immediately questioned how much they were being asked to pay towards my upkeep and sharply told them to mind their own business. I don't think perhaps that Dad really understood himself that a good education meant power in all sorts of ways and not just in procuring a good job.

The expression "good job" has always both amused and annoyed me as everybody put their fourpennyworth in on the definition of a "good job". Bertie Wilson had a "good job" - he was a London policeman. Cousin Ernie had a "good job" - he worked in a typewriter shop. I am not decrying their jobs, but I do question whether they were happy in them. It would seem their definition of a good job was one as far away as possible from the agricultural environment - a job where you had to dress up in order to go to work. Well, according to that maxim, I never had a good job in all my working days, but one thing I do know, I never stayed in work that I didn't enjoy, thus making my working life a happy one.

Anyway, as recorded earlier in this chapter, I continued with my education at the grammar school with the gap between myself and my fellow age group in the village getting wider, due to the conflict of interests. What the local people failed to realise was that I didn't really enjoy the

Back in the Groove

company of farmers' schoolboy sons and wanted nothing better than to be one of the local lads. But my terrible shyness left me to walk a very lonely path; Michael and John were my sole companions, but being older than them meant that my early teenage years were spent in schoolboy pursuits, rather than stepping out into the real, adult world. Not that we didn't enjoy ourselves, because we did. The pursuit of rabbits took up much of winter spare time, and games of cricket gave much fun in the summer. When Swaffham Breck was down to grass we played out there on most evenings; my own participation was limited to one hour before my massive homework took precedence. It was very hard to pore over books in the front room and hear the shouts of exuberant sportsmen from across the road. If ever a boy suffered in the field of education, it was me during those summer evenings. Still, without those hours of swotting, I would never have achieved my academic successes, even if the certificates gained remained in a drawer from that day to this.

In the holidays and on Saturdays, we three lads took our sports equipment to the park where we practised, using a real cricket ball. Both John and Michael bowled quite fast, and as we had no pads, my legs took a fair amount of bruising, due mainly to my failure to get bat on ball. As I fancied myself as a bit of a spin wizard, their legs remained almost unscathed, due this time to the lesser speed and greater skill with the bat. No one from the Hall ever minded our presence quite near their home, but there, cricket was very close to their own hearts, especially with Captain Harry Birkbeck who played for Norfolk on several occasions. Some Sunday evenings saw a different venue, that being the Squires Field when Uncles Will and John joined Dad and we boys in a game that was always very enjoyable. Having extra fielders was a big bonus after hours of fetching and retrieving in our three man games.

As field cropping mainly followed the age-old tradition of four year rotation, our cricket venues had to fit in with the year of the hay crop, as wheat, barley, or sugar-beet failed to lend themselves to the making of a good wicket. The park, of course, had by this time been returned to permanent pasture after its wartime excursion into arable cropping. One feature of the park not mentioned was the flint-stone, walled haha round the wooded western side. Now for the uninitiated, a "haha" is a ditch backed by a retaining wall which prevents animals from jumping out whilst giving an uninterrupted view from within the park. Quite why this idea had been used in this case is far from clear as the Hall didn't have a view in this direction and with the wood behind the wall, the view would have been interrupted anyway. I've no idea of the age of this man-made barrier, but, in places, large tree roots had pushed out the wall and stones had fallen into the ditch. Double, heavy, metal gates sealed the private road running into the park from the Pretoria direction and also at the top end leading out towards Castleacre. A lighter, single gate, known as the Anmer gate, shut up the park from the High House road, and this was where Dad always gathered his first bunches of spring violets carried home for my mother. In later years, as more traffic came to the Hall, cattle grids were constructed across the roads enabling cars to proceed straight through the white-painted gates propped open for free passage. Our cricket pitch was on the green road leading from Anmer gate to the Mowing Ground, as this provided a good, sound surface for the budding, fast bowlers to dig the ball in at high speed and frighten the life out of their older, but much less skilled, companion.

As I have mentioned, Grandad and family moved from Rats Hall to No 9 Pretoria in 1947. Aunt Ivy had become very disenchanted with the lonely life at Rats Hall and made frequent pleas for a move nearer a hard road. Eventually her pleas were heard and the house of Walter Wilson was allocated when Blustrous and his wife retired to live in the old laundry house beside the Methodist Chapel in Westacre village. Dick Welham took over the cowman's job at Soigné, replacing Walter, and he brought his wife Phyllis and daughter Mavis also from Rats Hall to live next to Charlie Wilson at Soigné. The outgoing incumbent there had been a Mr Simmonds who worked as a gardener for Colonel Carlyon at the farmhouse.

Before Ivy moved house, new curtains had to be measured for and run up as the Pretoria windows were huge compared with those in the Rats Hall cottages. I volunteered to help my Aunt measure up and we did it one Sunday afternoon. The Wilsons had the taste for an uncoordinated colour scheme of very bright distempers. Blue, yellow and green seemed to clash with each other as the sun shone through the large, uncurtained windows and my eyes soon began to ache, as did my head, and a severe bilious attack developed. We did manage to complete our measuring task, but I was violently sick immediately afterwards.

The houses at Rats Hall housed other people after the Bumfrey and Welham exodus, but with the departure of two such long-standing Rats Hall names, the days of human habitation there were numbered, and by the 1960s the three cottages and two bungalows had been condemned and razed to the ground. The huge barn remained, but may by now have become a victim of the ravages of time along with its extensive bullock yards where the cattle chewed the cud to fatten and Grandad used the soft water from their roofs to fill the copper for the Monday wash.

The male Bumfreys were very sorry to leave Rats Hall, but Ivy saw a little more of life at Pretoria, although she was still only on the fringe of civilisation. Drinking water still had to be carried from the bottom of the hill in buckets, the lavatory bucket contents buried in the garden, and the oil lamps filled and trimmed every day. Pretoria was not to be modernised just yet, but there was hope for better amenities in the future whilst activists like my mother were around, but there were occasions when progress seemed to be in reverse, as poor management on the Estate meant even more primitive conditions for the residents. One prime example was when the Pretoria water supply from the deep bore at the Hall suddenly ceased to flow, due to a corroded galvanised pipe in the underground system. An emergency supply came from Soigné in the form of a horse-drawn water cart which sloshed its contents into the storage tank under George Wright's chicken run, washing down mud and droppings as it went. My mother was appalled and bombarded both Charlie Wilson and Willie Thaxton with a request for urgent action on the restoration of supply from High House. Nothing came of this, so my mother met Major Birkbeck and raised the matter with him. "Do you expect me to dig up the pipe myself, Mrs Bumfrey?" was his tart reply. "No", said my mother, "but I thought that perhaps you had sufficient authority to get the job moving". With this exchange, the two parties went their separate ways with feathers well ruffled, but the pure water supply was restored within a short time, so no more needed to be said.

One thing this incident did underline was the fact that the huge estate vessel was drifting dangerously, without one really effective hand on the tiller. The Major, being heavily involved in banking with Barclays, was forced to leave the day to day running of the Estate in hands that were totally unqualified for the changing times forced on it by the Second World War. The old order was being eroded by progressive thinking of ex-servicemen who were so right in believing their country owed them a better life in return for their wartime efforts. They had seen the land fit for heroes promised after the great war, and didn't wish to see a repeat performance in the late 1940s.

Not that I lay any fault for the pre-war debacle at the door of our Estate, for as was mentioned previously their pre-war record on tenant care stood in a fair light, but at this new, crucial time of change no one of vision came to the fore. Frantic papering over the cracks seemed to be the number one policy as the incumbent leaders fought to hold the vast and often unwieldy estate machine together. People like my mother, who were determined to better the lot of tenant families became an embarrassment as they asked for basic domestic improvements, such as electricity and running water. Where was the money coming from to finance such schemes? Improved efficiency and a central policy were needed, but nothing came forth, until the life blood had almost ebbed away and apathy became a way of life which permeated through the whole Estate community.

Back in the Groove

Of course, writing in retrospect makes it very easy to comment on the action of others, but I try to make the points in explanation of my mother's frustration, in that direct action never came to bear on any problem, and it did seem to require constant prodding and carping to produce any action at all. I must also point out that my mother wasn't only an embarrassment to the Estate hierarchy, but also to my own father who was quite content with the status quo and who would hardly ever voice a complaint on his own behalf, except if the welfare of his stock was threatened. This didn't mean he failed to get things done if he wanted, but his methods were much less direct and somewhat quieter than my mother's. Dad was a peaceful, country man, but Mum never took no for an answer and would fight tooth and nail for any cause she really believed in, winning a large percentage of her battles along the way.

Chapter 20
All the Odds and Endings

At the end of the war in Europe, Billy and Bob Thaxton were freed from the German prisoner of war camps and came home to High House once again amidst much rejoicing. At Soigné, the Richardson family still clung to the hope that their son, Leslie, would be found alive once the Japanese were defeated. The atomic bombs in August 1945 abruptly ended that conflict in favour of the allies and after a long wait the wonderful news came through telling of Leslie's safe release and rehabilitation in New Zealand. Eventually he returned to Soigné, a shadow of the healthy young man who had left several years before, but thankfully well enough to recover under the care of his family and friends.

After the war ended, our trips to King's Lynn became more frequent, and catching the bus at the corner became less of a traumatic event for me, and I could spend the day without incurring a sick headache. The small, green Bedford bus would appear round Shortrow corner at about twenty minutes to ten, having picked up passengers at Westacre. I would try to get a seat by the window, so as not to miss any of the interesting, country pursuits along the way. The well-filled vehicle would slowly make its way up the incline towards High House, with the engine making its own peculiar whine and the sliding door rattling as numerous potholes were passed over. Billy Carter was at the controls, chatting away to the passengers in the seat right at the front, keeping one eye on the empty road ahead and the other on their spicy piece of gossip. Mrs Eves sat directly inside the door where she could collect the fares and keep a watchful eye on Billy should he be too engrossed in the gossip to notice potential passengers running along a side lane at the last minute. As they had travelled this route every week, year in and year out, they knew everyone, where they lived and all their private circumstances as well. The lady in question had been engaged to young Billy Carter before he had gone to France in World War I. After he was reported missing, presumed dead, May married Bert Eves. Billy Carter returned at the end of the war with the result that Bert and himself became partners in a bus business, with May Eves organising the financial side and providing us with a Tuesday bus service for many years. They were based at Marham, about ten miles from Westacre.

On one occasion, a Westacre passenger left a parcel of fish in the bus. The loss of a fish tea in times of food rationing was horrendous so the deprived person did no more than get out their bike and pursue the errant parcel of fish. Imagine their dismay when they arrived perspiring at the

190

All the Odds and Endings

Eves' door only to find May frying the fish for Bert and Billy's tea. Whether they all sat down to fish and chips I don't know, but great hilarity was engendered through the telling of the tale.

Let us return to the bus which was proceeding up the High House road, under the trees which occasionally slapped on the bus roof where the weight of their leaves pulled them down low. Occasionally, a servant from the Hall waited opposite Anmer gate, but more often Mrs Curl and Mrs Chase got on at the High House turn, then it journeyed on past Honeypot, Eighteen Acres and Little Ash Breck, where we looked out at the men working there. Any workmen within view always stopped their labours to watch the bus from the moment it came into sight until it disappeared in the distance as it might be the only moving thing to break the monotony until its return in the afternoon. Down the hill to the Mink's Corner it went, turning left alongside Massingham Heath and then down Norwich Hill where Mrs Smith almost always waited by the New Buildings, and a few hundred yards on to the Milestone where Mrs Easter and others from Rats Hall would join the passengers; then it travelled on to the Patch Corner, bearing left to Gayton Thorpe village where "Stocks" Raspberry and his son, Vessie, were regular customers. The tiny, round-towered Saxon church always intrigued me since I knew that my Granny Bumfrey and Uncle Stanley lay at rest there. The road through the village led on to join the East Walton to Gayton road where Sonny Smith, our late neighbour at High House, now lived in a cottage adjacent to the junction. Incidentally, Sonny was one of the older sons of the large Smith family whose mother boarded the bus at New Buildings. A right turn took our conveyance to the main road, into and through the village of Gayton, and past the silver sand workings at Bawsey. The Sandboy public house stood waiting for passing trade but got none from us as we sped on towards Gaywood which was on the Lynn outskirts.

Round the famous Gaywood clock, the bus slowed for increased traffic as the town centre was reached. We were dropped just off Norfolk Street where our shopping began in earnest, with a certain visit to Catleughs, the large, gents' outfitters, where young Geoffrey Wood served us with a smile and efficiency from behind his glass-topped counter, with trusty tape measure hung round his neck. Geoffrey was a good and keen cricketer, but was only able to play on Wednesday afternoons, which was early closing day for the Catleugh emporium and the town centre generally. Kirklands was another gents' outfitters in Norfolk Street, but our visits there were only undertaken if, on rare occasions, Catleughs failed to supply our need.

Another early call was to Stan Riches, the fishmonger, as no outing to Lynn was complete without some fish for Dad's tea. The large fishmonger, resplendent in blue and white striped apron, would be at the head of his

191

All the Odds and Endings

large, marble fish stall and he usually sold the best and freshest fish in Lynn. At the bottom of Norfolk Street at its junction with High Street stood Woolworth's, and to the right Marks and Spencer; these two fairly modern shops were always a must. Woolworth's was, or had been, the threepenny and sixpenny store. Then we went back up Norfolk Street to the Sandringham fish and chip restaurant for lunch before completing our shopping in the High Street at Boots the Chemist, Scotts the furnishers, Belfast Linen and probably last, but not least, W.H. Smith the bookseller. Here I loved to browse through the bird books.

Our bus left the extensive Tuesday Market at a quarter to three. There were a large number of stalls on the market with the traders yelling one against the other in an effort to attract custom. I liked watching the experts on the china stall as they juggled with dinner services, piling everything in their arms and then tossing them into the air to catch again, without dropping even a single item. A Dutch auction would ensue with eager customers thrusting their one pound notes in the air to purchase these wonderful bargains. Mum always maintained there was some trickery afoot and never succumbed to their antics. Her crockery came from Scotts and never failed to live up to expectations until dropped accidentally on the brick pantry floor. Dad was slightly more susceptible, as was proved on one occasion when he watched a salesman pulling hard on a pair of leather boot laces which he claimed would pull up the stiffest of boots. Dad, having bought half a dozen pairs, did quite a lot of swearing next day when he put one pair into his boots and found they were as rotten as muck. Mum likened his intelligence to that of a village idiot for being taken in so easily and Dad retired in a huff to his shed until the duff laces could be forgotten.

At 2.45 Billy Carter would mount the step of his bus and call, "Everyone here?". As all his passengers knew one another, any missing face was soon identified and Billy would wait until the perspiring passenger, usually laden with bags, appeared, to take his or her seat, venting anger at some slothful shop assistant who had held things up. Billy would laugh and take up his seat ready for the off. The only change to this routine was if we came to Lynn in the last two weeks in February, when the Lynn Mart, or annual fair, took over the Tuesday Market and alternative arrangements were made. If the Mart was there, a walk round and the purchase of some rock rounded off the afternoon. Much chatter over various bargains and purchases ensued between the passengers on the return journey, and loud "Cheerios" were exchanged as each party alighted to trek back along their own cart track to resume their rather quiet and mundane existence in the heart of the countryside. We would be indoors before four o'clock, with time to stir up the fire and get the frying pan on to cook the fish before Dad came home from work. Over tea, there would be plenty to tell about our day at Lynn, for a trip out was still something a bit special, and not an everyday occurrence as it would be today. Dad loved his fish teas and a couple of fresh herring with bread and butter was his idea of a perfect tea. Such a simple pleasure was his to enjoy and mine too, I might add, even to this day.

Comics played quite a part in our rural lives. The first one I had was "Radio Fun", where all the favourite radio stars were depicted in cartoon form. Cyril Jones had "Film Fun", and then we exchanged copies during the week. I then passed on the "Film Fun" to Dilbury in exchange for the Dandy, I think. I remember on one occasion I fell out with Cyril over something and he came to the door demanding the return of his threepenny comic. As I had already passed it over to my Soigné-based mate, he went home empty-handed. As my reading quality advanced, Douglas Wilson introduced me to "The Champion" and the exploits of Rockfist Rogan, Sexton Blake and other worthy characters. Douglas was the son of the policeman, Bertie Wilson, and was evacuated from London to stay with his Aunt Eva in the village. "The Champion" helped to improve my reading enormously and as I enjoyed the stories, I remember convincing myself that I would surely continue to read comics throughout my adult life. Only a short time later, I also remember thinking what childish mentalities the American soldiers must have had as they received comics as part of their provisions from home. How quickly our thinking changes as we grow up. However, in the ration book era, a nice slice of Desperate Dan's cow-pie with a horn sticking out wouldn't have gone amiss, if only the Dandy cartoons could have been brought to life.

On the subject of food I am reminded of the heavily-pastried pies allocated to manual workers as extra rations. They were instigated by Lord Woolton, Minister of Food, and continued to be delivered by Jack the Baker for quite some time after the war. Mum took in those which were allocated to Ivy's family and we boys carried them further up the hill on a tray with a nice white tea cloth over the top to keep off the dust. On one such journey I tipped the tray, and a couple fell off into the road. Michael just managed to grab them up before Waggs got her doggy jaws on to them. We blew the dust off and placed them back under their snow-white cover and continued our delivery as if nothing had happened. I hope Uncle Will didn't get too much dirt between his teeth as he sat eating dinner in the field on the morrow.

Charlie Wilson, the Soigné Farm foreman, was renowned for his love of fires. On one occasion he sent two men to burn thorn hedge cuttings on Swaffham Breck, the field immediately in front of Pretoria. There would seem nothing strange in this, except it was on a Monday morning,

All the Odds and Endings

washday, and the wind was due south and carried the smoke into the washing lines. This very slight indiscretion sent my mother hurtling across the road to berate the two unfortunate workmen unmercifully. They in turn blamed their foreman but were sent back to the farm with instructions to inform their stupid superior that Mrs Bumfrey would be expecting him round to rewash her smutty sheets. Discretion being the better part of valour meant that we saw nothing of Charlie for a week or two and no thorns were burned until a stiff, northerly wind took the resultant smoke away across open fields. As the farm grew much straw which was surplus to requirements, whole stacks of stiff wheat straw were often burned to clear the land. Charlie Wilson was the man who lit the match to start the inferno and many a scorched hedge or tree bore witness to his enthusiasm.

On one occasion he started a fire, then discovered that his little terrier was ratting in the straw. Charlie scorched his eyebrows and lost his trilby hat as he rescued the poor little dog. Riding into the farmyard with a white handkerchief tied over his bald head caused some comment and much ribald laughter, especially amongst the younger element of his staff. His biggest gaffe with fires was on the Twenty Five Acres where carrots were grown and left for a second year to run up to seed. After careful cutting and binding, a 15 x 6 yards stack was set out and the straw bottom covered with old binder canvases to catch any fallen, valuable seed. Wheat had been grown on a small part of the field nearest the farm, but stacked near to the carrot seed in the White Gate Corner. After the wheat-stack had been threshed, Charlie decided (he must have been mad!) to burn the resulting straw-stack. Within minutes of the conflagration catching hold, a spark set the tinder-dry carrot stalks ablaze. Charlie, in sheer panic, leapt in his cart, drove hell for leather to High House, collected Lou Abel and flew back just as fast as his horse would go. Quite what Lou was to do, no one knew, but by the time the imagined fire-fighter arrived, the stack of precious carrot seed was engulfed in flames. How Charlie escaped the sack, only the gods and Willie Thaxton knew, but my mother's comment as to his sanity cannot, for legal reasons, be printed here!

When the ashes were all cold, we walked the site, viewing the scores of crispy rat carcasses lying around. If Lou Abel could have doused those flames, he would have been as famous as our present day Red Adair, oil-well fire fighter. Mum said that when Charlie's chariot rushed past, Lou was hanging on for dear life as the rocking cart threatened to leave the road. We did see life at Pretoria sometimes!

Stepping back slightly to the time before I left Westacre school, the two most senior girls were June Thaxton and Grace Wilson. June we have mentioned before as being the youngest daughter of Willie Thaxton, the bailiff. Mrs Thaxton was quite clever with her hands and a beautiful

194

All the Odds and Endings

knitter and June followed closely in her mother's footsteps and was very neat in all her schoolwork. Grace was also a very nice girl, but the exact opposite to June in every way, being somewhat awkward, with everything she attempted fated to go wrong.

I remember both girls knitting white, all-in-one, baby garments. June's of course was pure in every way, but Grace made so many mistakes with subsequent pullings out, that hers was almost black and much derided. Some connection with these garments caused us to nickname her "Pilchards", but what the connection was I can't recall. To Grace's great credit, she never let her misfortunes get her down, always entering into jokes against herself. My only hope is that as her large family arrived in later years, they didn't have to depend on Grace's knitting prowess to provide their clothes!

One warm afternoon, Mrs Clark asked June to open the window; up blundered Grace and stood on the seat making enough noise and clatter to wake the dead. "How long has your name been June Thaxton, Grace Wilson?", cut in Mrs Clark's stern voice. Down crashed Grace again, to an eruption of laughter from the rest of the class. Good old Grace, she could always be relied upon to unintentionally liven up any day of classroom boredom.

It was after her two children had grown up, that Mrs Carlyon, who lived in the Soigné farmhouse, decided it was high time their nursery and toy cupboards were cleared out. Being a lady of generous nature, she sorted all the toys, and distributed them to the local children. Somehow my name was omitted from the initial list, and only came to mind after the toys had gone out. Full of apologies, she arrived with a large tin filled with cigarette cards. Being a cigarette card buff, I was thrilled to bits as I sorted through my newly acquired treasures. The sets depicted British birds and animals and they were the first ones to come out. Then sportsmen, especially footballers and cricketers, were separated into bundles and kept together with elastic bands. Some larger cards spring to mind, especially those depicting cries of Old London - piemen with trays on their heads carrying their wares, black-faced sweeps offering their services alongside men with singing birds in cages slung on canes across their shoulders. No toy could have given me the hours of pleasure those cards did. The birds were stuck into a red note book with the information copied from the reverse side before the sticking took place. This was my most valued possession ranging alongside my birds' egg collection.

When the MCC cricket team went out to Australia in 1946, I kept a record of all their matches, and stuck a picture card in as well, where appropriate. As the war had decimated our national side, we suffered terribly at the hands of the rampant Aussies, who took great pleasure in

All the Odds and Endings

reaping revenge on our batsmen for all the hostility generated by Larwood and Voce in the notorious 1933 Body-line tour. Bill Voce went on the 1946 trip, but as his age had advanced by thirteen years, his firepower had all but disappeared. Wally Hammond did his last stint as Captain, with Norman Yardley, the Yorkshire amateur, as Vice-Captain. Len Hutton, Cyril Washbrook, Bill Edrich, Denis Compton, Godfrey Evans, Paul Gibb and Alec Bedser, were all gifted cricketers who were match winners in their day, but either seemed to be too old or too young to produce the goods when all in the same team. They made up cannon-fodder for Ray Lindwall and Keith Miller at their fastest and rampant best. I little realised at the time how often during my life our cricketing fortunes would follow the same pattern of disaster, but eventually how sweet was the victory to come in 1953 when Len Hutton finally led us to an Ashes victory. I wish I still had my two little illustrated notebooks, but they have been lost in the times when far greater things monopolised my life, though strangely, none of these momentous things that replaced them spring to mind so clearly as do my boyhood treasures almost fifty years on.

The long-since banned gin trap was used very widely on the Estate, both for rabbit and rat catching. The keepers set them under half round ridge tiles, covered with turf, in the corners of fields and woods. Animals classed as vermin would pass through the tunnel and get a foot in the trap as their weight on the flat, metal plate covered with some loose earth sprung the steel tooth jaws around the leg. The poor creature would pull at the trap and suffer agony until the keeper called next day to check his traps. The rat, stoat, weasel and hedgehog would be killed with a boot or stick and then hung on the keeper's gibbet. A line of rotting corpses meant a hard-working gamekeeper stalked the land, and a few rooks, magpies or jays also indicated his skill with the gun. Sometimes, the animal would bite through the trapped leg and limp away, leaving the severed stump in the jaw of the trap.

We boys went through a period when we felt sorry for any animal trapped in such a cruel manner, so a plan sprung to mind as to how we might alleviate the suffering. Arming ourselves with a number of rabbits' feet cut from the animals Mum had skinned for dinners, we set off on our errand of mercy. Finding some traps set in rabbit burrows situated on the Abbey side of Middle Thirty Acres, we prodded the plate with the stiff hind foot, jumping back as the jaws clamped shut and leaving the foot upside down in the trap. One or two more were located and treated in the same manner, a stiff wing feather from a pigeon finishing the final one for us. Very proud of our achievements and so sure Clem Softley would think the animals had pulled their feet off to escape, we set off home completely oblivious to the numerous footprints left in the soft, sandy soil around the burrow entrances. In the ensuing days, nothing was said, and we forgot our latest craze and went on to other things. One evening, the smoke from Clem's smelly bonfire of ferret cage dirty litter drew us to a game of running through the smoke. We dashed backwards and forwards, attempting to hold our breath whilst in the smoke, and settling a wonderful odour deep into our woollen jerseys. A whiff of this odour would confirm the truth of the saying, "stink like a polecat". Why this pungent smoke should be such an attraction I don't know, but our noisy pastime drew Clem from his garden and out into the belt. "I suppose you are the ones who messed about with my traps", came suddenly to our ears and cut short our hilarity. "I've a good mind to kick your backsides, and I will if I catch you near them again!" With red ears and faces we slunk away before any more interrogation could take place, silently cursing our stupidity at going anywhere near the keeper's house. Needless to say, we kept well out of his way for a bit and hoped he wouldn't mention our humane actions to our parents, who, in turn, would see no wrong in country practices which had been in place almost since the dawn of time.

Thankfully, the age of the cruel gin trap was almost at an end, as a humane rabbit trap was being perfected, and this led to a ban on the gin trap coming into force soon after. Pet cats were often caught in traps, especially before Clem became the local keeper. It wasn't unknown for a keeper to set traps for a cat and then secretly kill the trapped animal and dispose of the evidence. On one occasion I was walking the woods by myself, when a loud rustling drew me to a lovely, black cat dragging a dreaded iron trap by its leg. With no thought of a bite or scratch I went up and released the stiff jaws of the trap by treading on the spring. The injured animal fled on three legs, and I had no idea whose it was. Maybe it was a wild feral cat as occasionally domestic cats turned wild. I do remember flinging the trap as far as I could into a bramble thicket.

A few years on saw us with a cat who had lost her front paw in a trap. She bobbed along on three legs and a stump, so came to be known as Bob. How or when her accident occurred I don't know as a new neighbour, Bill Johnson, arrived with two cats; both these animals decided to move one house up the hill and eventually we had two cats and Bill had none, but such are the habits of cats, and we humans have to go along with them. But before Bill Johnson came to live at No 5 Pretoria, the Deasley family moved from Hilborough. Ernie Deasley had been gamekeeper on the Estate there before the war and had served in the army during hostilities, suffering burns to the face when his petrol tanker was hit in North Africa; Ernie had a shrivelled ear and some scars to show the world, but these things did not affect his sense of humour and he enjoyed many a practical joke when he worked for a time on Soigné Farm. May, his wife, was very friendly with Mum, as Gerry and Colin, the sons, were friendly with us. When Clem Softley eventually retired, Ernie took up his natural keeper's trade and moved up to No 7 on the other side of us. But this move came after I had left school, so really belongs to another story.

To backtrack slightly, let me explain how No 5 first became vacant for the Deasleys to move into. George Hall, who had been our neighbour since the time of our move from High House and all through the war, was a vigorous character who, above all else, needed promotion, and when no opening was offered on the Estate, he decided to move up to Leicestershire into a foreman's post. After his move, we lost track of him, but I am sure he made a good job of his foremanship, being a natural leader of men. My father welcomed Ernie Deasley as a neighbour, if only for the fact that he kept no beehives. I am sure Dad felt that Leicestershire was very welcome to George and his bees. When the Lawrence family moved from No 4, Diddie Frost returned after a short time away from the fold, not this time as a groom, but, like Ernie, as a labourer on the farm. No 3 also saw changes when the Mann family departed and a new butler came in, whose name for the moment escapes me.

So, as the curtain begins to fall on my story in 1949, the Pretoria contingent looks like this: No 1 still housed George Wright, head gardener, and No 2 Jimmy Reynolds the Estate worker; as just mentioned, No 3 was the butler's residence, with Diddie Frost at No 4, Ernie Deasley at No 5 and we Bumfreys at No 6; Clem Softley remained as keeper at No 7, with Cyril and Peggy Goose, John Thaxton's mother and stepfather, at No 8; Grandad Bumfrey, Will, John and Ivy resided at No 9, and Frank Clarke completed the list at No 10. Apart from the few changes of tenants, life continued in much the same vein as it had all the time at Pretoria. We all cycled around, with the exception of Frank Clarke who was motorised, and provided a taxi for our holiday jaunts.

The Estate make-up changed after the war as the farms were once more let out to tenant farmers. In 1947 Leslie Cameron came to live at Abbey House and took over the running of the Estate and the Abbey Farm under Captain Harry Birkbeck. Soigné and High House Farms remained under the guidance of Willie Thaxton and foreman Charlie Wilson. Major Birkbeck retained full control of these operations, and could often be seen in his grey Opel car, with his faithful, black labrador in the seat beside him. The Major's wife, Mrs Sybil Birkbeck, passed away whilst staying with her eldest daughter, Patience, at Nekuru, Kenya in 1948. Major Boone took over farming at The Warren, the Cross brothers did likewise at Gayton Thorpe, and the Abbey Farm and Summer End Farm at East Walton also went out to tenants. So the Estate pattern had reverted to the kind of set up of 1930 when Major Birkbeck inherited it from his father.

All the Odds and Endings

The entire shoot of the Estate came under the Major, with four under-keepers and Fred Welham, the head keeper. Seemingly, the tremendous upheaval of the war had little effect upon our lives in and around Westacre, but small changes were taking place as the outside world made tiny inroads on the status quo of many years. To quote Captain Birkbeck's own words, "After the war, the Estate had many problems, cottages with leaky roofs, no running water, and no indoor sanitation". Four new houses were built by the Estate just after the war, and four pairs of semi-detached council houses went up behind the village hall at Westacre, which was something of an innovation. Apart from this, and an increase in mechanised power at work in the fields, very little had changed in Westacre during my schooldays. The Squire and his Estate entourage still led the village, and the vast majority of villagers were more than content to be thus led. My father was amongst the majority, but my mother was one of the foremost in the minority, and made her voice heard very strongly in the case for much-improved living conditions in the cottages.

Before I end my narrative, I must look once again at one or two local characters and the amusing happenings connected with them. Sam Askew lived at Castleacre and had at some time in the First World War helped to save Major Birkbeck's life. Sam had not escaped unscathed as his mouth was badly twisted by a malfunctioning gun exploding during action. Employment was found for him in and around the Hall and Dad saw a lot of him at High House. It seemed Sam wasn't too good at gardening, especially when someone gave him some French beans to plant in the spring. Well, these beans were of course bush-beans, but Sam thought sticks would be needed, so he pushed his bike all the way to Castleacre with a huge faggot of nut sticks resting on the machine. Imagine the ribald comments when neighbours viewed Sam's garden with six-foot sticks against twelve inch bean plants! The tale stretched to such extremes that it was reputed that Sam blocked the whole road getting his bundle of ten-foot poles home for the French beans.

Another tale circulating at the time told of Sam, with severe lumbago, getting his wife to iron his back over a sheet of brown paper using an ordinary flat-iron. Part way through the operation, a knock at the door drew Mrs Askew's attention, causing her to depart leaving the iron flat on her husband's back. The resultant severe burning sensation caused Sam to leap off the table with a very quick cure for his lumbago.

Just after the war, one of Major Birkbeck's daughters was coming to stay at the Hall with her baby. Someone remarked on this subject to Dick Everard who was working up there for a time. "She's going to have a nanny as well", continued Dick's informant. Very put out, Dick spluttered, "Then she can milk the b***** as well, 'cos I shan't!". I am sure

All the Odds and Endings

the proposed children's nurse would have been thrilled to have been mistaken for a nanny goat, had she known. The misunderstanding led to some pretty tough leg pulling for Dick after that.

On another occasion, Geoffrey Thaxton tied the end of a binder string ball to Dick's bicycle carrier strut when it was parked in the High House cart shed. The unsuspecting Dick set off home to Soigné, drawing the string gently from the centre of the paper-covered ball and trailing it down the farm drive. The next morning, Geoff told him Willie Thaxton wanted to know why he was stealing binder string in such a crafty manner. It was a trick that could have misfired badly if the string had fouled up causing the elderly man to fall from his bike. Luckily no mishap occurred to mar the joke. The Thaxtons were always up to some leg-pull or other, and Mr Thaxton wasn't averse to backing them up on occasions. During the many years he worked at High House, Freddie often had to suffer a snowball behind the cap, or a tied up door which he could only undo by going right round to the other side of it.

We still continued with our annual holidays at Briston. Granny and Grandad Eke enjoyed reasonable health in their retirement, and were always glad to see us. My introvert shyness didn't improve, and continued to hold me back from showing any potential, especially at school and in future career moves.

As mentioned previously, I gained my Cambridge School Certificate in July 1949. I had no idea of what I would like to do as a job, and someone mentioned a career in the RAF. This I jumped at and allowed my tutors to map out a sixth form curriculum to fit me for the entrance exams at the end of the school year. Returning to the grammar school in September at almost 17 years old, I realised just what a fraud I was by allowing my parents to spend their very limited finances on keeping me. I had no interest in the RAF and certainly no more interest in additional learning. I was mentally swotted out and getting further and further out of my academic and social depth. I had reached my watershed and had no inclination to run down the other side. So, by mid-October I plucked up courage to ask for my sixth form course to be terminated. I was determined to follow all my natural inclinations and go into farm work. Dad asked Mr Thaxton if I could begin work as a labourer at Soigné and the answer was, "Yes". Everyone threw their arms in the air, except my parents. The new headmaster looked down his nose at my utterly wasted education. Never had a grammar school boy left to become a farm labourer. I could never understand why so worthy an occupation should be regarded with such low opinion by so many, not least of all those who were farm workers and much too highly skilled to be classed as "labourers".

Some relatives and know-it-alls almost wept at the lost opportunity to

All the Odds and Endings

gain a "good job". Fortunately, the relatives and friends who really cared for me took it all in their stride and perhaps were secretly glad that I would stay very much as one of them, and not become part of an alien world with a good, but non-productive, job.

And so it was I put away my books and pens, donned my thick boots, working clothes and cap and settled down to my roots, beginning a very hard apprenticeship for real life amongst the large family of men employed at Soigné Farm. It was a move I have never regretted, although in later years I yearned for a larger stage upon which to set out my life. As my thoughts return to that late October morning when I pointed my trusty bike towards Soigné, memories flood back of the next ten years which saw such tremendous changes take place on that farm and farming in general. I feel it would be nice to share the times of fun and the times of frustration in another book, so if ever the opportunity arises then perhaps we can share the 1950s in true Norfolk village style.